Gender Politics in
Post-Communist Eurasia

Gender Politics in Post-Communist Eurasia

EDITED BY Linda Racioppi AND Katherine O'Sullivan See

Michigan State University Press • East Lansing

♾ The paper used in this publication meets the minimum requirements of ANSI/NISO
Z39.48-1992 (R 1997) (Permanence of Paper).

Michigan State University Press
East Lansing, Michigan 48823-5245
www.msupress.msu.edu

Printed and bound in the United States of America.

18   17   16   15   14   13   12   11   10   09   1   2   3   4   5   6   7   8   9   10

LIBRARY OF CONGRESS CATALOGING-IN-PUBLICATION DATA
Gender politics in post-communist Eurasia / edited by Linda Racioppi and Katherine
O'Sullivan See.
p. cm. — (Eurasian political economy and public policy studies)
Includes bibliographical references and index.
ISBN 978-0-87013-866-9 (pbk. : alk. paper) 1. Women—Europe, Eastern. 2. Women—Asia,
Central. 3. Sex role—Europe, Eastern. 4. Sex role—Asia, Central. 5. Women's rights—Europe,
Eastern. 6. Women's rights—Asia, Central. 7. Post-communism—Europe, Eastern. 8.
Post-communism—Asia, Central. I. Racioppi, Linda. II. See, Katherine O'Sullivan.
HQ1590.7.G463 2009
305.4209509'045—dc22
2009001322

Cover photograph is "Pensive" by Bronwyn Irwin and is used with permission.
Cover design by Erin Kirk New
Book design by Charlie Sharp, Sharp Des!gns, Lansing, MI

g green Michigan State University Press is a member of the Green Press Initiative
  press and is committed to developing and encouraging ecologically responsible
INITIATIVE
publishing practices. For more information about the Green Press Initiative and the use of
recycled paper in book publishing, please visit *www.greenpressinitiative.com*.

Visit Michigan State University Press on the World Wide Web at *www.msupress.msu.edu*.

Contents

Acknowledgments

I n the early-to-mid-1990s, feminist scholars developed rich and extensive
empirical and theoretical analyses of the impacts of the transition from Communism on women in Eurasia. The genesis of this volume is in that literature
and in our desire to explore the ongoing consequences of the post-Communist
transitions for women and men. With an aim to assessing contemporary gender
politics in Eurasia, we invited a multidisciplinary group of feminist scholars
from Europe, Russia, Central Asia, and the United States to a workshop held in
Istanbul in June 2006. *Gender Politics in Post-Communist Eurasia* is the result of
an arduous but stimulating process that began in that workshop.

This volume could not have been produced without the generous support of
a number of institutions and individuals. The workshop was cosponsored by Koç
University and two Michigan State University units: the Center for European,
Russian and Eurasian Studies and James Madison College. The funding provided
by these institutions made it possible to bring together a remarkable group
of feminist scholars from across Eurasia and the United States to share their
expertise and discuss the dilemmas of women's empowerment more than a
decade into the transitions from Communism. We are particularly appreciative
of the extraordinary hospitality and organizational skills of Timur Kocaoglu of
the Center for Strategic Studies at Koç. He not only contributed to the intellectual
richness of the seminar, but he also served as an exceptional host. The workshop
and the volume would not have been possible without the leadership of Norman
Graham, director of the Center for European, Russian and Eurasian Studies. He

recognized the importance of gender for contemporary politics in Eurasia, secured the lion's share of the funding for the workshop, and provided logistical support for the production of the volume. We are indebted to Alane Enyart, who helped organize the workshop, transcribed its proceedings, and formatted contributions for submission to Michigan State University Press. This volume would have been immeasurably more difficult to produce without her efforts. We are also grateful to Sherman Garnett, dean of James Madison College, for his support for the project and his participation in the workshop.

A number of people were crucial to the research and editing processes. We want to acknowledge the assistance of Terri Tickle Miller, Michigan State University's outstanding Slavic Collections librarian and head of Area Studies Collections and of International Documents. Terri's efficiency and expertise in locating critical documents made our work so much easier. We also want to recognize our professorial assistants at James Madison College, Tanya Rodriguez, Ryan Wyeth, and Katie Klante. Their important work on this project was funded by the Honors College at Michigan State University. The two anonymous reviewers for Michigan State University Press made useful suggestions for which we are especially appreciative. Finally, we are indebted to Michael Kamrin, whose culinary and editorial skills sustained us throughout this project.

Above all, we want to thank workshop participants and volume contributors. The critical insights they raised in workshop sessions, developed during informal conversations in Istanbul, and continued over e-mail have generated a shared sense of purpose and sustained us through the long process of completing this volume. Their contributions to this volume enrich our understanding of gender politics in Eurasia and reveal the myriad ways in which the transition from Communism continues to have important consequences for women and men today.

Gender Politics in Post-Communist Eurasia

Linda Racioppi and Katherine O'Sullivan See

The transitions from Communism in the former Soviet Union and Eastern Europe have not only dramatically altered socialist economies and political systems, they have also transformed the gender politics of Eurasia. Male-dominated political economies, or, as they are sometimes called, maleocracies, have continued unabated, as women have lost ground in the public sphere with the demise of quota system representation in government and as they have been frequently disadvantaged in processes of privatization. But the transitions have provided unprecedented opportunities for women to mobilize: politically—forming parties and participating in electoral politics, lobbying organizations, and interest groups; socially—organizing women's groups and religious and cultural associations; economically—seeking to establish businesses, pressing to protect women's labor rights, and enhancing women's human capital through training and education.

Gender Politics in Post-Communist Eurasia explores the range of transitions in Eurasia and the gender politics entailed in them. Differences in political authority and control, economic development, and sociocultural diversity during the Communist era left distinctive legacies and challenges for reforming or replacing the political orders, developing market economies in the face of economic globalization, responding to international norms of gender equality, and interacting with transnational and international organizations. Understanding how women have been affected by and addressed these complex challenges is central to the story of the transitions. The chapters in this volume reveal that there has been no single path in the gendered transitions from Communism. They address gender politics through case studies of Romania, Russia, and Tajikistan; comparative analyses of Azerbaijan, Kazakhstan, Kyrgyzstan, Tajikistan, and Uzbekistan; and regional examinations of Eastern and Central Europe and Central Asia. Many focus explicitly on transnational contexts and their gendered consequences, taking up such issues as the influence of global and regional norms on women's rights, the impact of the international political economy on women's social and economic positions, and the implications of international and regional migration and human trafficking for women's lives. Altogether, these chapters highlight the multiple and distinct gender politics across post-Communist Eurasia while also pointing out the commonalities.

This introduction aims to provide a framework for the ensuing chapters in two ways. First, it discusses the political dimensions of the transitions in Eurasia and provides an overview of trends in formal and informal politics. It illustrates the variations and similarities in gender politics through four cases from across Eurasia: the Czech Republic, the Russian Federation, Georgia, and Tajikistan. Second, it describes the transnational context for gender politics, particularly the changing global economy and the developing norms of gender equity and international institutions promoting these norms, and suggests how these transnational forces may interact with national and local contexts, once again drawing on the four case studies. The four cases represent distinct regions and political and economic contexts for the gendered transitions. The Czech Republic is interesting because its quick accession to Western European institutions, such as the North Atlantic Treaty Organization (NATO) and the European Union (EU), and relatively smooth passage to liberal democracy provide a "best case" scenario for women's empowerment. At the same time, its rapid integration into the European economy has had profound effects on women's socioeconomic standing. In Russia, the largest of the post-Communist states, the transition has been choppy: its turbulent economic growth has had widely disparate consequences and has fostered a feminization of poverty; at the same time, the development of "autocratic democracy" has jeopardized the vitality of civil society, where women had been particularly active in the early years of the transition. Georgia's emerging regime was plagued by a civil war, separatist claims, and internal turmoil for much of the 1990s. This political instability, compounded by population displacement, massive economic decline, and increased poverty, has been particularly difficult for women. Finally, Tajiki-stan is important for thinking about how women's rights and political agency have developed in a case in which civil war, economic underdevelopment, and resurgent religious traditionalism have circumscribed women's autonomy.

This introduction and the volume as a whole build on the rich feminist scholarship of the early-to-mid-1990s that chronicled the multiple impacts of the transitions from Communist rule on women. That literature underscores the necessity to comprehend post-Communist gender politics in their specific national sociopolitical contexts; it makes clear that women took different routes to address the consequences, challenges, and opportunities present in the early phase of transition. At the same time, the literature reveals the commonalities that women in post-Communist countries faced. Regional and local studies have delineated the ways in which the uneven shift to market economies throughout the post-Communist world jeopardized the position of women in the labor market, constrained their participation in the development of business firms, reinforced vertical and horizontal segregation and occupational stratification, contributed to a spike in gendered unemployment, and tolerated pervasive sexual harassment and discrimination in hiring and promotion. They show that the social welfare provisions of the Communist era (child care, pension schemes, secure employment, family supports) were increasingly subject to privatization, a process that assigned the tasks of social reproduction to women and reinforced the fragility of their labor market position. These works on the early transition recorded the backlash against the state emancipation of women that had been part of the Communist project, a backlash that discredited the language of women's emancipation and revived arguments about women's natural roles as mothers. And this scholarship called our attention to the gendered dimensions of nationalist revivals and their invocation of women as reproducers of the nation. But if the scholarship laid out a trajectory of immense challenges facing women in the post-Communist era, it also illuminated a broad range of women's mobilization, as democratization opened up spaces for political and civic activism. Women engaged in feminist critique, mobilized as mothers and workers, pressed for political inclusion, sought to stave off the loss of family and child-care benefits, and explored new forms of civic engagement. The extent and forms of women's activism varied from place to place, shaped in part by the particular histories of their countries, in part by the legacy of the official women's organizations, and in part by the process and local challenges of market reform, democratization, and party politics.[1]

As NATO and EU expansions proceeded apace, as the global economy was rocked by the Asian and Russian financial crises, and as global support for civil society and women's rights intensified in the late 1990s, feminist scholars turned to a more explicit focus on the international environment and its influence on and interaction with the gender politics of transitional societies (Einhorn 2006; Hemment 2007; Henderson 2003; Nikolic-Ristanovic 2002; True 2003). *Gender and Politics in Post-Communist Eurasia* contributes to efforts to comprehend the gender politics of the transitions through a lens that is simultaneously global and local. In this introduction, we frame the volume by addressing the national and international dimensions of gender politics and the linkages between them. We begin with the arena of politics, examining women's representation as members of nations and as formal participants in government and exploring the consequences of these for gendered constructions of citizenship. We then turn to the economic aspects of transitions, including women's experiences in the labor market in the context of economic regionalism, labor migrations, and globalization. We conclude with discussions of the international legal, normative, and organizational contexts for understanding gender politics at the local and regional levels.

Women and Political Transition

As these opening comments suggest, the story of the move from Communist political rule to new political orders has been complex and diverse. Although the language of democratization seemed dominant throughout Eurasia in the early post-Communist years, there was great variability and uncertainty in the process of building new systems of government. Today, democratic regimes in post-Communist Eurasia run the gamut from solidified liberal democracies such as those in the Czech Republic and Lithuania to emerging or unstable governments such as those in Bosnia and Herzegovina. But democracy has not taken hold everywhere, and authoritarian regimes have reconsolidated in countries like Belarus, Kazakhstan, Turkmenistan, and Uzbekistan. Some regimes faced secessions, civil war and paramilitary mobilization, and ethnonationalist and religious movements. Throughout the region, a broad range of political groups has sought to define and delimit the parameters of political participation. Obviously, the problem of constructing a post-Communist political order has been complex and has varied across Eurasia. But everywhere it has been deeply gendered.

The legacies of Communism for the development of state institutions and building of national solidarity have infused and shaped gender politics. Certainly, women's participation in government before the collapse of Communism in Eastern and Central Europe and the Soviet Union can best be described as limited and tentative. On the one hand, most of the Communist party states had quota system representation that ensured the political visibility, if not the voice, of women in governance. On the other hand, like many men, women were alienated from the political process and understood that despite their physical presence in the Communist state apparatus, real power lay with a male elite (Buckley 1990; Lapidus 1978; Wolchik and Meyer 1985). The uneasy and ambivalent relationship of women to political power in the Communist system could be seen in the reform movements of the late 1980s.

At the same time that reformers reiterated the importance of women to the development of new policies and politics, they often invoked essentialist views of women. Mikhail Gorbachev's famous observations about perestroika in 1987 reflect such ambivalence about women's role in political reform. He seemed to embrace the necessity of women's political participation, arguing that "democratization of society, which is the pivot and guarantor of perestroika, is impossible without enhancing the role of women, without women's active and specific involvement, and without their commitment to all our reforming efforts" (Gorbachev 1987, 102–103). Yet he also pointed to Soviet women's equality as the source of many social problems, arguing that it was necessary to resolve "the question of what we should do to make it possible for women to return to their purely womanly mission" as guardians of the family (Gorbachev 1987, 103). Though the most famous instance of such a contradiction, Gorbachev's views were not unique. As Jacqui True notes for the Czech Republic, this essentialist view of women as possessing a "purely womanly mission" was evident after the Velvet Revolution when the Civic Forum embraced a stance that the "disproportionate economic activity of women" should be reduced so that there would be a "rehabilitation of the family and better conditions for raising children" (2003, 59). Essentialist stances proliferated in media representations of women's rights, which "constantly portrayed gender differences as 'unchanging facts of nature,' and typecast gender equality as either a foreign or former Communist artifice" (True 2003, 53). From the perspectives of both Gorbachev and the Civic Forum, the woman as worker-mother was to be replaced by the woman as citizen-mother. A counterpoint was offered by some reformers reacting to the Communist view of women as worker-mothers: a construction of women as ungendered individuals, unaffected by social circumstances and interchangeable with men. Thus, for some politicians, the abandonment of quotas and social supports was legitimated as part of a democratization process where no special privileges would be accorded to individual citizens. Yvonne Corcoran-Nantes, for example, quotes an Uzbek government minister expressing such a view: "Under the previous system . . . women . . . were given many privileges and in this way men were disadvantaged. . . . Now this has to stop. We are now a democracy and women will have to compete equally with men for their place in society, politics and the labor force, just like the West. If they do not compete well, if they are unable to achieve similar positions to men, then it will be because they do not have merit" (2005, 161). In her chapter in this volume, Barbara Einhorn notes a similar rhetoric in Central and Eastern Europe, one that views women's rights as individuated and unrelated to the gendered realities of social and political power. Across the region, at the same time that reformers have viewed women as citizens who should participate in the political processes, the question of *how* they would be understood as equal citizens has generated distinctive and sometimes contradictory responses that reflect ambivalence about women's place in the body politic.

The nationalist movements that emerged in many Soviet republics and in some Eastern European countries often were also ambivalent about women's roles. In many of these movements, the past has figured prominently in rearticulations of gender roles. Regime changes and nation building almost always involve selective claims about the past to support contemporary political assertions, and these often entail gendered claims about that past (Racioppi and See 2000). The chapter in this volume by Timur Kocaoglu, for example, reminds us that in the transition to Soviet rule, Lenin invoked a myth of docile and subordinated Central Asian women to legitimate his claims about the ways in which communism would emancipate women. This myth belied the reality of the political reform movements in Central Asia that promoted women's equality; yet the myth has persisted, even informing many contemporary claims about women in this region.

Among nationalist invocations of the past have been imaginings of the nation as a collective family and neotraditionalist calls for a return to the "authentic" national forms of family life. Many nationalists embrace essentialist views that posit women as symbols and mothers of the nation whose destiny is to reproduce and socialize children for the national collectivity (Albanese 2006; Racioppi and See 1994). The most extreme case is that of the former Yugoslavia. As its component republics dissolved into conflict, Yugoslavia became synonymous with intensely gendered nationalism that ranged from pronatalist rhetorics and policies to the mass ethnic rape during the Bosnian war. However, nationalism has not inevitably led to violence, to pronatalist reproductive politics, or to a view of women as the mothers of the nation. Doina Pasca Harsanyi points out that during the early years of the Romanian transition, "In spite of the rampant nationalism, the triad women-mother-nation is absent from the Romanian rhetoric. . . . The new emphasis on individual rights, values, and achievements and the collectivist mentality proper to the traditional patriarchal society are in open contradiction, but for the time being both enjoy equal prestige and equally large audiences" (1993, 50). Still, although there may be no cohesive rhetoric that associates women with motherhood in Romania, nationalist discourses and national policies do draw ethnonational distinctions among women. Thus, as Enikö Magyari-Vincze illuminates in her chapter, Roma women are frequently written out of the new polity as the discourses and practices among policy makers reveal a particular gendered and ethnic vision of the nation. Gendered nationalisms are also variable in Central Asia, as Ayşe Güneş-Ayata and Ayça Ergun discuss in their chapter. By adopting arguments that the nation needed to break with the Soviet past and distinguish itself from the West, nationalists in Azerbaijan and Uzbekistan have sought to (re)construct a classic patriarchy in which women would return to their responsibilities in the home and define themselves as mothers and daughters. Yet this vision of the patriarchal nation has not been a central aspect of the politics of nation building in Kazakhstan and Kyrgyzstan. Thus, Güneş-Ayata and Ergun show how gendered nationalisms are very much a product of the particular historical legacies, sociodemographic realities, and political dynamics of individual states and societies.

Given the ambivalence about and different conceptions of women as participants in the nation and the state, it is not surprising that women's representation in formal politics appears, at first blush, to be quite varied: some countries have seen individual women emerge as political leaders—for example, Biljana Plavšić in Serbia, Yulia Tymoshenko in Ukraine, and Angela Merkel in Germany—while in many other countries, virtually no women can be found in the political elite. Nonetheless, the emergence of individual leaders across the array of regimes that have developed should not obscure the reality that in the arena of formal politics, women in post-Communist Eurasia have been frequently pushed out of the political sphere, raising questions about the gendered meaning of political representation. The "exit" from formal politics has had substantial implications for women's social and economic positions, raising questions about their rights as citizens of the new post-Communist states and about what kind of voice they will have in public discourse.

POLITICAL REPRESENTATION

The quota systems of the Communist era that reserved some legislative and administrative positions for women generally shifted in the post-Communist period to multiparty systems in which women's inclusion depended on party leaders and structures. In the name of democratization and pluralism, the number of women visible in parliamentary politics in the emerging democracies has dissipated substantially in many places. What Barbara Einhorn observes about Eastern and Central Europe is relevant for many of the post-Communist states of Eurasia: Women's political clout has been diminished by "[s]tructural factors such as the nature of the electoral system, the lack of quotas in most countries and political parties, the arbitrary and unpredictable influence of political party list gatekeepers on women's inclusion on electoral slates, women's lack of public profile or of the networks of influence that constitute political capital, and the unfavorable positioning of women on electoral lists" (2006, 52). A review of the electoral data bears out that there has indeed been a substantial decline in women's formal political representation. Nonetheless, it is prudent to be cautious in interpreting the meaning and significance of this decline. As we have already indicated, quota representation for women did not deliver real political power for women in any of the Communist countries because important decision making occurred at levels in which men overwhelmingly dominated (such as the Politburo in the Union of Soviet Socialist Republics [USSR]). Moreover, current levels of representation are often no lower than those found in Europe or North America. Still, the dramatic drop in women's formal participation in the post-Communist legislatures has accentuated men's monopoly of political power in a very visible way. It has also reinforced ideological assumptions and public perceptions about the "natural" propensity of men for political life.

In the Soviet Union of 1984, women comprised 31% of one of its two chambers in parliament and almost 35% of the other; in Czechoslovakia in 1986, women held slightly over 29% of parliamentary seats (Inter-Parliamentary Union 1987, 44, 110). A decade later, as quotas disappeared, women's share of the upper and lower houses of legislative bodies had fallen drastically: in Russia to 8% and in the Czech Republic to 10% (UNDP 1995, 60). Women tended to be better represented in lower chambers of the legislature and in local government. However, the more recent data reveal that even here women have not fared well in the post-Communist period. The extent of the decline in women's political representation has varied from country to country, but a pattern of loss remains almost everywhere. For example, in Russia, women elected to the State Duma fell from 10.2% in 1997 to 7.7% in 1999, rising only slightly in 2003 to 9.8% but increasing to 14% in the fifth State Duma (2007–2011). In Georgia, the percentage of women in the lower chamber hovered around 7% (6.9% in 1996 and 7.2% in 1999), also rising slightly to 9.4% in 2004. In the Czech Republic, the percentage of women in the lower chamber of parliament has been incrementally higher at 15% in 1996 and 1998 and 15.5% in 2006. But in Tajikistan, where the president reimposed some quotas, women's participation has increased substantially from 2.8% in 1995 to 15.7% in 2000 to 17.5% in 2005, where it remains (Inter-Parliamentary Union 2008).

Women are rarely represented at the ministerial and executive levels. In 1994, there were no women at these levels in Russia, the Czech Republic, or Georgia, and they comprised only 3% of government ministers in Tajikistan. Estonia was unusual among the post-Communist countries at this time, having 15% of its ministers who were women (UNDP 1995, 60–62). By 2005, Russia remained with no female ministers and Tajikistan with 3.1%. The Czech Republic and Georgia, however, had improved considerably to 11.1% and 22.2%, respectively (Inter-Parliamentary Union 2008). The presence of women in the government at all levels, though only one measure of women's political participation, suggests the continuing accuracy and applicability to all of Eurasia of Anastasia Posadskaya's early claim about Russia that "the democratization of society turned out to be a male project in which women are assigned the role of objects, not subjects of social reform" (1994, 165). Posadkaya's assertion about the early reform years in Russia is echoed in the chapters by Nadezda Shvedova and Amanda Sloat. Shvedova's findings for the more recent Russian political scene reveal that the lack of meaningful presence of women in government has stalled efforts at developing policies that will attend to women's rights and foster gender equality. Sloat's chapter stresses that women's political participation in government has been low even in the Eastern European states that have acceded to the EU, limiting the adoption of policies that would achieve the gender equity promoted by the EU.

CITIZENSHIP AND SOCIOECONOMIC RIGHTS

Most Communist states had instituted policies and benefits to encourage and support women's labor force participation, including maternity leave, child-care facilities, summer camps, family allowances, and medical and health care. In the immediate aftermath of the collapse of Communist regimes, states across Eurasia began to reduce support for those arenas of social policy critical to women's participation in the public sphere. They ended or sharply reduced family subsidies, while at the same time celebrating the importance of the family to the building of the nation. One Russian legislator from St. Petersburg, who was also a member of the Joint Committee on Women's Affairs and Protection of the Family, Mother and Child, bluntly said in relation to cutbacks in social services: "It is a pity, but in times of crisis we must sacrifice the women and children" (Racioppi and See 1997, 47). Of course, particular articulations of the retreat from social services have varied across Eurasia, but in general, structural adjustment policies promoted by international lenders and financial institutions have fostered privatization in the services that had been provided by the states. Thus, as Barbara Einhorn delineates in her chapter, the liberal individualist policies enacted in Eastern and Central Europe have delimited women's citizenship rights, deflecting social rights into the realm of civil society. In a distinctly different response, some Central Asian governments have tended to shift state responsibilities for social welfare to reconstituted community organizations that contain elements of community-based soviets and traditional neighborhood *mahallas* (small communities) (Kamp 2004). The chapter by Zulaikho Usmanova shows that in Tajikistan, the *mahallas* have become increasingly responsible for social control and welfare functions—from distributing aid to the needy to mediating domestic disputes. The structure of authority within the *mahallas* is often patriarchal, based on principles of gender and age. But Usmanova's work reminds us that although women are underrepresented on *mahalla* councils, they are nonetheless able to exercise some agency in life-cycle events and rituals.

Across Eurasia, many women have responded to the reality of reduced child-care benefits and social services by seeking part-time jobs or work in the informal sector so that they can manage the dual obligations of family and wage labor. In their respective chapters, Eleanora Fayzullaeva and Nadezda Shvedova point to the heavier burdens carried by women in Russia and Central Asia. They suggest that where social protection benefits are privatized and tied to formal employment, women in part-time or informal-sector jobs must rely increasingly on family members or individual strategies for subsistence. The erosion in state support, the privatization of many social services, and the frequent tying of benefits to employment have thereby posed serious public health challenges for men and women, though this, too, has varied over time and throughout the region. Not surprisingly, all of the countries have witnessed a decline in fertility, but population growth rates vary considerably, with the most precipitous decline seen in Tajikistan. Both Georgia and Russia experienced negative population growth in 2005.[2]

The gender politics of reproduction have been shaped not only by resources but also by the discourses of national leaders as they have interpreted the health challenges and advocated particular policy approaches. As we have already seen, during the early years of the transition, low or declining population and birth rates fueled pronatalist movements across a significant portion of Eurasia, as politicians argued that women must embrace motherhood for the good of the nation. And male politicians frequently represent the duties of women as coterminous with maternity and reproduction. Enikö Magyari-Vincze moves beyond this observation in her chapter to show how ethnonationalism underlies the discourses and practices of health care in Romania, making evident dominant views of which women are considered full citizens of the "nation" and which women are seen as marginal or nonmembers.

Abortion was the primary means for contraception in many Communist states, and access to abortion has continued to be important for women's reproductive control. But policies have shifted in some countries. In Albania and Romania, abortion was legalized in the early post-Communist period, whereas in Poland, the procedure was made illegal. In Germany, political discord over abortion policies threatened to stall unification, as reconciliation of liberal German Democratic Republic (GDR) laws and restrictive Federal Republic of Germany (FRG) policies seemed impossible; the resultant policies allowed abortion only in very limited circumstances (Einhorn 1993; Marx Ferree 1993). Data on the prevalence of contraceptive use again reveal great variability across Eurasia. United Nations (UN) data from 2005 document that modern contraceptive methods are employed by close to two-thirds of women in the Czech Republic (62.6% aged fifteen to forty-nine), a little over one-fourth of women (27.6%) in Tajikistan, and less than one-fifth of women (19.8%) in Georgia, the lowest in any of the former Soviet Republics (UNFPA 2008). Indeed, in Georgia, a survey by the Centers for Disease Control and Prevention (CDC) indicated that "fifty-two percent of women who have been pregnant in the past five years reported that their last pregnancy was mistimed or unwanted. The survey found that the induced abortion rate was 3.1 abortions per woman" (CDC 2005). Although such current data are not available for the Russia Federation, public reports and survey results from the mid-1990s indicate a high dependence on abortion, despite the fact that nearly three-quarters of couples reported employing modern contraception (CDC 1996). Thus, women across Eurasia face very different contexts as they seek a greater voice in their own reproductive lives, ranging from resource constraints on effective contraception to limited availability for abortion to strongly pronatalist discourses and politics. And in many cases, politicians and policy makers have framed the politics of reproduction in ethnic and nationalist terms. Enikö Magyari-Vincze's chapter illuminates how the intersection between women's rights to reproductive health care and ethnic/national minority rights has often been fraught; women from ethnic minorities such as the Roma do not have the same de facto rights or resources as the ethnic majority. Hence, any consideration of the gender politics of reproduction must take into account the intersectionality of gender, ethnicity/nationality, and social class.

From celebrations of the norms of liberal individualism to invocations of traditional family structures and values, beliefs that governments should keep their "hands off" the private arena of the family have proliferated across post-Communist Eurasia. Such attitudes have meant not only increasing reliance on women to absorb the social services and care-giving that the state was relinquishing, but in some cases it has also meant that issues like violence against women and abuse within families have been seen increasingly as private problems. Although reliable data on the extent of domestic violence across Eurasia are only now emerging, available studies indicate that women across the region face substantial exposure to physical and sexual abuse in intimate relations.[3] For example, in the Czech Republic, 38% of women respondents in a 2004 study reported that they had experienced physical or sexual abuse by a male partner, but only a quarter of those women sought help (Hoy 2007). Similarly, studies of physical and sexual abuse in Georgia indicate that a significant minority of women have experienced violence in the home; in one study, 55% of respondents asserted that such "family problems" should not be made public (UNDP Country Team in Georgia 2006, 6). The Asian Development Bank cites data reporting that 30% of women in Tajikistan had experienced domestic violence in 2004 and that the rates of sexual harassment in public places were even higher (2006, 38). In the Central Asian republics more generally, traditional cultural norms mitigate against reporting domestic violence to the police and encourage women to turn to the leaders in the *mahalla*, who promote reconciliation to hold together a family unit (Corcoran-Nantes 2005, 146–156). In many cases, women see themselves as responsible for handling problems of domestic violence, and lawyers and law enforcement officials are not well informed about women's rights protection. At the same time, across post-Communist Eurasia, women activists, nongovernmental organizations (NGOs), and international governmental organizations have mobilized to challenge the idea that such violence is a private affair. And acceptance of domestic violence as a private matter is shifting. For example, in the Czech Republic, a poll in 2001 indicated that 43% of respondents viewed domestic violence to be a private family affair, whereas in 2006 this number had declined to 28%. In response to pressure by women activists and women legislators, the Czech government in 2007 adopted measures endorsing and supporting police intervention into domestic abuse situations (Hoy 2007). The government of Georgia has also responded to national and international pressure by adopting a law in 2006 to provide legal and social protection to victims. Nevertheless, the belief that the family is somehow off limits to gender equality is evident in the resistance to such laws and in weak enforcement. According to Keti Makharashvili, the legislator who introduced the law in Georgia, "Thirty or forty percent of the comments we received were that this law is breaking up our families" (UNDP 2006, 8).

Finally, in Central Asia, some traditional practices, such as polygamy and bride kidnapping, that had been wiped out during the Soviet era (and that remain illegal) have begun to return in some areas. As the chapter by Eleanora Fayzullaeva indicates, these practices have been exacerbated by poverty, civil war, economic stress, and labor migration. But economic changes have also produced class realignments that have contributed to neotraditionalism. For example, some research indicates that postindependence efforts to legalize polygamy in Kyrgyzstan, Kazakhstan, and Uzbekistan have come from newly affluent men for whom having several wives is considered a measure of status (Corcoran-Nantes 2005, 150–151).

The Gendered Political Economy of Transition

The collapse of Communism and the movement from socialism occurred at and contributed to a specific moment in global economic history, a moment when the role for global financial institutions in economic trade and development (for example, the World Bank and International Monetary Fund [IMF]) was great; when global foreign direct investment (FDI) and securities markets were expanding; when regionalism was intensifying, particularly in Europe; and when labor migration was globalizing. The closed markets of Eastern Europe began to open up at a time when there were more economic opportunities but at the same time more vulnerability to the exigencies of the world market. While the transitions in the Eastern and Central European countries that eventually joined the EU were in many ways smoother than those of other states, global capitalism wrought inequality and economic insecurity across the region.

The transition from socialism entailed two major economic disruptions: marketization, the move from a planned economy to a market-driven economy; and privatization, the shift from state ownership to private ownership. Different regimes chose particular methods to marketize and privatize, with varying levels of success. In general, the states of Central and Eastern Europe adopted relatively quick marketization and privatization approaches and became market economies in the early 1990s, whereas it took Russia until 1996 and the Central Asian states much longer (Oatley 2004, 384). Some scholars insist that it is important to examine the differences within subregions to understand both the timing and the consequences of their privatization approaches. For example, the

GDR, Poland, and Russia pursued early "shock therapy" strategies, while Hungary and Uzbekistan took somewhat more measured paths, but with different results (Graham 2006, 2–3). Neil Robinson argues that Russia had little choice but to pursue shock therapy because "radical reform was the best way of accessing international resources. . . . The only source of . . . aid for Russia was the global economy" (2004, 23). Central Europe, on the other hand, could more easily rely on the EU for its infusion of resources.

As might be expected, the states of Central and Eastern Europe were generally more successful in reorienting to trade with the West than were their former Soviet counterparts, and they also enjoyed more FDI in their economies. From 1989 to 1999, Central and Eastern Europe and the Baltic states had total FDI inflows of $74 billion, whereas the total FDI inflow to the Commonwealth of Independent States (CIS) countries was $28.3 billion, of which almost $18 billion went to two countries: Kazakhstan and Russia. More important as a gauge of the impact of FDI, the per capita FDI inflows to Eastern Europe in 1999 were $135, as contrasted with $25 to the CIS. The only CIS country that approached Eastern Europe's level was Kazakhstan, at $106 (Bradshaw and Swain 2003, 62). Of course, by the middle of the 1990s most of the Eastern European countries had applied for membership in the EU. The historic expansion of the EU that occurred in 2004 was preceded by the intensification of economic linkages. In order to comply with the EU's Single Market Plan of 1992, the new states had to meet its goals of free movement of goods, services, capital, and people (Balaam and Veseth 2005, 253). By the turn of the century, it was clear that EU accession was having a major impact on economic developments in Eastern Europe: not only was its FDI booming in comparison with that of the CIS, but as Oatley points out, trade patterns also differed markedly, with the EU accession states uniformly targeting the vast majority of their exports to industrialized countries—an indicator of their international competitiveness—while no CIS country was doing so (2004, 389).

The percentage of exports to industrialized countries as a component of total exports varied from a low of 59% to a high of 94% among the Central and Eastern European countries, whereas in the former Soviet bloc the range was a mere 11% to 49% (Oatley 2004, 389). The upshot is that the economic reforms and openness to the global economy had widely differing effects throughout the former Communist world. The contrasts are vivid among the four countries we selected for illustration: in 1995, the Czech Republic received $2.56 billion in FDI (5% of its gross domestic product [GDP]); by 2000 that had increased to $4.99 billion, or 9% of its GDP. The three CIS countries had much lower FDI rates since the collapse of the USSR, though here there has been some variance as well. Russia has had substantial amounts of FDIs, but these remain a relatively small part of its entire GDP—for example, net inflows in 1995 were $2.06 billion (only 1% of its GDP); by 2005 FDI amounted to $15.2 billion (2% of its GDP). Georgia has increased its FDI from a more modest $6 million in 1995 (barely discernible as a percentage of GDP) to $450 million in 2005, and the proportion of such investment as part of its GDP has grown to 7%. And Tajikistan, like Russia, has had an increase in the amount of FDI from $10 million in 1995 to $54 million in 2005, but it remains a small portion of its GDP, moving from 1% to 2% over this period (World Bank 2008).

Despite this variability, no country escaped the transition unscathed, and each faced challenges in coping with the processes of marketization and privatization. Very generally, the initial years often witnessed an economic downturn. All but one country faced a significant drop in real GDP between 1990 and 1997. In Russia, for example, the GDP dropped as low as 57.9% of its former level by 1996; in Tajikistan, it was 32.7% by 1997; and in Georgia, it plunged to 36.5% in 1993 but recouped to about 50% in 1997. Even in the much more favorably placed Czech Republic, the GDP fell to just over 80% in 1993 (UNDP 1999, 14). The dramatic downturns of the 1990s have slowly begun to be reversed, but the reversals have been uneven, and differences persist across the region, as is evident in the four cases. Between 1995 and 2005, the GDP per capita PPP (purchasing power parity in constant 2000 international dollars) in the Czech Republic increased from $14,273 to $18,545. Russia reached its lowest GDP in 1999 at $6,236 but has improved steadily in the new century, rising to $11,974 in 2006. The situation in Georgia evokes less optimism. Its GDP is low, and although this, too, has improved from $1,998 in 2000 to $3,366 per capita in 2005, Georgia has not yet returned to its 1990 GDP rate of $4,606 per capita. Neither has Tajikistan, with the lowest GDP of these four cases: its GDP per capita, which was $2,470 in 1990, plunged to $808 in 2000. Growth across the last several years raised the GDP to $1,191 per capita in 2005, but this amount is still less than half the GDP per capita in the very early years of the transition (World Bank 2008). Average annual GDP growth rates between 1990 and 2005 make it clear that these countries have faced and continue to address very different economic challenges. The rate for the Czech Republic over this period was 1.9; for Georgia, it was 0.2; for Russia, it was a negative 0.1; and Tajikistan faced a negative 4.0 (UNDP 2007, 277–279).

Not surprisingly, the initial economic crises across the region had devastating effects on the population, and many of these effects have persisted. Indeed, in the early 1990s approximately 20% of the population of transitional economies were living in absolute poverty, and even today more than 60 million people live in poverty and 150 million are economically vulnerable (Asad et al. 2005, 2). Val Moghadam argues that "unemployment, a decline in real wages, and the breakdown of the socialist welfare systems led to the rapid impoverishment of what in some countries was a majority of the population, particularly that part of it living in rural areas and small towns" (2005, 23).[4] Over the last decade, the situation of most of the Central and Eastern European countries has differed dramatically from that of many of the CIS states. The Czech Republic, like most of the EU accession states, has seen a decline in the percentage of its populace living below $2 a day, from 2% in 1996 to negligible absolute poverty. Russia has faced significant poverty despite a substantial decline in those living under $2 a day, from 23% in 1996 to 12% in 2002. Tajikistan also has seen improvement in the reduction of poverty, from 23% living at $2 a day in 1996 to 12% in 2002. Georgia's poverty, on the other hand, has increased substantially, from 9% in 1996 to 25% in 2003 (World Bank 2008). It is important to stress the limits of such statistics for comparing across the region, as the figures for "absolute" poverty do not take into account the variable cost of living. Perhaps more important is the increasing stratification of income, and the literature on the economic aspects of the transition has documented dramatic increases in income inequality. But even in this arena, there are substantial differences across post-Communist Eurasia: according to Norman Graham, income inequality, as measured by the Gini index, is highest in Russia (with a score of 45.6) and lowest in Albania (with a score of 23), and in general the Central and Eastern European countries display less income inequality than the states of the former Soviet Union (2006, 18–19).

Given the differences in economic growth, productivity, and poverty across the region, it should not be surprising that women's experiences of economic changes have also varied according to country and region. But as we will suggest, there are also some powerful similarities. Women's economic activity relative to that of men has generally declined across Eurasia, suggesting that women are dropping out of the labor market. Figures from the United Nations Development Program (UNDP) indicate that in 2005, the economic activity rate for women between the ages of fifteen and fifty-four was 51.9% in the Czech Republic, 54.3% in Russia, 50.1% in Georgia, and 46.3% in Tajikistan. As important, women's labor force participation has declined significantly in all four countries since 1990: by 15% in the Czech Republic, 10% in Russia, 27% in Georgia, and 11% in Tajikistan. And the decline has been greater for women than for men in all four cases: in 2005 women's economic activity was 77% that of men in the Czech Republic, 80% in Russia, 66% in Georgia, and 74% in Tajikistan (UNDP 2007). Together, these data suggest that gender infuses every aspect of economic activity in post-Communist Eurasia, disproportionately moving women from remunerative economic activity and often back to the home and making them more reliant on state subsidies or family members for support. As the chapter by Ayşe Güneş-Ayata and Ayça Ergun clearly shows, the synergy between declines in state support for care-giving activities and traditionalist and nationalist calls for women to return to the home constricts women's labor market position.

For those women who do remain in the labor market, unemployment has been a challenge. Feminist scholars like Valentine Moghadam point to a feminization of unemployment in the first half of the 1990's. Drawing on International Labor Organization (ILO) data, she concluded that in "the mid-1990s, some 66.3 percent of the unemployed in eastern Germany were women; in Poland it was 54–58 percent, in Romania 60 percent, and in Russia 68 percent (down from a high of 72–80 in the early 1990s)" (Moghadam 2005, 23). However, by the mid-1990s the unemployment situation became more complex. In some countries, such as the Czech Republic, the disparity between women's and men's unemployment rate remained high: in 2003, for example, it was 9% for women compared to 6% for men (World Bank 2008). In contrast, in Georgia and Russia, the unemployment rate for men and women has been virtually the same since 2000.[5] Nonetheless, as Shvedova's chapter here documents for Russia and scholars have pointed out for Eastern Europe, women make up a disproportionate percentage of the long-term unemployed (Einhorn 2006, 152). Moreover, according to one World Bank report on gender discrimination in labor markets, even when women are formally employed, they "have less access to self-employment . . . [and] . . . higher chances of moving out of the labor force if they lose their formal job" (2005, 95).

As important, the gendered wage differentials that existed in every post-Communist country in the early 1990s continue to be problematic in more recent years (Moghadam 2005, 136). Women earn less than men across the entire Eurasian region. According to the 2008 Gender Empowerment Measure, the ratio of women's earned income to men's ranges from a high of 0.69 in Lithuania to a low of 0.33 in Georgia, this despite the fact that women make up more than half the professional and technical workforce in all countries in Central and Eastern Europe and the former Soviet Union for which data are available (UNDP 2007, 330–331).[6] There is no single explanation for these gendered wage differences. As Shvedova and others suggest for Russia, it can be attributed in part to the persistence of gendered occupational segregation in which women are located in jobs that tend to be paid less, regardless of training or skill level (Paci 2002, 28). Studies in the Czech Republic suggest that pay differences within particular establishments are more important in explaining wage gaps, even as gendered occupational segregation has increased since the end of the Communist regime (Valentova et al. 2007). And in Georgia and Russia, researchers have documented rampant employment discrimination against women (ABA/CEELI 2003, 44–45). Mihaly Simai found that women in late transition economies (that is, Russia and much of the CIS) are at risk for poverty. He observes that "single-parent households are much more likely to be poor compared to other types of families. More than 90 per cent of such households are headed by women" (Simai 2006, 12). Simai continues that women are among the "losers" in the transition. All of these observations are supported by the declining measures of gender equality across the region. For example, the Czech Republic's GDI ranking dropped from 15 in 1995 to 29 in 2008, while Russia's dropped from 29 to 59. Only one post-Communist country for which data were available (Lithuania) had an improved GDI ranking in these years (UNDP 1995, 76–77; 2007, 329). These findings point to the real consequences of patriarchy in its many forms: the assumption that women should be primarily responsible for the home and family undermines their equal participation in the market and in politics.

The opening of markets in post-Communist Eurasia had an additional human corollary as the boundaries between states became more porous and labor migration increased significantly. In response to internal conflicts but even more to the economic problems generated by the uneven impacts of marketization and privatization, men and women moved in large numbers. However, the kinds of movement that occurred varied among the post-Communist states. The Czech Republic, Hungary, and Slovenia, following the pattern of much of Western Europe, had a net population gain through immigration, whereas Romania and Poland lost population to emigration (Informal Network 2002, 57–76; Muenz 2006). Not surprisingly, much of the migration from the Central and Eastern European states that did occur went to Western Europe. For example, in 1999, 57.9% of the foreign workers in Austria came from four Balkan states (Bosnia Herzegovina, Croatia, Macedonia, and the Federal Republic of Yugoslavia); in Germany, 20.4% of all foreign workers came from the Balkans, Poland, and Russia; in Italy, 21.4% were from the Balkans, Romania, and Poland; and in Sweden, 17.5% came from the Balkans, Poland, and Russia (Informal Network 2002, 60).

In the former Soviet Union, Russia and Kazakhstan became net receivers of migrants. Most of the migrants to Kazakhstan have been seasonal laborers. Russia's situation, however, is more complex. Within the first year of the USSR's collapse, some 2 million people arrived in Russia, which has remained the largest destination country in the CIS and second only to the United States in the world (Ivakhnyuk 2006, 3). Most of the migrants come from Ukraine and Central Asia; many of these were ethnic Russians, reacting to nationalism and anti-Russian hostility in post-Soviet countries (Kosmarskaya 1999; Pilkington 1998). Although Russia is the largest recipient state in the region, it also sends more workers abroad than any other country: estimates range from 2 to 3 million annually (Ivakhnyuk 2006, 4). Estimates of emigrants from Georgia during the 1990s range from 300,000 to 1.5 million (vanSelm 2005). Current estimates for Tajikistan are that 600,000 Tajiks leave the country annually to find seasonal or temporary work. Aaron Erlich claims that "between 17 and 30 percent of the working-age population of any given Tajik district is a labor migrant in another country" (2006).[7]

As the chapter by Eleonora Fayzullaeva in this volume powerfully demonstrates, labor migration has had quite varying significance, given different types of emigration. Among emigrant streams have been highly qualified and younger workers who sought better opportunities and jobs; unskilled and low-skilled workers in agriculture, construction, and service work; and workers who commute for very temporary and day jobs across proximate borders. Fayzullaeva carefully explores the parameters and gender consequences of the substantial migrations involving Central Asia. The gendered dimensions of migration are evident across Eurasia. In Russia, men constitute the overwhelming number of emigrants (90% or higher in the late 1990s and 2000), but women are slowly entering the migrating workforce, increasing from 1.2 million to 5.8 million between 1996 and 2000 (Tiuriukanova 2005, 103). As Elena Tiuriukanova observes, "The feminization of migration is recognized by experts as a new stage characteristic of international labor migration. In large part this is related to structural changes in the world economy accompanying the globalization processes: relative reduction of the industrial sector . . . and the growth of the service sector. . . . The dominance of the service sector . . . resulted in a growing demand of developed nations for women-migrants for employment and unskilled jobs" (2005, 98). She points out that almost all Russian women migrants abroad seek work in the low-wage service sector. Further, recent data from the Russian Academy of Sciences reinforce this observation, as among poorly paid (under $500/month) migrants the proportion of women to men is 3:1, whereas among well-paid (over $1,000/month) migrants it is 1:3 (Tiuriukanova 2005, 100). While the Russian pattern of women seeking low-wage service sector jobs abroad applies as well to Georgia, the composition of the migrant pool is quite different in this case, with the overwhelming majority of migrants being men and just 37.4% of international migrants being women (IOM 2007a). In the Tajik case, according to the International Organization for

Migration (IOM), approximately 90% of all migrants head to Russia, often as irregular workers, and more than half the migrants are women (57.8%) whose irregular status makes them more vulnerable to work in illegitimate occupations such as prostitution (IOM 2007b).

Indeed, human trafficking, particularly sex trafficking of women, is one of the most blatantly gendered aspects of migration (van den Anker and Doomernik 2006). The chapters by Mary Buckley and Eleanora Fayzullaeva document that the collapse of Communism and its attendant social, economic, and legal dislocations permitted the rapid expansion of sex trafficking across the post-Communist successor states. As they note, getting a handle on the exact numbers of women trafficked is difficult, in part because this global problem is not always well policed. The U.S. government estimates that approximately 800,000 individuals are trafficked each year, and the overwhelming majority, 80%, are women who will work in the sex trade (Office to Monitor and Combat Trafficking in Persons 2007). These data do not include women trafficked within countries, only those trafficked across international boundaries. Prior to the 1990s, sex trafficking had been particularly associated with Asia and Latin America; however, according to the Coalition against Trafficking in Women (CATW), the former Soviet Union has now "matched or overtaken" both those areas as a main source for women, earning traffickers approximately $7 billion per annum (CATW 2008b). Citing a *Moscow Times* report, the CATW claims that "two-thirds of the 500,000 women trafficked for prostitution worldwide annually come from Eastern Europe" (2008a). While trafficking patterns vary across states of Eurasia, Mary Buckley's chapter shows that there are some commonalities: persistent poverty and lack of economic growth mean some women will be forced to emigrate for work, and organized crime is ready to step in to take advantage of this situation, entrapping women in global prostitution webs.

Thus, in the relatively affluent Czech Republic, some women are still trafficked into Western Europe, and the country itself has become a destination for individuals trafficked from other areas of Eastern Europe and the former Soviet Union. Dire economic circumstances elsewhere, however, prompt women to seek work overseas. That is certainly the case for Georgia, where, according to the Trade Environment Database (TED), "Women are often recruited by agencies offering work abroad as a waitress or in childcare, however once abroad women find themselves in the sex industry with little recourse due to the fact that traffickers take their passports" (Murtha 2003). This situation is also the case for Russian and Tajik women who migrate. Buckley's chapter cites data estimating that between 20,000 and 60,000 women are trafficked each year from the Russian

Federation, most lured by promises of employment in Western Europe and other areas. In the case of Tajikistan, an IOM report claimed that 1,000 women were trafficked in one year; once again, most of these were tricked into thinking they were taking legitimate jobs or accepting marriage proposals (IOM 2001). The organized crime rings that run many of the prostitution networks often control women by confiscating their passports and forcing them into debt bondage.

Sex trafficking may be the starkest reminder of the gender consequences of the dramatic economic changes in Eurasia, but as this section has tried to suggest, it is not the only example of how the transition has been gendered in ways that have disempowered women. The economic disruptions faced by the peoples of Eurasia have been extensive, and the attendant difficulties (for example, women's unemployment or underemployment, migration and displacement, trafficking) have called out for regulation at the level of the state and of the international system. Women have responded to these challenges by mobilizing at the grassroots level and by lobbying governments to generate and implement policies, and here, too, the impact of globalization is evident. Activists and policy makers committed to applying a gendered lens on the political and economic problems of the post-Communist regimes have relied on existing and emerging international norms of gender equality to help legitimize their claims.

The International Normative and Legal Environment for Gender Equality

The dissemination of principles of gender equality by the UN, regional bodies, NGOs, and nongovernmental networks has generated a normative framework for pressuring individual states and evaluating sex policies in relation to gender equity. Across Eurasia, the UN Convention on the Elimination of Discrimination against Women (CEDAW) has been the underpinning for these norms, as it provides general principles of gender equality and equal opportunity, as well as specifying the meaning of these principles in various domains. At the regional level in post-Communist Central and Eastern Europe, the EU legal framework of common obligations and responsibilities of member states (the *acquis communautaire*) has been especially important in setting the context for gendered political claims.

CEDAW was promulgated in 1979 and entered into force in 1981. CEDAW defines discrimination against women as "any distinction, exclusion or restriction made on the basis of states which has the effect or purpose of impairing . . . the exercise by women, irrespective of their marital status, on a basis of equality of men and women, of human rights and fundamental freedoms in the political, economic, social, cultural, civil or any other field" (CEDAW n.d.). CEDAW has made three intertwined contributions to the normative globalization of women's rights. First, in its emphasis on the fundamental rights and freedoms of women, it obligates signatory states both to eliminate discriminatory laws and to institutionalize administrative mechanisms by which the state would remedy violations of women's rights in the private and public spheres. Second, it emphasizes the interplay between women's rights to reproductive autonomy and their rights in other spheres, thereby underscoring the connection between rights in the family and participation in public life. Third, CEDAW stresses the interrelatedness of culture and women's rights, explicitly arguing that cultural traditions should not be invoked to justify customary practices and prejudices that reinforce gender superiority or inferiority. Hence, countries that have signed the Convention agree to commit themselves to adopt and implement measures to ensure that women have equal opportunities in political and economic life, education, employment, health, and reproductive rights and to reject cultural claims that would legitimate women's inequality as a component of national identity. By November 2006, 185 states—over 90% of the members of the UN— had ratified the treaty, including all of the post-Communist states. CEDAW is, thus, a crucial document affirming the international norm of gender equality and establishing an international bill of rights for women. It also provides an important basis for institutionalizing those rights, often through the development of national machineries to advance women's status.

The chapter by Ayşe Güneş-Ayata and Ayça Ergun demonstrates that the national machineries for ensuring nondiscrimination and for implementing women's rights have become important spaces where women's NGOs can exercise pressure. Moreover, every four years the signatories must submit national reports that document their compliance with the thirty provisions of the Convention. The reports provide a way of assessing the implementation of these rights in each of the countries that is a party to the Convention and a basis for pressure for NGOs and activists. These reports are reviewed and responded to by the Committee for the Elimination of Discrimination against Women. As our descriptions earlier in this chapter suggest, however, states across post-Communist Eurasia have not evenly conformed to CEDAW norms. In August 2006, for example, the third report by Georgia was reviewed and critiqued for the absence of a permanent national machinery to monitor discrimination and specify measures to provide equal opportunity. Georgia was faulted for the limited training of lawyers and judges on gender equality law; the absence of statistical data on the gender impact of economic restructuring, including data on women's employment in public, private, formal, and informal sectors; the lack of statistics on domestic violence and other violence against women; and the failure of the state to "address the root causes of trafficking by increasing its efforts to improve the economic situation of women" (CEDAW 2007c).

Similarly, the committee recently completed a review of Tajikistan's combined first, second, and third reports. The UN expressed concern about the insufficient national machinery for the advancement of women and the absence of remedies for violation of antidiscrimination laws. It encouraged the state to adopt measures that would address the "resurgence of patriarchal attitudes subordinating women and of strong stereotypes regarding their roles [as] . . . a root cause of . . . the continuing existence of polygamy, domestic violence and the high dropout rates of girls from schools" (CEDAW 2007a). In the case of the Czech Republic, the committee recognized the advances in women's rights made as a consequence of the EU accession process and in working toward the goals of the Convention; however, it also noted the need for better implementation, monitoring, and enforcement of antidiscrimination laws and policies (CEDAW 2007b). The most recent committee review of the Russian Federation's report was in 2002 and was based on data submitted in 1999. The committee lamented the underdevelopment of legal measures and national machinery to address issues of sex discrimination; the underrepresentation of women in public life; violence against women; the deteriorating situation of women in employment, politics, health care, and family planning; and the escalation in prostitution and human trafficking. CEDAW has provided a normative basis on which women's rights can be asserted and government compliance monitored; however, the impact of CEDAW has been variable.

For the ten former Communist states that sought to enter the EU (Bulgaria, Czech Republic, Estonia, Hungary, Latvia, Lithuania, Poland, Romania, Slovakia, Slovenia), the *acquis communautaire* established an additional normative context for gender politics. Each had to accept the *acquis* and show that its government had the capacity to implement EU norms in relation to gender equality. The EU explicitly stipulated that the promotion of democracy "requires the participation of all citizens, women and men alike, to participate and be represented equally in the economy, in decision-making, and in social and political life. . . . The promotion of gender equality is an important element of the EU's external relations and of its development cooperation policies and, in particular, the promotion and protection of women's rights is an integral part of the EU's human rights policies in third countries" (European Commission 2000).

The *acquis* includes primary laws that obligate countries to promote equality between men and women, to combat sex discrimination, to support equal labor market opportunities, and to ensure equal pay for equal work. It also includes secondary laws that incorporate equal opportunity directives in the areas of pay, treatment in the workplace, social security schemes, and maternity and parental leaves (European Women's Lobby 2005). The *acquis* is not as strong in its normative language as CEDAW, but it does provide an additional set of political and institutional resources for pressing gender equality. In her chapter on Romanian policy practices and their implications for Romani women, Enikö Magyari-Vincze points out the role played by EU standards in efforts to secure women's reproductive health rights. Similarly, Amanda Sloat reveals the effects of the *acquis* on maternity leave policies and sex discrimination laws in the accession states. And Barbara Einhorn underscores the mixed and complex impact of EU accession on gender equity. All three authors demonstrate that the EU's legal/normative framework has been influential but insufficient in fostering gender equity.

Additional international legal and normative regimes exist that are especially relevant to gender politics. Among the most significant for the former Communist countries is the Convention for the Suppression of the Traffic in Persons and of the Exploitation of the Prostitution of Others (1951), the more recent Protocol to Prevent, Suppress and Punish Trafficking in Persons (2003), and the UN Declaration on the Elimination of Violence against Women (1993). The first two instruments specifically identify trafficking for purposes of sexual exploitation as illegal and commit the signatories to protect victims and to adopt measures that require law enforcement agencies to cooperate in detecting and punishing traffickers. The third instrument resulted in the appointment of a special UN Commission on Human Rights rapporteur, Radhika Coomaraswamy, who was responsible to investigate "violence against women and report to the Commission with proposals for addressing the issue, [and to provide] . . . a framework for monitoring progress on the Declaration" (Antrobus 2004, 93). But these are not the only mechanisms in place to combat trafficking. As Mary Buckley's chapter aptly demonstrates, the sharing of information and linkages between antitrafficking institutions are critically important: the U.S. State Department's Trafficking in Persons initiative, the Organization on Security and Cooperation in Europe (OSCE), the UN Office on Drugs and Crime (UNODC), and the UN Interregional Crime and Justice Research Institute (UNICRI) have all been crucial to developing and coordinating an international antitrafficking strategy.

UN Conferences and Women's Mobilization

Since the collapse of the Communist regimes in Eurasia, women throughout the region have contributed to and benefited from the globalization of women's activism, as international women's networks and transnational women's organizing have increased in scope and variety. The transitions occurred in the context of a developing global women's movement that has had some impact on gender politics in the region.

The UN institutions and initiatives contributed greatly to this development. Moving from its early phases of seeking to secure women's legal equality through the development of international instruments to recognize and protect women's political rights (1952 Convention on the Political Rights of Women) to its efforts in the 1970s to address women's economic and social position (evident in CEDAW and the International Women's Year in 1975), the UN has given legitimacy to efforts to address women's rights in a global context. As important, its conferences related to the International Women's Decade (1975–1985) and the subsequent Beijing Conference in 1995 were instrumental in establishing a base for women's networking and the development of understandings and perspectives on local, regional, and global dimensions of gender politics. The political and ideological conflicts among women's groups within the early conferences (Mexico City, Copenhagen) over different perspectives about feminism helped to inform women about the need to bridge the multiple and overlapping hegemonies shaping women's positions and perspectives. They also inspired the development of networks of women to address the gendered impact of globalization: from Development Alternatives with Women for a New Era (DAWN) to Women's Environment and Development Organization (WEDO). The NGO forums, especially at the UN conferences in Nairobi and Beijing, which drew in large numbers of women's organizations, further fostered transnational networks for identifying issues, and building bases for support and mobilization. At the Beijing Conference in 1995, more than 1,700 NGOs were present, but only 46 of these came from post-Communist states (UNDPCSD n.d.). Women's caucuses were formed within the major UN conferences of the 1990s, ensuring that all summits would have gendered analyses and providing women the opportunity to further frame economic, environmental, and population issues in terms of women's concerns and to foster women's global networking.

World conferences were preceded by local, national, and regional meetings that brought women together and illuminated critical differences but also generated "reciprocal recognition . . . of the validity of various claims" (Bunch 2001, 29). The UN Conference on Human Rights in Vienna in 1993 was a great example of this. The run-up to the conference included a campaign to get the UN to recognize women's rights as human rights, a series of leadership institutes to bring together human rights activists and specialists to link their local work to global organizing, efforts to coordinate actions and strategies on women's rights so that these would be placed at the center of the meetings in Vienna, and the development of the Global Tribunal on Violations of Women's Human Rights at the conference, which drew together organizations and networks from around the world. Representatives from more than 1,500 NGOs attended the Vienna conference (Nowak 1994, 6–7). As Peggy Antrobus notes, "an outcome of the experience leading up to the conference and at the Forum and conference itself was the strengthening of work on women's human rights networks in all regions. The assertion that 'women's rights are human rights' and the expansion of the rights framework to incorporate explicitly sexual and reproductive rights, along with economic and social rights, provided a solid base for further advocacy by the emerging global women's movement" (2004, 93–94).

Hence the conferences, the NGO forums, and the campaigns related to these conferences have provided a basis for the development of global networks and the "possibility of organizing that builds on the specificity that women have developed around particular identities and takes account of diversity but also creates a broader political analysis from that place" (Bunch 2001, 135). UN institutions also contributed to this globalization of women's activism. UN institutions such as the International Research and Training Institute for the Advancement of Women (INSTRAW) and the United Nations Development Fund for Women (UNIFEM) helped to lay a research basis for the development of international norms. They also became a basis for establishing international and multinational standards that are particularly helpful under the forces of globalization. Framing women's rights as universal rights, argues Charlotte Bunch, "challenges the contention that the human rights of women (or any group) can be limited by religious or culturally specific definitions of their role" (2001, 140).

Civil Society, International Nongovernmental Organizations, and the Gender Politics of Transition

If gender politics in Eurasia have been affected by emerging norms of gender equality and by the many initiatives and conferences and treaties on women's issues sponsored by the UN and other international institutions, they have also been influenced by the activities of national and international nongovernmental organizations (international NGOs) with interest in women's status and issues. CEDAW, the UN Conference on Human Rights in Vienna in 1993, and the Beijing Conference in 1995 all facilitated the forging of global feminist alliances. Such transnational organizing has historically been the hallmark of women's movements, and Timur Kocaoglu reminds us in his chapter that activist reformers in Central Asia in the early twentieth century had strong links transnationally and a sense of women's rights that were international in scope; but they defined their goals and strategies in ways that were understanding and respectful of local cultures. In the contemporary context, the need to understand women's perspectives in their local contexts has increased, as international NGOs and actors have had to recognize the complexity of gender politics in post-Communist Eurasia.

Early in the transition, across the formerly Communist world, women's groups arose to try to address the deteriorating position of women and their families and to provide some of the social services left vacant by the state. With the collapse of the Communist-led regimes, established women's groups as well as new groups in the transitional states were able to build from existing international ties and develop relationships with a wide range of activists. For example, in Russia, the Union of Women of Russia, the official women's organization of the former USSR, continued to pursue contacts with women's groups from around the world. And new and more overtly feminist women's associations, like the Gender Studies Center of the Academy of Sciences and the Women's League, extended the reach of women's activism, provided wide-ranging critiques of women's situation, and developed their own linkages with transnational women's groups (Racioppi and See 1997; Sperling 1999). Similarly, in Kyrgyzstan, the Forum of Women's Non-Governmental Organizations was established in 1994 in the run-up to the Beijing Conference to coordinate women's activism. Building from a small number of groups, it includes more than eighty organizations and has increased its activism both nationally and internationally, becoming a central part of the Asian Pacific Forum on Women, Law and Development (APWLD) and also part of the Minnesota Advocates for Human Rights Project to stop violence against women. It has secured resources from the Soros Foundation to support its efforts to develop organizational capacity and promote gender equality. Thus, national NGOs have sought to use international and transnational networks to legitimate the political agendas of local women's organizations, to provide leverage in pressuring government officials, and to extend their resources.

The networking possibilities afforded by linkages with international and transnational women's organizations have thus been significant. In the area of trafficking, for example, women's organizations came together in 1995 to found La Strada International—a trilateral initiative of feminists that has developed into a Europe-wide network of antitrafficking organizations. It works with "national and international organisations, national governments, European institutions and UN bodies" (La Strada International n.d.). La Strada activists in Prague work with women trafficked from Bulgaria and Romania and collaborate with the La Strada sister organizations throughout Europe; they also lobby for legal reform and consult with Czech police to improve prevention of trafficking (La Strada 2003).

Another influential example is the Network of East-West Women (NEWW). NEWW was established in Dubrovnik in 1991 as an "international communication and resource network supporting dialogue, informational exchange and activism among those concerned about women's situation in Central and Eastern Europe and the former Soviet Union" (NEWW). It went online in 1994, and has provided an important opportunity to link women's organizations and activists from around Eurasia with their counterparts in the United States and Western Europe. Originally headquartered in Washington, D.C., NEWW continues to operate today, offering programs, networking services, and organizing conferences, out of its relocated headquarters in Poland. If NEWW was the most prominent of the major networking organizations, it was not the only one to take advantage of the networking possibilities afforded by the Internet: Open Women Line (OWL) is a Russian-language information portal for news about women's activism and their position in society.

A very different kind of transnational activism was promoted by the American Bar Association, whose Rule of Law Initiative, a public service project, established a Central Europe and Eurasian focus, one component of which took up issues of women's rights. The Central European and Eurasian Law Initiative has developed a CEDAW assessment tool "to uncover the legal obstacles that frustrate the achievement of greater gender equality . . . and provide capacity-building . . . for local nongovernmental organizations" (ABA/CEELI n.d.). Based on scholarly research and interviews with experts, their reports are widely disseminated and help to legitimate activists' concern with gender equity. The interactions between the new women's groups and relatively resource-rich and often well-established, well-connected Western-based organizations have helped support women's mobilization in Eurasia. However, as networked groups have struggled to find a common language and interests on which to cooperate, it is probably inevitable that the direction of influence would be lopsided.

Relatively resource-rich Western organizations such as the Soros, MacArthur, Mott, Ford, and Winrock foundations have been active in promoting civil society. Of course, these donors were not just interested in women's activism and position during the transition: they have funded a wide range of economic, political, and social initiatives intended to ease the transition for ordinary citizens of countries in Eurasia and facilitate projects on the ground. Writing about post-Communist Armenia, Armine Ishkanian argues that such funders "were motivated to fund NGOs, because they were perceived as panaceas for the political cynicism, apathy, disaffection, and overcentralization that marked post-Soviet societies. Of course, NGOs also counted as the fundamental signs of democratization" (2004, 264). Indeed, funders and many Western governments see a strong civil society, with a rich culture of NGOs, as crucial for a successful transition from Communism (Henderson 2003; Ishkanian 2004). Not all funders have operated the same way, but the largest international NGOs frequently have had a physical presence in the former Communist states. For example, Soros's Open Society Institute has maintained its central organization in New York but also established national Soros foundations whose "priorities and specific activities are determined by a local board of directors and staff in consultation with George Soros and OSI boards and advisers" (Soros Foundation 2008).[8] The Ford Foundation set up an office for Eastern Europe, now in Sofia, and one for Russia in Moscow.[9] The existence of in-country donor offices ostensibly has enabled Western international NGOs to assess the needs of the country and to work with local activists to identify and support worthy projects; however, it also has enhanced the already hefty influence of donors with big pocketbooks. Studies by Henderson (2003), Hemment (2004), and Rivkin-Fish (2004) indicate that the lure of substantial resources as well as the visibility afforded by connection to the foreign international NGOs could induce local NGOs to craft initiatives that they know would be attractive to the donor.

The effects of international funding have not been sufficiently examined to make definitive conclusions, but some observations can be made. Many of the large international NGOS identified above did have specific programs to target women in civil society and were keen to work with emerging and established grassroots women's groups. Women's NGOs across Eurasia no doubt would have had a far more difficult time surviving the transition and accomplishing their goals without the resources and visibility brought by the international NGOs. On the other hand, women's organizations have had to work within the constraints imposed by their funders. It would be going too far to generalize that local women's organizations changed their agendas to fit donor interests, but it has not been uncommon to contour projects to take into account the funding priorities and organizational-operational styles of Western funders. One clear result of this process is that large, established NGOs, especially those with English-speaking and foreign-trained staffs who were familiar with the grant-writing process, have had an advantage over smaller, less internationally experienced groups (Henderson 2003). Further, groups that could couch their projects in terms of their contribution to the broader goals of democratization have also found favor with donors. But particularly in more authoritarian states, ties with international NGOs could be problematic, as governments that were already concerned about domestic civil society actors were even more troubled by both the image and the reality of external actors meddling in politics and society.

In a civil society environment of resource constraints, the ability to secure support from international organizations and international NGOs could mean the difference between the success or failure not only of specific projects or local NGOs but of the more general drive for gender equality. At the same time, organizers had to be chary about cultivating international linkages that would either control the trajectory of women's mobilization, thus replacing Communist directives with donor demands, or raise the ire of an authoritarian state, thus jeopardizing women's ability to press their interests. As several of the chapters in this volume demonstrate, the growth of civil society and especially of women's organizing in post-Communist societies evidences that women were not simply victims or subjects of tumultuous transitions; they were important agents crafting responses to the many challenges presented by the social and economic upheavals and resisting as well as maintaining ideologies about women's proper place in postsocialist states. In many countries, international organizations (IOs) and international NGOs played a part in this process, and linkages with them facilitated the development of transnational networks that included women from the post-Communist transition states as important voices in the global women's movement.

Transitional Sites, Transnational Politics

The chapters that follow illustrate both the great range and the shared features of women's experiences in the post-Communist transition throughout Eurasia. They also reveal, explicitly or implicitly, how historical legacies, contemporary "domestic" politics and economics, and transnational forces interact to produce distinctive contexts for women's responses and mobilization across the region. The volume is divided into two sections, one that examines the gender politics of transitions in Eastern and Central Europe and a second that focuses on Russia, Central Asia, and the Caucasus. On the one hand, the division is too facile: just as local, national, and international/transnational gender politics are not easily segmented, a shared Communist past and interactions across regions belie regional integrity. On the other hand, proximity to Western Europe and particularly the potential for EU accession has had important consequences for Central and Eastern Europe that differentiate the experiences of many of the countries of this region from those of the former Soviet Union. Together, these sections capture the particularities of specific countries and regions at the same time that they illuminate the interplay between the local and the global in gender politics.

Barbara Einhorn's chapter, "Democratization, Nationalism, and Citizenship: The Challenge of Gender," addresses the problems of democratization and nation building for women in the EU accession states of Central and Eastern Europe in the face of global economic liberalization and the enduring role of the neoliberal paradigm in the transformation process. Einhorn reveals how gendered citizenship is being reconstructed in a context in which liberal democracy and nationalism compete. She argues that liberal individualism rejects social entitlement and rights, with dire consequences for women as "the primacy of the market ... tend[s] to overshadow the political subject." Nationalism counters liberal democracy's individualism, but its collective vision of the nation as a family, replete with a gendered hierarchy of roles, also leaves women as secondary citizens. And given the influence of neoliberalism, the role of NGOs has been problematic, both filling a gap between the state and society and trapping women in an arena that is often politically discounted. Thus, Einhorn concludes that transitions to liberal democracy have been fraught with gendered problems in defining the post-Communist citizen.

Amanda Sloat also examines the EU accession states in "The Influence of European Union Legislation on Gender Equality in Central and Eastern Europe." Sloat looks carefully at the legacy of women's rights under Communism and implications for women's political consciousness, arguing that the wide array of entitlements disguised women's secondary status. With the collapse of Communism, these entitlements eroded; however, accession to the EU promised an enhanced standard of living and democratic rights for citizens in many countries of Eastern and Central Europe. The accession process required states to meet principles of economic liberalization but did not necessarily maintain the entitlements that women had under Communism. Sloat closely examines EU policies on maternity leave and sex discrimination and their implementation in the accession states to determine whether they have advanced women's rights. She concludes that their impact has been mixed: even as a political norm across the accession states, gender equality has not yet been realized. Further, until attitudes associating women mainly with the private sphere are changed, legislation alone will be insufficient to advance women's equality.

In her chapter, "Public Policies as Vehicles of Social Exclusion: The Case of Romani Women's Access to Reproductive Health in Romania," Enikö Magyari-Vincze undertakes a political anthropology. She documents the extensive policy changes in post-Communist Romania in the sphere of reproductive health, including the liberalization of abortion, the development of family planning networks, and the availability of contraception. However, in a context of pervasive ethnocentrism and discrimination, the Roma minority have been wary of the new policies, often viewing them as attempts at population control. Magyari-Vincze places the ethnogender politics of reproduction within the Decade for Ethnic Roma Inclusion, a Europe-wide initiative, supported by the World Bank and Open Society Institute, to advance Roma rights. Drawing on her fieldwork, she describes health care providers' attitudes and practices toward Roma women and Roma women's attitudes about reproductive health. In emphasizing how ethnicity is gendered and gender is ethnicized, Magyari-Vincze reminds us of the complex intersections among social identities in realizing women's rights and of the many ways in which ethnonationalist views can be gendered.

The next two chapters take up the case of post-Communist Russia. "Human Trafficking in the Twenty-first Century: Implications for Russia, Europe, and the World," by Mary Buckley, begins with an examination of rising international interest in the problem of human trafficking, particularly sex trafficking. After delineating the scope of global trafficking, Buckley provides an in-depth analysis of trafficking to and from Russia. Using select individual narratives, she discusses how individuals get drawn into trafficking. She describes the process by which sex trafficking was framed as a policy problem in Russia, acknowledging the key roles played by the United States and by transnational and national NGO activists. She explores state-level responses, most particularly Russia's legislative and policy actions but also those of other European states, and international responses and efforts at cooperation, such as those by the UN, NATO, and the OSCE. Buckley's analysis reveals the necessity of coordination between states and international NGOs as well as the obstacles to success in combating trafficking.

In "Gender Politics in Russia," Nadezda Shvedova uses the Millennium Declaration to frame her analysis of women's empowerment in post-Communist Russia, suggesting the importance of international norms and frameworks for securing gender equality. She emphasizes that Russia is different from other developing countries, given its high levels of industrialization and female employment and education. She then explores the extent of and reasons for women's unequal representation in politics, in the economy, and in society at large, and she builds a case for the full implementation of the proposed Gender Strategy for Russia. Such a strategy is necessary because women's continuing inequality in Russia is rooted in gender stereotypes that limit women's political voice, reproduce their secondary position in the market, and create a political environment in which women's contributions are discounted.

"The Past as Prologue? Challenging the Myth of the Subordinated, Docile Woman in Muslim Central Eurasia," turns to Central Asia, where Timur Kocaoglu provides a historical vantage point for the contemporary transition by examining another critical political transition, the one to Soviet rule. Countering the Soviet-cultivated myth of the subordinated Muslim Central Asian woman found in both academic writing and literature, Kocaoglu shows that indigenous reformist movements for women's rights predated the Soviet era and thus provide a model for contemporary gender politics. This chapter also contributes a valuable emphasis on the crucial role that intellectuals and novelists played in imagining the gendered state and representing gender identities and relations both before and during Soviet rule.

The subsequent chapter by Ayşe Güneş-Ayata and Ayça Ergun, "Gender Politics in Transitional Societies: A Comparative Perspective on Azerbaijan, Kazakhstan, Kyrgyzstan, and Uzbekistan," undertakes a comparative analysis of transitions in the Caucasus and Central Asia. The authors argue that despite a shared Soviet past, there are important differences in gendered nation building that have to do with the individual histories, economic development, and current demographic realities of these four states. In particular, they argue that Azerbaijan and Uzbekistan have reinstated classic patriarchies in which gender is a core component of national identity, while in Kazakhstan and Kyrgyzstan, where there are sizable minorities, patriarchy is less prominent, and gender identity is more associated with ethnicity than nationality. Their chapter concretely describes the situation for women and analyzes the gender dimensions of the nation-building process in each of the four cases and examines the interplay between civil society and the international community in shaping state policies.

"Labor Migration in Central Asia: Gender Challenges" is the topic of the next chapter. Here, Eleanora Fayzullaeva explicates how the transition from Communism precipitated waves of migration throughout the former Communist countries, as peoples responded to the exigencies of economic collapse and reconstruction and to more porous borders between East and West. Such migration has shaped social relations at the local level, as families and communities cope with human in- and out-flows, and has generated particular burdens for women in Central Asia. Fayzullaeva explains how women and men in Kazakhstan, Kyrgyzstan, Tajikistan, and especially Uzbekistan have adapted to the transition in the context of a globalizing economy and resulting opportunities for international migration. She emphasizes the complexity of the gendered impact of migration, both providing women with opportunities for empowerment and reinscribing male dominance.

In the concluding chapter, "The Complexity and Multiplicity of Gender Identities in Central Asia: The Case of Tajikistan," Zulaikho Usmanova probes the multilayered and intersecting cultural and gender identities evident in contemporary Tajikistan. Drawing on ethnographic fieldwork and bibliographic research, Usmanova documents the myriad challenges that Tajik women have faced, from civil war and economic turmoil to the resurgence of Islam and traditionalism. She explains that while traditionalism has revived and attempts have been made to push women into traditional roles within the home, the transition has also witnessed social changes that have increased women's visibility in the public sphere, particularly in urban areas. She looks especially to the roles that women play in the *mahallas* as evidence of their continuing agency in the face of change. This chapter reminds us of the many domains of women's activism and of the importance of understanding the ways in which women reinforce and reinstantiate gendered traditions in the face of change. This, too, is a crucial part of the politics of transition.

Together, these chapters illuminate the continuing centrality of gender to every dimension of the post-Communist transitions: from political representation and rights of citizens to invocations of national identity, from privatization and economic opportunity to social equality. They document that the legacy of the Communist past has interacted with efforts to construct a post-Communist future across Eurasia. These efforts—whether liberal individualist, nationalist, or "traditionalist"—have sought to define new regimes and societies against the

Communist past in ways that have frequently constrained public commitments to women's socioeconomic rights and political voice. However, the chapters also delineate that the prospects for gender equality vary across countries, shaped not only by their distinctive histories and by local politics, economics, and demographics but also by their relationship to regional and international structures and processes. Global and regional norms and institutions such as the EU's equality agenda, CEDAW, and the Global Program against Trafficking in Human Beings (GPAT) have provided resources for women to mobilize and address issues of gender equality in their local contexts and transnationally. Thus, the volume provides clear evidence that the synergy between the international and the local will be at the heart of gender politics in Eurasia for the foreseeable future.

NOTES

1. See, for example, Bridger et al. 1996; Buckley 1992, 1998; Einhorn 1993; Fong 1993; Funk and Mueller 1993; Gal and Kligman 2000a, 2000b; Jacquette and Wolchik 1998; Johnson and Robinson 2007; Marsh 1996; Moghadam 1993; Posadskaya 1994; Racioppi and See 1997; Rai et al. 1992; Rueschemeyer 1998; Rule and Noonan 1996; Sperling 1999; Tokhtakhodjaeva and Turgumbekova 1996; Verdery 1996. More recent works that also cover the early years include Fodor 2003; Haney 2002; Harris 2004; Hemment 2007; Kuehnast and Nechemias 2004; Lukic et al. 2006; and True 2003.

2. In the Czech Republic, the population growth rate fell from 0 to -0.1 while the fertility rate decreased from 1.92 to 1.16 children per woman aged fifteen to forty-nine. In Georgia, population growth decline was more precipitous, from 0.6 to −0.9, and its fertility rate fell from 2.26 to 1.4. Russia experienced an equally dramatic decline from a population rate of 0.7 to a negative rate of −0.06 and a fertility decline from 2.13 to 1.14. Tajikistan was among the most significant of these, with a decline in population from 3.0 to 0.9 and in fertility from 5.41 to 3.06. It should be evident that these different shifts have distinct origins and pose equally distinct problems for social policy.

3. The UN Secretary-General's Study of Violence against Women relied on available studies done at the country level between 1993 and 2005. For post-Communist Eurasia, the findings on women ever having experienced intimate violence ranged from 5% in Georgia (based on a 1999 study) to 36% in Tajikistan. But there is a shortage of reliable methods of data collection, reportage, and statistical record keeping (United Nations Secretary-General 2006b; also see UNIFEM n.d.).

4. Numerous analysts point out the difficulties with comparing data in the post-Communist regions, as the point at which the transitions began varies from country

to country; as data are not available for all countries, particularly in light of the new state boundaries; and as national statistical offices have not collected the same data across the region or used the same measures. This is particularly problematic with social indicators.

5. No World Bank data are available on unemployment rates for Tajikistan.

6. With the exceptions of Kazakhstan and Kyrgyzstan, the Human Development Report contained no data on the gender ratio of professional workers in the former Central Asian Republics.

7. In addition to emigrants, both Georgia and Tajikistan experienced dramatic population shifts as a consequence of their civil wars. Georgia faced some 242,000 Internally Displaced Persons due to the conflicts in Abkhazia and South Ossetia, while Tajikistan's war produced between 500,000 and 600,000 Internally Displaced Persons as well as tens of thousands of minority ethnic refugees. See vanSelm 2005 and Erlich 2006.

8. Soros has foundation offices, known as Open Society Institute Foundations, in Albania, Armenia, Azerbaijan, Bosnia and Herzegovina, Bulgaria, Czech Republic, Estonia, Georgia, Hungary, Kazakhstan, Kosovo, Kyrgyzstan, Latvia, Lithuania, Macedonia, Moldova, Mongolia, Montenegro, Poland, Romania, Serbia, Slovakia, Tajikistan, Ukraine, and Uzbekistan (suspended) (http://www.soros.org/about/foundations).

9. The Moscow office alone has provided some $70 million in grants since its creation in 1996 (Ford Foundation 2008).

WORKS CITED

ABA/CEELI (American Bar Association and Central European and Eurasian Law Initiative). N.d. *CEDAW Assessment Tool.* Washington, D.C.: American Bar Association and Central European and Eurasian Law Initiative.

———. 2003. *CEDAW Assessment Tool Report: Georgia.* October. Washington, D.C.: ABA/CEELI. Http://www.abanet.org/rol/publications/georgia-cedaw-2003-eng.pdf.

———. 2006. *CEDAW Assessment Tool Report: The Russian Federation.* Trans. Olga Vovk. February. Moscow: ABA/CEELI. Http://www.abanet.org/rol/publications/russia-cedaw-eng.pdf.

Albanese, Patrizia. 2006. *Mothers of the Nation: Women, Families and Nationalism in Twentieth-Century Europe.* Toronto: University of Toronto Press.

Antrobus, Peggy. 2004. *The Global Women's Movement: Origins, Issues and Strategies.* London: Zed Books.

Asad, Alam, Erwin Tongson, Martha Murthi, and Ruslan Yemtsov. 2005. *Growth, Poverty and Inequality in Eastern Europe and the Former Soviet Union.* World Bank. Http://web.

worldbank.org/WBSITE/EXTERNAL/COUNTRIES/ECAEXT/0,,contentMDK:2062721
4~pagePK:146736~piPK:146830~theSitePK:258599,00.html.

Asian Development Bank. 2006. *Mainstreaming Gender in Poverty Reduction Strategies.* Country
Gender Assessment Report, Tajikistan. Asian Development Bank. East and Central
Asia Regional Department and Regional and Sustainable Development Department.
May. Http://www.untj.org/files/reports/Country_Gender_Assessment_Tajikistan_ADB.
pdf.

Balaam, David, and Michael Veseth. 2005. *Introduction to International Political Economy.*
3rd ed. New York: Prentice Hall.

Bradshaw, Michael, and Adam Swain. 2003. "Foreign Investment and Regional Development."
In *East Central Europe and the Former Soviet Union: The Post Socialist States,* ed. Michael
Bradshaw and Alison Stenning, 59–86. Harlow, England: Pearson.

Bridger, Sue, Rebecca Kay, and Kathryn Pinnick. 1996. *No More Heroines? Russia, Women
and the Market.* London: Routledge.

Buckley, Mary. 1990. *Women and Ideology in the Soviet Union.* Ann Arbor: University of
Michigan Press.

———, ed. 1992. *Perestroika and Soviet Women.* Cambridge: Cambridge University Press.

———, ed. 1998. *Post Soviet Women from the Baltic to Central Asia.* Cambridge: Cambridge
University Press.

Bunch, Charlotte. 2001. "Women's Human Rights: The Challenges of Global Feminism and
Diversity." In *Feminist Locations: Global and Local, Theory and Practice,* ed. Marianne
Dekoven, 129–146. New Brunswick, N.J.: Rutgers University Press.

CATW (Coalition against Trafficking in Women). 2008a. *Factbook on Eastern Europe.* Http://
www.catwinternational.org/factbook/EUeast.php.

———. 2008b. *Factbook on Russia.* Http://www.catwinternational.org/factbook/Russia.php.

CDC (Centers for Disease Control). 1996. *International Reproductive Health Surveys and
Comparative Reports: Russia.* Washington, D.C.: Department of Health and Human
Services. Http://www.cdc.gov/reproductivehealth/Surveys/SurveyList.htm#Russia.

———. 2005. *International Reproductive Health Surveys and Comparative Reports: Georgia 2005.*
Washington, D.C.: Department of Health and Human Services. Http://www.cdc.gov/
reproductivehealth/Surveys/SurveyList.htm#Georgia%20Republic%202005.

CEDAW (Convention for the Elimination of Discrimination against Women). N.d. Http://
www.un.org/womenwatch/daw/cedaw.

———. 2002. *Summary Record of the Fifth Periodic Report Federation to CEDAW. Twenty-sixth
Session,* February. Http://daccessdds.UNDOC/GEN/N02/231/14/PDF/N0223114.pdf?
OpenElement.

———. 2007a. *Concluding Comments of the Committee on the Elimination of Discrimination against
Women: Tajikistan.* Thirty-seventh Session, January 15–February 2, 2007. Http://www.

un.org/womenwatch/daw/cedaw/cedaw37/concludingcommentsAU/Tajikistan.

———. 2007b. *Concluding Comments of the Committee on the Elimination of Discrimination against Women: Czech Republic*. Thirty-sixth Session, August 7–25, 2007. Http://www. un.org/womenwatch/daw/cedaw/36sess.htm.

———. 2007c. *Concluding Comments on the Committee on the Elimination of Discrimination against Women: Georgia*. Thirty-sixth Session, August 7–25, 2007. Http://www.un.org/ womenwatch/daw/cedaw/36sess.htm.

Corcoran-Nantes, Yvonne. 2005. *Lost Voices: Central Asian Women Confronting Transition*. London: Zed.

Einhorn, Barbara. 1993. *Cinderella Goes to Market: Citizenship, Gender and Women's Movements in East Central Europe*. London: Verso.

———. 2006. *Citizenship in an Enlarging Europe: From Dream to Awakening*. London: Palgrave Macmillan.

Erlich, Aaron. 2006. "Tajikistan: From Refugee Sender to Labor Exporter." *Migration Information Source*. July 2006. Washington, D.C.: Migration Policy Institute. Http:// www.migrationinformation.org/Profiles/display.cfm?ID=411.

European Commission. 2000. *Community Framework Strategy on Gender Equality (2001–2005)*. Brussels: Commission of the European Communities. Http://europa.eu/scadplus/leg/ en/cha/c10932.htm.

European Women's Lobby. 2005. Http://www.womenlobby.org.

Fodor, Éva. 2003. *Working Difference: Working Women's Lives in Hungary and Austria, 1945–1995*. Durham, N.C.: Duke University Press.

Fong, Monica S. 1993. *The Role of Women in Rebuilding the Russian Economy*. Washington, D.C.: World Bank.

Ford Foundation. 2008. Http://www.fordfound.org/regions/russia/overview.

Funk, Nanette, and Magda Mueller, eds. 1993. *Gender Politics and Post Communism: Reflections from Eastern Europe and the Former Soviet Union*. New York: Routledge.

Gal, Susan, and Gail Kligman, eds. 2000a. *The Politics of Gender after Socialism*. Princeton, N.J.: Princeton University Press.

———. 2000b. *Reproducing Gender: Politics, Publics and Everyday Life after Socialism*. Princeton, N.J.: Princeton University Press.

Gorbachev, Mikhail S. 1987. *Perestroika: New Thinking for Our Country and the World*. New York: Harper and Row.

Graham, Norman. 2006. "Introduction and Overview." In *The Political Economy of Transition in Eurasia: Democratization and Economic Liberalization in a Global Economy*, ed. Norman Graham and Folke Lindahl, 1–41. East Lansing: Michigan State University Press.

Haney, Lynn. 2002. *Inventing the Needy: Gender and the Politics of Welfare in Hungary*. Berkeley: University of California Press.

Harris, Colette. 2004. *Control and Subversion: Gender Relations in Tajikistan*. London: Pluto Press.

Harsanyi, Doina Pasca. 1993. "Women in Romania." In *Gender Politics and Post Communism: Reflections from Eastern Europe and the Former Soviet Union*, ed. Nanette Funk and Magda Mueller, 39–52. New York: Routledge.

Hemment, Julie. 2004. "Strategizing Gender and Development: Action Research and Ethnographic Responsibility in the Russian Provinces." In *Post-Soviet Women Encountering Transition: Nation Building, Economic Survival, and Civic Activism*, ed. Kathleen Kuehnast and Carol Nechemias, 313–333. Washington, D.C.: Woodrow Wilson Center Press; Baltimore: Johns Hopkins University Press.

———. 2007. *Empowering Women in Russia: Activism, Aid, and NGOs*. Bloomington: Indiana University Press.

Henderson, Sarah. 2003. *Building Democracy in Contemporary Russia: Western Support for Grassroots Organization*. Ithaca, N.Y.: Cornell University Press.

Hoy, Hilda. 2007. "Domestic Abuse Law a Major Step." *Prague Post Online*, January 3. Http://www.praguepost.com/articles/2007/01/03/domestic-abuse-law-a-major-step.php.

Informal Network on International Migration in Central and Eastern Europe. 2002. *Transformation and Migration in Central and Eastern Europe*. Geneva: International Labor Office.

Inter-Parliamentary Union. 1987. *Distribution of Seats between Men and Women in National Assemblies*. Reports and Documents No. 14. Geneva: International Centre for Parliamentary Documentation. Http://www.ipu.org.

———.2008. *Women in National Parliaments*. Geneva: International Centre for Parliamentary Documentation Database. Http://www.ipu.org.

IOM (International Organization for Migration). 2001. *Deceived Migrants from Tajikistan: A Study of Trafficking in Women and Children*. August. Http://www.iom.tj/publications/trafficking_2001.pdf.

———. 2007a. Georgia Facts and Figures. July. Http://www.iom.int/jahia/Jahia/cache/offonce/pid/781.

———. 2007b. Tajikistan Facts and Figures. November. Http://www.iom.int/jahia/Jahia/pid/508).

Ishkanian, Armine. 2004. "Working at the Local-Global Intersection: The Challenges Facing Women in Armenia's Nongovernmental Organization Sector." In *Post-Soviet Women Encountering Transition: Nation Building, Economic Survival, and Civic Activism*, ed. Kathleen Kuehnast and Carol Nechemias, 262–287. Washington, D.C.: Woodrow Wilson Center Press; Baltimore: Johns Hopkins University Press.

Ivakhnyuk, Irina. 2006. "Migration in the CIS Region: Common Problems and Mutual Benefits." International Symposium on International Migration and Development,

Turin, Italy. June 28. Http://www.un.org/esa/population/migration/turin/Symposium_Turin_files/P10_SYMP_Ivakhniouk.pdf.

Jacquette, Jane, and Sharon Wolchik. 1998. *Women and Democracy: Latin America and Central and Eastern Europe*. Baltimore: Johns Hopkins University Press.

Johnson, Janet Elise, and Jean C. Robinson. 2007. *Living Gender after Communism*. Bloomington: Indiana University Press.

Kamp, Marianne. 2004. "Between Women and the State: Mahalla Committees and Social Welfare in Uzbekistan." In *The Transformation of Central Asian States and Society*, ed. Pauline Jones Luong, 29–58. Ithaca, N.Y.: Cornell University Press.

Kosmarskaya, Natalya. 1999. "Post Soviet Russian Migration from the New Independent States: Experiences of Women Migrants." In *Engendering Forced Migration: Theory and Practice*, ed. Doreen Indra, 177–199. New York: Berghan Books.

Kuehnast, Kathleen, and Carol Nechemias, eds. 2004. *Post-Soviet Women Encountering Transition: NationBuilding, Economic Survival and Civic Activism*. Washington, D.C.: Woodrow Wilson Center Press; Baltimore: Johns Hopkins University Press.

Lapidus, Gail Warshofsky. 1978. *Women in Soviet Society*. Berkeley: University of California Press.

La Strada International: European Network against Trafficking in Human Beings. N.d. *Information La Strada International*. Http://www.lastradainternational.org/?main=informationlsi.

———. 2003. Interview with authors, La Strada Headquarters, Prague, July.

Lukic, Jasmina, Joanna Regulska, and Darja Zavirrsek. 2006. *Women and Citizenship in Central and Eastern Europe*. Burlington, Vt.: Ashgate.

Marsh, Rosalind, ed. 1996. *Women in Russia and Ukraine*. Cambridge: Cambridge University Press.

Marx Ferree, Myra. 1993. "The Rise and Fall of 'Mommy' Politics: Feminism and Unification in (East) Germany." *Feminist Studies* 19(1) (Spring): 89–115.

Moghadam, Valentine M., ed. 1993. *Democratic Reform and the Position of Women in Transitional Economies*. Oxford: Clarendon Press.

———. 2005. "The 'Feminization of Poverty' and Women's Human Rights." In UNESCO, *Social and Human Sciences Papers in Women's Studies/Gender Research*, No. 2, July 2005. Http://portal.unesco.org/shs/en/files/8282/11313736811Feminization_of_Poverty.pdf/Feminization%2Bof%2BPoverty.pdf.

Muenz, Rainer. 2006. "Europe: Population and Migration 2005." *Migration Information Source*. June. Washington, D.C.: Migration Policy Institute. Http://www.migrationinformation.org/Feature/display.cfm?ID=402.

Murtha, Danielle. 2003. *Sex Trafficking in Georgia*. TED Case Study 680. Washington, D.C.: Trade Environmental Database (TED). Http://www.american.edu/TED/child-sex-georgia.htm.

NEWW (Network of East-West Women). Http://www.neww.org.pl/en.php/about/historia/o. html.

Nikolic-Ristanovic, Vesna. 2002. *Social Change, Gender and Violence: Post Communist and War Affected Societies*. Dordrecht: Kluewer Academic.

Nowak, Manfred, ed. 1994. *World Conference on Human Rights: Vienna, June 1993, The Contribution of NGOs: Reports and Documents*. Vienna: Ludwig Boltzmann Institute of Human Rights.

Oatley, Thomas. 2004. *The Global Economy: Contemporary Debates*. New York: Longman.

Office to Monitor and Combat Trafficking in Persons. 2007. *Trafficking in Persons Report*, 12. June. Http://www.state.gov/g/tip/rls/tiprpt/2007/82809.htm.

Paci, Pierella. 2002. *Gender in Transition*, 12. World Bank. Http://ec.europa.eu/employment_social/employment_analysis/gender/gend_in_trans.pdf.

Pilkington, Hilary. 1998. *Migration, Displacement and Identity in Post-Soviet Russia*. London: Routledge.

Posadskaya, Anastasia, ed. 1994. *Women in Russia: A New Era in Russian Feminism*. London: Verso.

Racioppi, Linda, and Katherine O'Sullivan See. 1994. "The 'Woman Question' and National Identity: Soviet and Post-Soviet Russia." In *Women in International Development Annual*, vol. 4, ed. Rita Gallin and Ann Millard, 173–202. Boulder, Colo.: Westview Press.

———. 1997. *Women's Activism in Contemporary Russia*. Philadelphia: Temple University Press.

———. 2000. "Engendering Nation and National Identity." In *Women, States and Nationalism: At Home in the Nation?* ed. Sita Ranchod-Nillson and Mary Ann Tetreault, 18–35. London: Routledge.

Rai, Shirin, Hilary Pilkington, and Annie Phizacklea, eds. 1992. *Women in the Face of Change: The Soviet Union, Eastern Europe, and China*. New York: Routledge.

Rivkin-Fish, Michele. 2004. "Gender and Democracy: Strategies for Engagement and Dialogue on Women's Issues after Socialism in St. Petersburg." In *Post-Soviet Women Encountering Transition: Nation Building, Economic Survival, and Civic Activism*, ed. Kathleen Kuehnast and Carol Nechemias, 288–312. Washington, D.C.: Woodrow Wilson Center Press; Baltimore: Johns Hopkins University Press.

Robinson, Neil. 2004. "A Fickle Benefactor: Russia and the Global Economy as a Resource for Change." In *Reforging the Weakest Link: Global Political Economy and Post-Soviet Change in Russia, Ukraine and Belarus*, ed. Neil Robinson, 22–45. Burlington, Vt.: Ashgate.

Rueschemeyer, Marilyn, ed. 1998. *Women in the Politics of Post Communist Eastern Europe*. Armonk, N.Y.: M. E. Sharpe.

Rule, Wilma, and Norma Noonan, eds. 1996. *Russian Women in Politics and Society*. Westport,

Conn.: Greenwood Press.

Simai, Mihaly. 2006. *Poverty and Inequality in Eastern Europe and the CIS Transition Economies.* DESA Working Paper No. 17, ST/ESA/2006/DWP/17. UN Economic and Social Affairs. Http://www.un.org/esa/desa/papers/2006/wp17_2006.pdf.

Soros Foundation. 2008. Http://www.soros.org.

Sperling, Valerie. 1999. *Organizing Women in Contemporary Russia: Engendering Transition.* Cambridge: Cambridge University Press.

Tiuriukanova, Elena. 2005. "Female Labor Migration Trends and Human Trafficking: Policy Recommendations." In *Human Traffic and Transnational Crime: Eurasian and American Perspectives,* ed. Sally Stoeker and Louise Shelley, 95–113. Lanham, Md.: Rowman and Littlefield.

Tokhtakhodjaeva, Marfua, and Elmira Turgumbekova, eds. 1996. *The Daughters of Amazons: Voices from Central Asia.* Trans. Sufian Aslam. Lahore, Pakistan: Shirkat Gah Women's Resource Center.

True, Jacqui. 2003. *Gender, Globalization and Post-Socialism.* New York: Columbia University Press.

UNDP (United Nations Development Program). 1995. *Human Development Report.* New York: Oxford University Press. Http://hdr.undp.org/en/media/hdr_1995_en.pdf.

———. 1996. *Human Development Report.* New York: Oxford University Press. Http://hdr.undp.org/en/media/hdr_1996_en.pdf.

———. 1999. *Regional Transition 1999: The Human Cost of Transition.* New York: UNDP.

———. 2007. *Human Development Report 2007/2008. Fighting Climate Change: Human Solidarity in a Divided World.* New York: Palgrave Macmillan. Http://hdr.undp.org/en/media/hdr_20072008_en_complete.pdf.

UNDP Country Team in Georgia. 2006. *Domestic Violence and Child Abuse in Georgia.* Tblisi: Institute for Policy Studies; Minneapolis: Minnesota Advocates for Human Rights. Http://www.stopvaw.org/sites/608a3887-dd53-4796-8904-997a0131ca54/uploads/Domestic_Violence_and_Child_Abuse_in_Georgia_-_web_version.pdf.

UNDPCSD (United Nations Department for Policy Coordination and Sustainable Development). N.d. *List of Accredited Non-Governmental Organizations Who Were Present at the Fourth World Conference on Women.* New York: UNDPCSD. Http://www.un.org/esa/gopher-data/conf/fwcw/ngo/attendee.txt.

UNFPA (United Nations Population Fund). 2005. *Country Profiles for Population and Reproductive Health.* Population Development and Indicators. New York: UNFPA. Http://www.unfpa.org/profile.

———. 2008. *Population, Health and Socio-Economic Indicators.* New York: United Nations. Http://www.unfpa.org.

UNIFEM (United Nations Development Fund for Women). N.d. *Life Free of Violence:*

Regional Public Awareness Campaign in CIS and Lithuania. Http://www.nasilie.net/main.php?lang=en.

United Nations Secretary-General. 2006a. *Background Documentation. Item 60(a) on Advancement of Women*, 53–55. A/61/122/Add.1 61st Session of the General Assembly, July 6. Http://www.un.org/womenwatch/daw/vaw/violenceagainstwomenstudydoc.pdf.

———. 2006b *Ending Violence Against Women: From Words to Action*. United Nations. Http://www.un.org/womenwatch/daw/public/VAW_Study/VAWstudyE.pdf.

Valentova, Marie, Iva Krizova, and Tomas Katrnak. 2007. "Occupational Gender Segregation in the Light of the Segregation in Education: A Cross National Comparison." IRISS Working Paper Series 2007–04, IRISS at CEPS/INSTEAD, revised. Http://ideas.repec.org/p/irs/iriswp/2007-04.html.

van den Anker, Christien, and Joroen Doomernik, eds. 2006. *Trafficking and Women's Rights*. London: Palgrave Macmillan.

vanSelm, Joanne. 2005. "Georgia Looks West, but Faces Migration Challenges at Home." *Migration Information Source*. (June). Washington, D.C.: Migration Policy Institute. Http://www.migrationinformation.org/Profiles/display.cfm?ID .=314.

Verdery, Katherine. 1996. *What Was Socialism, and What Comes Next?* Princeton, N.J.: Princeton University Press.

Wolchik, Sharon, and Alfred G. Meyer, eds. 1985. *Women, State, and Party in Eastern Europe*. Durham, N.C.: Duke University Press.

World Bank. 2005. *Enhancing Job Opportunities in Eastern Europe and the Former Soviet Union*. World Bank. November. Http://web.worldbank.org/WBSITE/EXTERNAL/COUNTRIES/ECAEXT/0,,contentMDK:20678241~pagePK:146736~piPK:146830~theSitePK:258599,00.html.

———. 2008. *World Development Indicators*. Http://devdata.worldbank.org.

PART 1

Gender Politics in Central and Eastern Europe

1

Democratization, Nationalism, and Citizenship: The Challenge of Gender

Barbara Einhorn

This chapter rests on the premise that gender equality is a necessary condition for socially just societies. Given the fundamental economic, political, and social transformations in Central and Eastern Europe since the collapse of state socialist regimes, the region provides an important case study for the exploration of this proposition. The chapter focuses on the competing and contradictory forces of nationalism and liberal democracy in the region and considers the potential of both as vehicles for gender equitable outcomes. It is argued that citizenship continues to provide the most helpful conceptual and practical tool for the achievement of gender equality, not least because of its emphasis on the importance of mainstream political engagement. Since the macropolitical context is dominated by the impact of European Union (EU) enlargement on gender equality norms and practices in Central and Eastern Europe, it makes sense to focus in the main upon new EU member states in the region, with some reference to non-EU member states.[1]

The situation of formerly state socialist countries in Central and Eastern Europe is very different today than it was in the early, mid, or even late 1990s. The central plank of the transformations ushered in by the fall of state socialist regimes has involved a dual process of economic and political liberalization. Yet the resulting changes exhibit not only differences in the speed of adoption of economic market principles between individual countries. Politically, too, some inter- and intracountry tensions have emerged between openness toward the West and a desire to "return to Europe," on the one hand, and a more closed, inward-looking focus on the reestablishment of national identity and culture, on the other.[2] Gerard Delanty and Patrick O'Mahony see the EU as a potentially integrative counterbalance to the disintegrative force of nationalism and point to the dangers inherent in nationalism's tendency to be exclusionary (2002, 137, 139, 145).

The symbolic strength of the European idea as the supposed cradle and epitome of parliamentary democracy has been reduced to the hope of joining the EU. However, far beyond accession representing merely membership in an economic market and supranational institution of governance, Europe—in this case equated with the EU—is imagined as a club claiming "sociopolitical advancement and superiority that rests upon an image of women's freedom and a particular kind of gender order between women and men" (Lewis 2006, 92–93). This contrasts starkly with the notion of the nation based on a conception not of an equitable gender order, but on the reestablishment of traditional, hierarchical gender relations within the individual family unit and the national family unit.

Accession has become overlaid with powerful imaginings not only of material improvements and greater mobility for individual citizens within the boundaries of the EU but also of increased progress toward societies characterized by individual empowerment in general and greater gender equity in particular. Concrete grounds for such hopes were justified by the history of the EU's success in forcing national states to amend their legislation in order to conform with European standards. An example is provided by the 1979 proceedings in the European Court of Justice instigated by the European Commission. These successful proceedings obliged Belgium, Denmark, Luxembourg, Germany, France, the Netherlands, and the United Kingdom (UK)—all of which had refused to implement the 1975 Equal Pay Directive—to reform their domestic legislation (Walby 2005, 16; on the legislative advances made via the EU, see also Gerhard 2006, 44–45; Hoskyns 1996).

Yet there have already been disappointments and disillusionment. First, the EU set entry conditions in 1993 for prospective members from the region, stating that "membership requires that the candidate country has achieved stability of institutions guaranteeing democracy, the rule of law, human rights and respect for and protection of minorities" (cited in Kenney 2006, 150). As Padraic Kenney points out, this ensured that "the new post-communist members were not welcomed as equals, but as pupils, made to accept various limitations of membership that have given them a kind of second-class status within the Union" (2006, 150, 154).

Second, despite the inclusion of human rights, widely held to encompass women's rights as human rights, the language in which these conditions are couched heralds a fatal flaw with regard to gender politics, namely the narrow emphasis on *institutional* readiness for membership. As various scholars have pointed out, this has enabled candidate countries to adhere to the letter, but not the spirit, of the entry conditions (Einhorn 2006a; Miroiu 2004; Steinhilber 2002; True 2003b).

Third, on the question of the relationship between the EU and individual nation states, there is a direct contrast in this relationship between those countries that joined in 2004 or 2007 and existing member states. The European Commission was able in 1979 to force individual member countries retrospectively to adjust their national legislation in line with EU directives. In the run-up to accession in 2004 and 2007, by contrast, individual candidate countries were obliged to pass antidiscrimination legislation—and to institute national women's machineries dedicated to its implementation—in advance, as a precondition for attaining membership status. Yet implementation has not followed, and the institutional mechanisms are weak, leading analysts from the region to conclude that there is a lack of government commitment or political will (Bitušiková 2005; Jezerska 2003; Taljunaite 2005). An example is that of Slovakia, where the Concept on Equal Opportunities for Men and Women was adopted by the Slovak government in 2001 in response to the need to fulfill EU requirements prior to accession. Alexandra Bitušiková has argued that it remains a purely formal and bureaucratic paper commitment, adopted in a top-down process that lacked the dialogue with social partners that is formally specified by the EU. Thus, in practice, its impact on the adoption of improved gender norms in society remains negligible (Bitušiková 2005).

A further disappointment has been that the EU's narrow focus on labor market integration limits the extent to which other aspects of political and social citizenship rights are addressed (Barendt 2002; Lohmann and Seibert 2003). Nor has failure to implement EU gender directives delayed or impeded accession, as shown particularly by evidence from the Czech Republic and Poland (Bretherton 2001; Chołuj 2003; Graff 2002; Jezerska 2003; Karat Coalition 2005; Lohmann and Seibert 2003; Marksová-Tominová 2003; Regulska 2001, 2002; Steinhilber 2002; True 2003a, 99–100).

The potential and the constraints of the EU's gender mainstreaming policy are discussed more fully elsewhere (Einhorn 2006a; Gerhard 2003; Hoskyns 1996; Rai 2003; Sloat this volume; Stratigaki 2005; True 2003b; Verloo 2002). Of particular concern for the future is the current trend for the EU to move away from its earlier striving for gender equality to a broader brush approach to multiple inequalities, in particular gender, race or ethnicity, sexual orientation, and class. This could mean a shift away from a high-profile single focus on gender equality toward a more diluted or more dispersed policy of equal opportunities. The danger here is that, as Mieke Verloo points out, "compared to gender and sexual orientation, class and race/ethnicity are represented more as firmly located in the public sphere, in the spheres of citizenship and employment"—in other words, in those spheres to which EU policy is primarily addressed (2006, 216, 218). Sylvia Walby maintains that the EU has often taken the lead on equal opportunity issues (2004, 23); nevertheless, she warns that "support for gender equality is seen as ebbing, because the draft of the new Constitution for the EU by the Convention proposed that gender equality was merely an objective and not the higher-order value" (Walby 2004, 7).

These examples illustrate some of the ways in which the dream of belonging to the EU as guarantor of Western democratic ideals, and in particular the promise of greater gender equality, has already been dented.

Nationalism

It has been argued in the introduction to this chapter that there are tensions in some Central and Eastern European countries between the aspiration to accede to the EU as the embodiment of liberalization and democracy, and countervailing nationalist tendencies to resist what is perceived as the threat rather than the promise of new supranational forms of governance. This hesitation or even suspicion of supranational institutions can be explained in part by the recent memory of Soviet hegemony, coupled with a fierce reassertion of national autonomy and difference after the experience of being the guinea pigs in a homogenizing social experiment.[3]

In the postsocialist era, then, the countries of Central and Eastern Europe have reinvented themselves as sovereign nation-states, liberated, as they perceive it, from the yoke of the Soviet empire. In this process, and as a reaction to the repressive regimes experienced in these countries prior to 1989, nationalism as the expression of the desire for "radical freedom" (Delanty and O'Mahony 2002, 160) is perhaps not surprising. However, what is potentially—and in some cases has been actually—dangerous and destructive is the exclusionary and xenophobic character of the radical forms of nationalism to have emerged in the post-Communist period (Delanty and O'Mahony 2002; Einhorn 2006b).

The question thus remains whether the political forms that the new nation-states of Central and Eastern Europe have adopted can be read as signs of postcolonial independence, emergent pluralistic democracies, or backward-looking isolationist nationalisms. Two revealing indicators are the extent to which these nation-states grant political subject status in relation to both ethnicity and gender. Christina Chiva points out that in Hungary and Romania, almost all women who have made it into parliament are from non-Roma groups, in other words, from the dominant ethnic groups (Chiva 2005, 971; see also Magyari-Vincze this volume).

Nationalist critiques of Western liberal democracy would see it as privileging the individual to the detriment of the community. Hence, nationalist discourses favor a more communitarian approach. Nationalism is thus "collective both as a form of identification and as an orientation to collective action—a kind of collective identity" (Delanty and O'Mahony 2002, 44). Graham Smith et al. argue that "throughout the multi-ethnic borderlands, there remains a predisposition among dominant national groups and minorities alike to recognise and overemphasise the importance of collective rather than individual actors as the constitutive elements of political community" (1998, 2). Ieva Zake states that in Latvia, "the state and the nation do not consist of individuals, but families" (2002, 634). In this way, nationalist discourse runs directly counter to the discourse of liberal democracy with its emphasis on the individual citizen.

Paradoxically, therefore, nationalism offers some sense of continuity with the recent past, in that both nationalist and socialist rhetoric require individuals to subsume their needs and aspirations to the larger collective interest. Whereas under state socialism, that collective interest was envisaged as a rosy future embodying hopes for equality and social justice, nationalist rhetoric privileges national culture and tradition based on an ethic of difference. This difference can be both individual and collective. In the former case, it is often defined through gender and/or sexual difference; in the latter, national difference is thought to be determined by ethnic/racial and/or cultural variance. In gender terms, nationalist discourse replaces the purportedly "gender-neutral" Soviet citizen-as-worker—or "citizen-as-worker-mother" in the case of women—with a starkly gender-differentiated hierarchy of roles within the individual family and the national family. In terms of sexuality, these families remain firmly heteronormative. Thus, the Latvian People's Party (Tautas Partija), "a neo-liberal political force, . . . uses the heteronormative, father-ruled, traditional family as a foundation of national statehood, political stability, and economic development" (Zake 2002, 634–635). On the issue of ethnicity, and the tendency of nationalist forces to become isolationist, thus potentially to some extent anti-European, Zake describes the "orientation of Latvian politicians toward building an enclosed, introspective and ethnically and gender stratified community" (2002, 636).

What is problematic is the way that nationalism instrumentalizes difference in order to proclaim itself as superior to individuals or groups defined as "others" who are then discriminated against or excluded on the basis of that otherness. Nationalism tends, in other words, to be exclusive rather than inclusive, and discriminatory toward minorities within and communities outside of the self-defined nation. Latvia is an example of several countries in the region that defined citizenship within the new nation-state along ethnically exclusionary lines, such that "citizenship in the post-Soviet Latvian state was defined and designed as an instrument of ethnic Latvians' survival, not of social integration" (Zake 2002, 633).

Nations thus tend to be imagined as a community of insiders defined less in terms of their distinctive identity than in contrast to putative "others" who do not share that identity, imagined as the social glue of the national group. These outsiders are commonly bordering nations, but often also minority groups within the nation itself, which—contrary to nationalist rhetoric—is usually neither homogeneous nor united (McClintock 1995). Such disunity within the national community reveals the struggle for the power to define what constitutes "authentic" national identity (Einhorn 2006b, 197). Such power struggles invariably involve discourses of gender, sexuality, and race. They set dominant "insiders" against "enemies within" (Kofman et al. 2000, 37). Such "outsiders," "others," or "enemies within" can be minority ethnic groups, immigrants, refugees and asylum seekers, gays and lesbians, or even women, hardly a minority (Allen 1998, 55; Dwyer 2000, 27–28). This is because, as Tamar Mayer asserts, the nation was "produced as a heterosexual male construct, whose 'ego' is intimately connected to patriarchal hierarchies and norms" (2000, 6). National communities are conceived of in simultaneously gendered, sexualized, and ethnic terms as extended families, as "metaphoric kinship" (Eriksen 1993, 108), or as "family-writ-large" (Golden 2003, 85).

In Ukraine, for example, "nation and family (the latter traditionally associated with women) are seen as cornerstones of a new Ukraine" (Taraban 2007, 119). Svitlana Taraban considers the widespread phenomenon of Ukrainian women who offer themselves as Internet brides accentuating "the qualities and attributes that portray them as pre-feminist, vulnerable and docile" (2007, 118). These women present themselves as offering reliably submissive wife and mother potential as well as the ability to fulfill the sexualized imaginings of the putative (Western) customer/husband. Taraban suggests that nationalism plays a (perhaps subliminal) role in their identity formation, in that "Ukrainian women come prepared to create their virtual selves in accordance with all-too-familiar to them traditional gender imagery" (2007, 121). That this is a tightly imbricated dialectical relationship is evident from the formulation of Tatiana Zhurzhenko, namely that "in the framework of Ukrainian neotraditionalism the solution of family problems is being linked to the revival of the Ukrainian nation, and vice versa—the revival of the nation starts within the family" (2001, 6).

The nation-as-family metaphor was also the assumption underlying the debate about reproductive rights in Poland during the 1990s. Several analysts have interpreted this debate as symbolizing much more than reproduction, namely contestations about the nature of democratization and the nation-state (Kramer 2005, 131; Zielińska 2000, 25). Susan Gal and Gail Kligman identify two crucial ways in which "reproduction makes politics," including the way that "narratives of nationhood rely crucially on reproductive discourses and practices to make and remake the category of 'nation' and its boundaries," and that, conversely, "debates about reproduction serve as coded arguments about political legitimacy and the morality of the state" (2000, 21–22).

Anne-Marie Kramer analyzes the way that the line taken by two different Polish newspapers on the abortion debate demonstrated two competing visions of the future Polish nation: as primarily Christian (Roman Catholic) or as international and secular (Western). In the course of this political (and highly politicized) debate, the local Polish weekly *Gosc Niedzielny* in 1996 reported the Polish pope John Paul II, stating in response to the second reading of a liberalization amendment to the abortion law in the Sejm (Polish Parliament) that "the nation which kills its own children, [is] a nation without a future" (Kramer 2005, 135). Here, as Kramer puts it, "the liberalisation of abortion comes to be read as a metaphor for the extinction of 'Polishness'" (2005, 135). The conflation of nation with family is particularly clear in this example.

In another example, Agnieszka Graff cites the "Normality Parade" held on June 18, 2005, in response to gay rights demonstrations. Some of the slogans used were "Boy + Girl = Normal Family," and "Paedophiles and Pederasts are Euro-Enthusiasts" (2009). These slogans neatly exemplify this equation of the heterosexual family with the nation, and the parallel construction of those who deviate from the "normality" of heterosexuality as undermining the Polish nation. Graff goes on to cite a speech in the Sejm by Roman Giertych, leader of the far right League of Polish Families (LPR) and subsequently Poland's minister of education, in which he derides antihomophobic teaching in schools, portraying it as an aberration, an invasion of the pure, family-orientated Polish nation by alien European forces—in his formulation, "German transsexuals" (Graff 2009).

These examples illustrate both the gendered and sexualized construction of the nation, and the conflation of nation with ideas of the "normal," traditional heterosexual family. They also illustrate the way that nationalist discourses can oppose ideas of the "pure" nation to Europe as the potentially polluting enemy. Graff identifies a paradox whereby "Poland has become more isolationist and confrontational under right-wing rule, but it is not . . . planning to leave the EU" (2009).

Anthony Smith argues that "the metaphor of the family is indispensable to nationalism. The nation is depicted as one great family, the members as brothers and sisters of the motherland or fatherland, speaking their mother tongue" (1991, 79). Smith—perhaps unconsciously—utilizes the language of gender difference to describe the nation. In the introduction to his book *National Identity*, Smith actually links recognition of gender as a key component in (individual and national) identity formation to relationships of unequal power within the nation, conceding that "if not immutable, gender classifications are universal and pervasive. They also stand at the origins of other differences and subordinations." Yet as Linda Racioppi and Katherine O'Sullivan See conclude in their cogent analysis of this work, Smith, while not quite sharing the gender blindness of most other mainstream theorists of nations, nationalism, and national identity, nevertheless "does not pursue . . . [his] . . . crucial insight about the centrality of gender" (2000, 26).

Given the way that nationalism both structures and is structured by rigid notions of gender, to leave it out of the equation is to downplay the potential threat posed by the East-West convergence not of democratic yearnings and awareness of gender equality as the fundamental prerequisite of full citizenship rights but of ultranationalist sentiments and extreme right political parties. It is important in this context to realize that the direction of influence between the EU and its constituent parts is two way. Nationalist discourses at the national level—and within the European Parliament—have the potential to undermine political commitment to, or impede the implementation of, gender equality norms and indeed other equal opportunity or human rights policies expressed through both EU directives and national legislation.

Liberalization and Democracy

The transformation process in Central and Eastern Europe has involved economic liberalization and privatization, on the one hand, and political democratization, on the other. It is significant that both elements have been constructed within the parameters of neoliberal understandings that privilege the economic over the political, and hence the individual economic actor over the citizen as political subject. Joseph Stiglitz describes liberalization as "the removal of government interference in financial markets, capital markets, and of barriers to trade" (2002, 59). What is known as the Washington Consensus is, according to Stiglitz, "based on a simplistic model of the market economy . . . [in which] there is no need for government—that is, free, unfettered, 'liberal' markets work perfectly." Stiglitz explains that this faulty assumption, namely that the market can operate as the sole and sufficient regulator of society, is the reason why the model is "sometimes referred to as 'neo-liberal,' based on 'market fundamentalism.'" Stiglitz points out that such policies "have been widely rejected in the more advanced industrial countries," and indeed that "today even the IMF agrees that it has pushed that agenda too far—that liberalizing capital and financial markets contributed to the global financial crises of the 1990s and can wreak havoc on a small emerging country" (2002, 74, 59). Nevertheless, the neoliberal paradigm was applied to the economic restructuring process in Central and Eastern Europe.[4] As a direct result of this model, the state has been forced to retrench, with the massive loss of social entitlements and public welfare provision in most countries in the region. The neoliberal paradigm as applied during the transformation process in Central and Eastern Europe is thus revealed to be based on an individualistic concept of citizenship and a market-centered economic model that together systemically tend toward social exclusion rather than social inclusiveness.

In the transformation process, although the civil and political rights associated with citizenship were discursively validated, in practice they became subordinated to the assertion of economic rights. This begins to explain the enormous increases in economic inequalities and social disparities between citizens discursively constructed as equal. It is important to understand how the economic changes were embedded in—and have themselves shaped—an altered political landscape, in which the discourses used to describe and understand the accompanying social and cultural changes have been fundamentally reworked. As already suggested, neotraditionalist discourses have been applied to legitimate these shifts.

Ruth Lister has pointed out that while civil and political rights are commonly "seen as a necessary precondition of full and equal citizenship . . . they are not, however, a sufficient condition, for they need to backed up by social rights" (1997, 33–34). This insight has formed the basis of much of my theorizing of citizenship in the context of democratization in Central and Eastern Europe, for the privileging of market mechanisms and the idea that the state should take a backseat have had severe consequences for the possibility of realizing gender equitable citizenship. I have argued elsewhere that without social entitlements to social welfare, for example, to publicly provided and affordable child care—in other words, without the enabling structures that link state, market, and household—the possibility of women accessing the marketplace as the arena in which citizenship is realized and thus exercising the citizenship rights they possess on paper on an equal basis with men is dramatically curtailed (Einhorn 2000, 2006a). These developments have also increased the differences *between* women in terms of their capacity to become active citizens.

Not only does the primacy of the market, and thus of the economic actor as citizen, tend to overshadow the political subject. Even within the sphere of democratic politics, there is also a hierarchization of citizenship status. External actors such as international agencies, Western governments, the EU, and international nongovernmental organizations (NGOs) have lauded civil society as the key instrument and measure of democratization. This has led to an underestimation of the extent to which in fact it is mainstream political representation that counts. This sphere has remained heavily masculinized, although there have been significant gains in the region.[5]

This relative underestimation of the importance of mainstream politics has particularly pernicious effects for ethnic minority women. In Hungary and Romania, as already mentioned, almost no Roma women have been elected to national parliaments. In both countries, Roma women's political participation takes place almost exclusively at the level of civil society activism. Yet in an illustration of my theory of the civil society "gap," Christina Chiva points to the "relatively marginal status of women's organisations vis-à-vis the governmental sector" and that "linkages with governmental bodies remain scarce" (Chiva 2005, 974; for the civil society "gap," see Einhorn 2006a). Even within civil society organizations, Chiva argues, few women hold leadership positions in the two countries, so that not only Roma women in particular but also women in general remain underrepresented both in civil society and in mainstream politics (2005, 974).

Suvi Salmenniemi notes the same phenomenon in Russia, where "political space, agency and citizen identities are gendered in such a way that civic activity is discursively constructed as feminine and institutional politics as masculine" (2005, 736; for an analysis of this phenomenon in the EU member states, see Sloat this volume). There is a danger that through this gendering—and simultaneous creation of a hierarchy—of the different spaces of political agency, women's citizenship status can be marginalized or weakened (for more on this phenomenon of the civil society "trap," see also Einhorn 2006a and Lister 2007).

Despite the neoliberal emphasis on market mechanisms, the power of the state to influence social rights has not diminished. Julia Szalai (2005) demonstrates—using an example from Hungary—that the national and the local state influence women's agency and capacity to become full citizens. The Hungarian example also illuminates the gulf opening up between women on the basis of both social class and ethnicity. Local Hungarian welfare officials acting in the name of the state have the power to discriminate against others in a weaker position. In arrogating to themselves the power to act as the arbiter of who qualifies as "deserving poor," these female welfare officials apply gendered and racist discourses against Roma women welfare claimants, labeling them as "irresponsible" mothers for having too many children (of the "wrong" kind, ethnically speaking). Following the logic of such discourses, the officials deny Roma women claimants their welfare entitlements, thereby excluding them from the social mainstream by denying them the social citizenship rights that could render them equal citizens with the majority Hungarian population. Szalai makes the strong argument that this example demonstrates how discourses of *cultural* (ethnic) otherness are translated into *structural* (socially) discriminatory practices (2005; see also Magyari-Vincze 2006 and this volume; and Woodcock 2007 for similar examples from Romania).

This example of the workings of the local welfare state illustrates the impact of the state on social citizenship rights, as well as its potential to open up divisions between women. It also serves to underline the fact that market, state, and household are intimately interlinked, not only in conceptualizations of national identity and definitions of who "belongs" to the national community but also in the practical possibilities of accessing the social entitlements that form the prerequisite of full citizenship status. Thus it highlights the ways in which the transformation process in Central and Eastern Europe has produced links, and simultaneously tensions, between the two potentially competing discourses of national identity, on the one hand, and democratization with its emphasis on citizenship, on the other. In the process, differences and inequalities (of gender, class, and ethnicity) have grown, leading to increases in discriminatory practices.

In effect, as Ieva Zake highlights, the three factors under discussion in this essay, namely "nationalism, new economy, and gender ideology . . . all work together to make political power inaccessible to women" (2002, 632).

Democratization and Citizenship

Pnina Werbner and Nira Yuval-Davis remind us that although historically coexisting within a single social field, democratic citizenship's overt stress on rationality, individuality, and the rule of law has frequently been in tension with, and even antithetical to, nationalism's appeals to communal solidarities and primordial sentiments of soil and blood. Furthermore, they argue that while nationalism is trapped in a backward glance, finding its legitimation in "past myths of common origin or culture, citizenship raises its eyes towards the future, to common destinies" (Werbner and Yuval-Davis 1999, 1, 3).

One of the strengths of citizenship as a concept relevant to the aspiration for gender equitable societies is precisely its stress on the importance of formal political participation as a key determinant of gender equality. In the context of Central and Eastern Europe, this sphere has until recently been relatively neglected. Anne Phillips reminds us of the importance of this sphere of action in her book *Democracy and Difference* (1993). She argues passionately that "we do need to reassert the importance of the specifically political; and we do need to campaign for more active involvement and control." In her view, "the value of citizenship lies in the way it restates the importance of political activity" (Phillips 1993, 87). Baukje Prins also insists that "a liberal democracy is a political community, whose common good cannot be found at the level of substantive beliefs, but must be located at the level of agreed-upon procedures for articulating conflicts and attaining temporary agreement" (2006, 246).

Similarly, Ruth Lister, in her influential book *Citizenship: Feminist Perspectives* (1997), argues that the concept of citizenship is useful in that it "is understood as both a *status*, carrying a set of rights including social and reproductive rights, and a *practice*, involving political participation broadly defined so as to include the kind of informal politics in which women are more likely to engage (1997, 196; see also 13–41). In other words, citizenship does not merely circumscribe a bundle of legally enshrined rights and responsibilities. Rather, the attainment of full citizenship status requires the active agency and political participation of citizens themselves.

Several authors argue that the state socialist notion of citizenship "put the gender-less working class above all other groups or interests" (Bitušiková 2005). Indeed, the 1960 constitution of the Czechoslovak Socialist Republic stated that "in the working class society each individual can reach full development of his/her own skills and interests only by active participation in the development of the whole society, mainly by taking part in work for the society" (cited in Bitušiková 2005).

The notion that the individual is worthless unless subsuming his or her own interests to the welfare and development of the entire society is one that has understandably been rejected since the collapse of state socialism. Such total subordination of individual needs and aspirations to social goals is extreme. It suggests an obvious corrective—one that has emerged since 1989—namely a focus on recognition of individual or group differences rather than on issues of economic redistribution, social justice, or political equality.

One of the central and immediate effects of economic liberalization and privatization in the region as expressed through the so-called Washington Consensus imposed by the World Bank and the International Monetary Fund (IMF) manifested itself in the disproportionate female share of high unemployment levels. Another was the embrace—by international agencies such as the UN as well as foreign governments and donor agencies—of civil society reconstruction as a—if not *the*—central plank of democratization. This led to the phenomenon I have called the civil society "trap," whereby women made redundant by economic restructuring step in to run NGOs and civil society associations that increasingly provide the social and welfare services from which the state, following neoliberal guidelines, has retreated (Einhorn 2000, 2006a). In other words, what we see here is a step backward from the assumption of full-time paid work for women as an accepted societal norm, to a situation where much of women's work is socially necessary but unpaid and thus rendered invisible. In addition, the reduction of civil society activism to a form of social provision contains the danger of blunting the political edge of potential feminist organizing that has an agenda of social transformation.

The invisibility of (unpaid) women's work is not simply a case of lacking recognition, but, as Nancy Fraser (2003, 215–216) has emphasized, rather the direct and systemic effect of neoliberal capitalist economic mechanisms that exclude many from the labor market altogether while discriminating on the basis of gender and other markers of difference against many of those within it. This insight is relevant to the analysis of the processes of structural adjustment occurring in the "transition" to capitalist market-based economies in Central and Eastern Europe. It is just as important for our understanding of the issues impeding genuine gender equality in civil and political participation in the region.

Fraser makes this argument in the context of a discussion with Axel Honneth about the relative merits of prioritizing issues of (cultural) recognition over questions of (economic) redistribution. She argues that "reducing all social subordination to misrecognition, rooted in hierarchies of cultural value," fails to allow for "distributive injustices that do not simply reflect status hierarchies." In her view, the attainment of social justice requires the adoption and application of a "*perspectival dualism*" that combines cultural recognition claims by particular social groups who are marginalized or discriminated against on the basis of gender, "race," class, or disability with "struggles for egalitarian redistribution" (Fraser 2003, 217). Similarly, Mieke Verloo argues that "struggles around gender and race/ethnicity are about both redistribution (equal pay, discrimination in the labour market) and recognition (revaluing care and cultural differences)" (2006, 221).

Fraser's acknowledgement of the need for a perspectival dualism that combines recognition claims with concerns for redistribution and social justice represents a shift from the "cultural turn" to a more balanced approach. Such a perspective has the capacity to reintegrate the cultural with the social and economic. It also, by extension, suggests a revalidation of the need for political activism to achieve both cultural recognition and greater social justice. Such an approach requires a critical reevaluation of fundamentalist market-based strategies that distract attention from the social and political arenas (in which issues of redistributive justice could be raised) by means of their singular focus on the individual (male, white, social- and economic-capital-rich) citizen defined as economic actor in the marketplace. In other words, it questions the globally dominant neoliberal paradigm that privileges the market and vilifies the state, historically the actor with the power to facilitate "egalitarian redistribution" and to improve levels of social justice. It also leads us to reconsider the arguments about the relative merits of a difference-based approach as opposed to one based on the quest for greater (gender and) social justice.

Conclusion

While it is true that the political uniformity imposed by state socialist regimes stifled interest group representation, it is equally true that the neoliberal focus on the individual (which one could regard as the swing of the pendulum to the opposite extreme) fragments interests and hinders the possibility of their recognition or representation. It also renders responsibility a purely individual concern; hence it minimizes the possibility of acknowledging or making claims for recognition of interests, not to speak of claims to correct systemic social injustices (which themselves tend to become invisible in this individualistic framework). One could argue that the cause of greater gender equity, whether it is presented as equal opportunities, gender equality, or gender mainstreaming, runs counter to the neoliberal paradigm itself. It is therefore structurally unlikely that gender equity can be adequately addressed by a system that prioritizes the market and economic development over gender-equitable political representation. Yet equality in civic participation and political representation is a necessary, though not sufficient, condition for the achievement of a fully democratic society incorporating social and economic justice in addition to civil and political rights.

NOTES

1. The countries that became members in March 2004 as part of the first round of enlargement were the Czech Republic, Estonia, Hungary, Latvia, Lithuania, Poland, Slovakia, and Slovenia. There followed, in January 2007, Bulgaria and Romania. Thus a total of ten countries from Central and Eastern Europe have now become EU member countries. This chapter does not refer explicitly to all new member countries, but uses some country cases as examples of trends.

2. The oft-cited "return to Europe" is in itself a problematic concept, first, in terms of what a "return" might connote, and second, because Europe itself is ill-defined: does it denote geographical boundaries, some nebulously defined notion of "the West," or even a fantasy about the presumed superiority of "Western" or "European" culture? Several writers have pointed to the contested nature of Europe in such connotations, resting, as it does, on an exclusionary and exploitative, racist, and imperialist history (Einhorn and Gregory 1998). Gail Lewis, for example, writes of "the symbolic struggle . . . over what it means to be European, where Europe begins and ends" as "a symbolic field in which that which is 'essentially' European is claimed as the originary site of progress and morality" (Lewis 2006, 89).

3. In fact, as Padraic Kenney points out, the experience of relative homogeneity in the states of this region was historically recent. Prior to World War I, most Eastern Europeans lived within the confines of the Russian, Ottoman, or Austro-Hungarian empires, all of them multiethnic in nature (Kenney 2006, 52).

4. Stiglitz's analysis was extremely prescient and has been proven correct in light of the more general discrediting of such market fundamentalism—and the acknowledgement of its failings by its own proponents—during the credit crunch and recession beginning in 2008.

5. Although none of the new EU member states can rival the levels of female representation in national parliaments demonstrated by the Nordic states (average 41.4% in lower or single houses), nevertheless levels of female political representation at the national level have been rising steadily in many of them in recent years. Of the ten new member states, five countries have achieved levels of representation in their lower houses exceeding the level of 19.5% in the UK in the 2005 elections, or the average of 19.2% achieved in European OSCE member states excluding the Nordic states. These are: Bulgaria, with 21.7% women representatives in the Lower House in 2005; Poland, with 20.2% in the Sejm in 2007; Estonia, with 20.8% in 2007; Latvia, with 20% in 2006; and Slovakia, with 19.3% in 2006. Lithuania's record slid backwards, from 22% female parliamentarians in the Lower House in 2002, to only 17.7% in 2008. Lagging behind are (somewhat surprisingly, given its long history of secular democracy) the Czech Republic, with 15.5% in 2008 (down from 17% in 2002); Slovenia, with 13.3% in 2008; Hungary, with 11.1% in 2006; and Romania, with 11.4% in the November 2008 elections (Inter-Parliamentary Union database on Women in National Parliaments, http://www.ipu.org/wmn-e/world.htm, last accessed 5 January 2009).

WORKS CITED

Allen, Sheila. 1998. "Identity: Feminist Perspectives on Race, Ethnicity and Nationality." In *Gender, Ethnicity and Political Ideologies,* ed. N. Charles and H. Hintjens, 46–64. New York: Routledge.

Barendt, Regina. 2002. "Women for Europe and Europe for Women: KARAT Coalition Lobby-Building, Network Creation, Building Alliances and Gaining Power." Paper presented at the conference "Europe's Daughters: Traditions, Expectations and Strategies of European Women's Movements," Berlin, June.

Bitušiková, Alexandra. 2005. *Women in Civic and Political Life in Slovakia.* Banska Bystrica: Research Institute of Matej Bel University.

Bretherton, Charlotte. 2001. "Gender Mainstreaming and EU Enlargement: Swimming against the Tide?" *Journal of European Public Policy* 8(1): 60–81.

Chiva, Christina. 2005. "Women in Post-Communist Politics: Explaining Under-Representation in the Hungarian and Romanian Parliaments." *Europe-Asia Studies* 57(7): 969–994.

Choluj, Bożena. 2003. "Die Situation der Frauen-NGOs in Polen an der Schwelle zum EU-Beitritt" (The situation of women's NGOs in Poland on the threshold of EU-accession). In *Europas Töchter: Traditionen, Erwartungen und Strategien von Frauenbewegungen in Europa* (Europe's daughters: Traditions, expectations and strategies of European women's movements), ed. Ingrid Miethe and Silke Roth, 203–224. Opladen: Leske+Budrich.

Delanty, Gerard, and Patrick O'Mahony. 2002. *Nationalism and Social Theory: Modernity and the Recalcitrance of the Nation.* London, Thousand Oaks.

Dwyer, Leslie K. 2000. "Spectacular Sexuality: Nationalism, Development and the Politics of Family Planning in Indonesia." In *Gender Ironies of Nationalism: Sexing the Nation,* ed. T. Mayer, 25–64. New York: Routledge.

Einhorn, Barbara. 2000. "Gender and Citizenship in the Context of Democratization and Economic Reform in East Central Europe." In *International Perspectives on Gender and Democratization,* ed. Shirin M. Rai, 103–124. London: Macmillan.

———. 2006a. *Citizenship in an Enlarging Europe: From Dream to Awakening.* Basingstoke: Palgrave Macmillan.

———. 2006b. "Insiders and Outsiders: Within and Beyond the Gendered Nation." In *Handbook of Gender and Women's Studies,* ed. Kathy Davis, Mary Evans, and Judith Lorber, 196–213. London: Sage.

Einhorn, Barbara, and Jeanne Gregory. 1998. "The Idea of Europe." Introduction to *The Idea of Europe,* special issue of *European Journal of Women's Studies* 5(3–4): 293–296.

Eriksen, Thomas Hylland. 1993. *Ethnicity and Nationalism: Anthropological Perspectives,* London: Pluto Press.

Fraser, Nancy. 2003. "Distorted Beyond All Recognition: A Rejoinder to Axel Honneth." In Nancy Fraser and Axel Honneth, *Redistribution or Recognition? A Political-Philosophical Exchange,* 198–236. New York: Verso.

Gal, Susan, and Gail Kligman. 2000. *The Politics of Gender after Socialism.* Princeton, N.J.: Princeton University Press.

Gerhard, Ute. 2003. "Frauenbewegung in Deutschland—Gemeinsame und geteilte Geschichte" (The German women's movement—shared and split history). In *Europas Töchter: Traditionen, Erwartungen und Strategien von Frauenbewegungen in Europa* (Europe's daughters: European women's movement traditions, expectations, and strategies), ed. Ingrid Miethe and Silke Roth, 81–100. Opladen: Leske+Budrich.

———. 2006. "European Citizenship: A Political Opportunity for Women?" In *Women's Citizenship and Political Rights,* ed. Sirkku K. Hellsten, Anne Maria Holli, and Krassimira Daskalova, 37–52. Basingstoke: Palgrave Macmillan.

Golden, Deborah. 2003. "A National Cautionary Tale: Russian Women Newcomers to Israel Portrayed." *Nations and Nationalism* 9(1): 83–104.

Graff, Agnieszka. 2002. "Lost between the Waves? The Paradoxes of Feminist Chronology and Activism in Contemporary Poland." Paper presented at the conference "Third Wave Feminism," University of Exeter, July.

———. 2009. "Gender and Nation, Here and Now: Reflections on the Gendered and Sexualized Aspects of Contemporary Polish Nationalism." In *Intimate Citizenships: Gender, Sexualities, Politics,* ed. Elzbieta H. Oleksy. New York: Routledge.

Hoskyns, Catherine. 1996. *Integrating Gender: Women, Law and Politics in the European Union.* New York: Verso.

Jezerská, Zuzana. 2003. "Gender Awareness and the National Machineries in the Countries of Central and Eastern Europe." In *Mainstreaming Gender, Democratizing the State? Institutional Mechanisms for the Advancement of Women,* ed. Shirin M. Rai, 167–185. Manchester: Manchester University Press.

Karat Coalition. 2005. "Institutional Mechanisms for Gender Equality: Despite a Formal Progress—Still Very Weak." Infosheet for Forty-ninth UN CSW session, New York, February 28–March 11, ed. Stanimira Kadjimitova, Kinga Lohmann, and Aleksandra Solik. Warsaw: Karat Coalition.

Kenney, Padraic. 2006. *The Burdens of Freedom: Eastern Europe since 1989.* London: Zed Books.

Kofman, Eleonore, Anne Phizacklea, Parvati Raghuram, and Rosemary Sales. 2000. *Gender and International Migration in Europe.* New York: Routledge.

Kramer, Anne-Marie. 2005. "Gender, Nation and the Abortion Debate in the Polish Media." In *Nation and Gender in Contemporary Europe,* ed. Vera Tolz und Stephenie Booth, 130–148. Manchester: Manchester University Press.

Lewis, Gail. 2006. "Imaginaries of Europe: Technologies of Gender, Economies of Power." *European Journal of Women's Studies* 13(2): 87–102.

Lister, Ruth. 1997. *Citizenship: Feminist Perspectives.* Basingstoke: Palgrave Macmillan.

———. 2007. "Inclusive Citizenship: Realizing the Potential." *Citizenship Studies,* 11(1), 49–61.

Lohmann, Kinga, and Anita Seibert, eds. 2003. *Gender Assessment of the Impact of EU Accession on the Status of Women in the Labour Market in CEE: National Study: Poland.* Warsaw: Karat Coalition with support from Norwegian Ministry of Foreign Affairs and Polish Ministry of Economy, Labour and Social Policy.

Magyari-Vincze, Enikö. 2006. "Romanian Gender Regimes and Women's Citizenship." In *Women and Citizenship in Central and Eastern Europe,* ed. Jasmina Lukić, Joanna Regulska, and Darja Zaviršek, 21–38. Burlington, Vt.: Ashgate.

Marksová-Tominová, Michaela, ed. 2003. *A Gender Assessment of the Impact of EU Accession on the Status of Women in the Labour Market in CEE: National Study: Czech Republic.* Prague: Gender Studies o.p.s with the support of UNIFEM and coordinated by the Karat Coalition.

Mayer, Tamar. 2000. "Gender Ironies of Nationalism: Setting the Stage." In *Gender Ironies of Nationalism: Sexing the Nation,* ed. Tamar Mayer, 1–25. New York: Routledge.

McClintock, Anne. 1995. *Imperial Leather.* New York: Routledge.

Miroiu, Mihaela. 2004. "Durzhavni muzhe, pazarni zheni: posleditsite ot leviya konservatism za politikata na pola v romanskiya prehod" (State Men, Market Women: The Effects of Left Conservatism on Gender Politics in Romanian Transition.) In *Zhenski identichnosti na Balkanite* (Women's identities in the Balkans), ed. Krassimira Daskalova and Kornelia Slavova, 95–111. Sofia: Polis.

Phillips, Anne. 1993. *Democracy and Difference.* University Park: Pennsylvania State University Press.

Prins, Baukje. 2006. "Mothers and Muslims, Sisters and Sojourners: The Contested Boundaries of Feminist Citizenship." In *Handbook of Gender and Women's Studies,* ed. Kathy Davis, Mary Evans, and Judith Lorber, 234–250. London: Sage.

Racioppi, Linda, and Katherine O'Sullivan See. 2000. "Engendering Nation and National Identity." In *Women, States and Nationalism,* ed. Sita Ranchod-Nilsson and Mary Ann Tetreault, 18–35. London: Routledge.

Rai, Shirin M. 2003. "Institutional Mechanisms for the Advancement of Women: Mainstreaming Gender, Democratizing the State?" In *Mainstreaming Gender, Democratizing the State? Institutional Mechanisms for the Advancement of Women,* ed. Shirin M. Rai, 15–39. Manchester: Manchester University Press.

Regulska, Joanna. 2001. "Gendered Integration of Europe: New Boundaries of Exclusion." In *Gender in Transition in Eastern and Central Europe: Proceedings,* ed. Gabriele Jähnert, Jana Gohrisch, Daphne Hahn, Hildegard Maria Nickel, Iris Peinl, and Katrin Schäfgen, 84–96. Berlin: Trafo Verlag.

———. 2002. "Women's Agency and Supranational Political Spaces: The European Union and Eastern Enlargement." Paper presented at the Annual Meeting of the American Association of Geographers, Los Angeles, March 20–24.

Salmenniemi, Suvi. 2005. "Civic Activity—Feminine Activity? Gender, Civil Society and Citizenship in Post-Soviet Russia." *Sociology* 39(4): 735–753.

Smith, Anthony D. 1991. *National Identity.* Harmondsworth: Penguin.

Smith, Graham, Vivien Law, Andrew Wilson, Annette Bohr, and Edward Allworth. 1998. *Nation-Building in the Post-Soviet Borderlands: The Politics of National Identities.* Cambridge: Cambridge University Press.

Steinhilber, Silke. 2002. "Women's Rights and Gender Equality in the EU Enlargement: An Opportunity for Progress." WIDE (Network Women in Development Europe) Briefing Paper. October.

Stiglitz, Joseph. 2002. *Globalization and Its Discontents.* New York: Penguin Books.

Stratigaki, Maria. 2005. "Gender Mainstreaming vs. Positive Action: An Ongoing Conflict in EU Gender Equality Policy." *European Journal of Women's Studies* 12(2): 165–186.

Szalai, Julia. 2005. "Cultural Diversity or Social Disintegration? 'Cultural Otherness' and Roma Rights in Contemporary Hungary." Paper presented at the conference "Gender Equality, Cultural Diversity: European Comparisons and Lessons," London, May 27–28.

Taljunaite, Meilute. 2005. "Gender Mainstreaming as a Strategy for Promoting Gender Equality in Lithuania." *Czech Sociological Review* 41(6): 1041–1055.

Taraban, Svitlana. 2007. "Birthday Girls, Russian Dolls, and Others: Internet Bride as the Emerging Global Identity of Post-Soviet Women." In *Living Gender after Communism,* ed. Janet Elise Johnson and Jean C. Robinson, 105–127. Bloomington: Indiana University Press.

True, Jacqui. 2003a. *Gender, Globalization, and Postsocialism: The Czech Republic after Communism.* New York: Columbia University Press.

———. 2003b. "Mainstreaming Gender in Global Public Policy." *International Feminist Journal of Politics* 5(3): 368–396.

Verloo, Mieke. 2002. "The Development of Gender Mainstreaming as a Political Concept for Europe." Keynote address to International Gender Learning Conference, Leipzig, September 6–8.

———. 2006. "Multiple Inequalities, Intersectionality and the European Union." *European Journal of Women's Studies* 13(3): 211–228.

Walby, Sylvia. 2004. "The European Union and Gender Equality: Emergent Varieties of Gender Regime." *Social Politics* 11(1): 4–29.

Werbner, Pnina, and Nira Yuval-Davis, eds. 1999. *Women, Citizenship and Difference.* London: Zed Books.

Woodcock, Shannon. 2007. "Romanian Women's Discourses of Sexual Violence: Othered Ethnicities, Gendering Spaces." In *Living Gender after Communism,* ed. Janet Elise Johnson and Jean C. Robinson, 149–168. Bloomington: Indiana University Press.

Zake, Ieva. 2002. "Gendered Political Subjectivity in Post-Soviet Latvia." *Women's Studies International Forum* 25(6): 631–640.

Zhurzhenko, Tatiana. 2001. "Free Market Ideology and New Women's Identities in Post-Socialist Ukraine." *European Journal of Women's Studies* 8(1): 24–49.

Zielińska, Eleonora. 2000. "Between Ideology, Politics and Common Sense: The Discourse of Reproductive Rights in Poland." In *Reproducing Gender: Politics, Publics, and Everyday Life after Socialism,* ed. Susan Gal and Gail Kligman, 23–57. Princeton, N.J.: Princeton University Press.

2

The Influence of European Union Legislation on Gender Equality in Central and Eastern Europe

Amanda Sloat

When the Soviet Union began to exert political influence over socialist countries across Central and Eastern Europe (CEE) after World War II, it imposed the Communist model of equality among all human beings without any distinction in class, sex, or ethnicity. Gender equality became one of the most important and successful elements of Communist propaganda, as the party sought to demonstrate how CEE women—unlike their Western counterparts—were not discriminated against: they could study, vote, and be voted for as well as achieve professional fulfillment (including participation in "masculine" jobs). Women (understood as "married working mothers") were seen to exemplify how socialism had overcome the bourgeois ideology that oppressed them, as they enjoyed the same rights as men. This perception was perpetuated by full employment for women, political representation (through quotas to bolster women's involvement), encouragement to attend higher education, and the provision of child-care facilities to aid women's contribution to the socialist economy. Yet despite the public proclamation of formal equality between women and men, hidden and visible acts of discrimination permeated all sectors of society. There was a discrepancy between women's presence in politics and the workplace and their lack of real influence at senior levels, as women remained vastly underrepresented in the upper tiers of economic and political decision-making bodies and often were not taken seriously given the tokenism of many of their positions. Consequently, socialist women had more duties than rights, while the constitutional principles of equality and nondiscrimination were never enforced by the socialist state (Eberhardt 2004).

In the years since the fall of the Berlin Wall, CEE countries have undergone vast structural reform into market economies and representative democracies. These efforts have been hastened and assisted by the quest for membership in the European Union (EU), a goal achieved by eight post-Communist countries in May 2004 and by Bulgaria and Romania in January 2007. By requiring all new member states to implement its entire body of legislation, the EU has been able to exert some influence over their development. This chapter examines the EU's role in shaping the gender configuration of the new politics of CEE, considering how the requirement to implement equality legislation has affected gender equality across the region. It draws on data collected from an EU-funded research project on women's political participation in ten CEE countries, utilizing desk research, statistical collection, and elite interviews.[1] It also uses two pieces of legislation—maternity leave and burden of proof in sex discrimination cases—as case studies to illustrate the complicated nature of gender relations in post-Communist Europe. Despite significant progress in reforming CEE societies, the chapter suggests that the complex political and socioeconomic transition process has uncovered new forms of discrimination against women along with the reemergence of patriarchal attitudes. This is exacerbated by the widely shared belief across the region that the socialist regime left a legacy of gender equality in place, which has complicated feminist attempts to mobilize women in pursuit of equal rights and EU efforts to introduce progressive social legislation.

Gender Equality under Communism

During the socialist period, key provisions declaring gender equality were contained in CEE constitutions modeled on the constitution and labor codes introduced by Joseph Stalin, the Soviet dictator. Both documents stressed that working for the benefit of society is a primary obligation and a primary right, as well as an issue of honor, for every citizen. The principle of equality of rights in the socialist society was used to support the social duties of women, who received their rights from their duty to work and bear children. Constitutional regulations provided women and men with equal rights in all areas of political, socioeconomic, and cultural life. The constitution prohibited any form of discrimination, gave citizens the right to work and choose their occupation freely, required equal remuneration for equal work, ensured the rights to rest and dignity, and guaranteed social security during sickness and after retirement. It also provided material and moral support for mothers and children, including the protection of pregnant women, paid leave of absence prior to and after giving birth, and a network of obstetrics facilities, nurseries, and kindergartens. Many of these entitlements (for example, free education, health care, paid sick leave, pensions) were wider and more generous than in Western capitalist countries. While the labor code entitled every employee (regardless of gender) to equal remuneration for work of equal value and obliged the employer to facilitate the improvement of employees' professional qualifications, it also contained detailed regulations protecting—and thereby limiting—women's work.

It could be argued that Communism hastened the legal codification of women's rights in CEE countries by implementing many equality measures in advance of Western Europe. However, the state socialist regimes simultaneously introduced provisions that discriminated against women in their effort to enable women to combine a professional career with a maternal role and to "protect" them as mothers or future mothers (see Fuszara 2004). Between 1946 and 1964, the Polish government—to take but one country example—annulled many regulations that discriminated against women on the basis of biological difference, introduced safeguards of equality of rights in regard to sex (emphasizing similarities between the sexes), and granted women the same rights as men in the political and socioeconomic spheres (see Zielińska 2002). The government also introduced protective regulations (for example, leave to care for an ill child, prohibition on pregnant women working at night) in the labor code that referred to biological differences between the sexes. Most of these women's "privileges" became a source of discrimination, particularly during the economic transition of the 1990s, when employers perceived women as more expensive and less effective employees. Women suffered from greater unemployment, faced difficulties finding work, experienced discrimination in terms of promotion and remuneration, and failed to enforce their rights given the threat of losing their jobs.

A widely shared belief across CEE is that the socialist regime left a legacy of gender equality in place. While many entitlements (for example, free education, health care, paid sick leave, pensions) were wider and more generous than in Western capitalist countries, the motivation behind them and their social effects were entirely different. For example, the socialist government could easily disguise unemployment by granting long parental leave; because mostly women requested this leave, their chances in the labor market were reduced. In reality, the constitutional principles of equality and nondiscrimination in the labor market were never actually enforced during state socialism. Although gender equality was part of the official socialist ideology, the methods of its implementation were neither satisfactory nor popular: politicians elected by quotas were not "real" legislators; there were insufficient places for children in often poor-quality daycare centers; and the requirement of full employment among the working-age population, which occurred amid the scarce availability of everyday goods and services, caused a "double burden" for women who retained primary responsibility for domestic life.

The economic uncertainty of the post-1989 transition period provided fertile ground for the revival of stereotypes that "a woman's place is at home," as nurseries were closing, unemployment was increasing, and old social practices were deteriorating. Furthermore, many people began to value security as one of the key aspects of a good job, and violations of women's labor rights increased. Although the concept of equality in the home was recognized, the traditional division of labor persisted as women suffered from the "double burden" of holding external employment and remaining responsible for the bulk of domestic chores. "During the Soviet period the rhetoric of equal rights and gender ideology towards the family and motherhood led to the maintenance of male dominance in the public sphere. The patriarchal structure of society was therefore maintained and the tradition of a gender-structured society was not interrupted" (Taljunaite 2004, 6). Yet women, as part of the system that apparently sustained their formal equality, did not always recognize the gendered basis of discrimination at that time; this continued lack of awareness has hindered efforts to construct a more egalitarian society today.

EU Accession Process

The political and economic reform process in post-Communist CEE was largely motivated by countries' desire to join the EU, which provided access to European markets, money for economic development, and a feeling of (re)connectedness with the West. Applicant countries were required by a decision of the European Council in Copenhagen in June 1993 to have stable institutions (including democracy, human and minority rights, and rule of law), a functioning market economy, and the ability to handle competitive economic pressure. In addition, aspirant governments were obliged to implement all social, economic, and legal "chapters" of EU legislation—known collectively in French as the *acquis communautaire*. There are a total of twenty-nine chapters, covering areas ranging from the environment and transport to culture and fisheries. While the *acquis* places relatively little emphasis on the equal opportunities of men and women, the candidate countries needed to implement ten directives within chapter 13 on "employment and social policy." These equality measures include: equal pay (75/117/EEC), equal treatment at the workplace (76/207/EEC), equal treatment with regard to statutory social security schemes (79/7/EEC) and occupational social security schemes (86/378/EEC), equal treatment for the self-employed and their assisting spouses (86/613/EEC), protection of pregnant workers (92/85/EEC), organization of working time (93/104/EC), parental leave (96/34/EC), burden of proof in sex discrimination cases (97/80/EC), and part-time work (97/81/EC). These directives eliminated the majority of discriminatory provisions remaining from the socialist period. They also introduced some novel measures: the equality of women and men is explicitly mentioned in law rather than primarily in the constitution; men are allowed to take paternity leave; employers must prove that they did *not* discriminate against a woman employee; and a voluntary pension insurance system has been established.

The equality *acquis* is reinforced by provisions within EU treaties that articulate the importance of gender equality. The Maastricht Treaty (1992) obliged member states to promote equality between the sexes and to ensure equal pay for equal work. The Amsterdam Treaty (1997) formally made gender equality one of the EU's main objectives, requiring member states to eliminate inequalities and promote equality between men and women. Legislative measures, such as equal treatment in social security schemes and parental leave allowances, are the method most frequently used in efforts to achieve equality and prevent discrimination in employment. The Amsterdam Treaty also empowered the EU's Council of Ministers to take "appropriate action" to combat discrimination based on sex (among other criteria) within and outside employment.

While EU provisions required CEE countries to address both antidiscrimination and gender equality, a study by the Open Society Institute (OSI) found that "the limited understanding of the differences and interrelation of the two concepts by candidate countries has led sometimes to the assumption that gender equality policy is covered by adopting anti-discrimination [legislation], and sometimes to the assertion that 'positive rights' for women contradicts the principle of non-discrimination" (OSI 2002, 16). Consequently, CEE countries have approached the implementation of the legislation differently. For example, Hungary and Bulgaria included gender equality by reforming their labor laws, Lithuania and Romania adopted a Gender Equality Act, and Romania and Bulgaria focused on general antidiscrimination legislation. However, as noted by OSI, such legislation does not necessarily cover gender equality sufficiently and can overlook the intended impact on equal treatment between men and women.

At the European Council in Berlin in 1999, EU leaders developed an action plan—known as Agenda 2000—to prepare for impending enlargement of the European Union. Among other measures, they decided that the European Commission would report regularly to the Council of Ministers on progress made by the candidate countries on meeting the accession criteria. These reports would serve as the basis for decisions on when countries would be deemed ready for EU membership. They describe the relations between the candidate country and the EU, analyze progress toward meeting the political and economic criteria, and assess the implementation of the *acquis*—focusing not only on the alignment of legislation but also on judicial and administrative mechanisms to implement and enforce the new laws. Progress is "measured on the basis of decisions actually taken, legislation actually adopted, international conventions actually ratified (with due attention being given to implementation), and measures actually implemented" (European Commission 2002, 10). The assessment is based on information provided by the candidate countries themselves, as well as by the assessment of the EU, nongovernmental organizations (NGOs), and other international organizations.

By December 2002, the EU had formally closed chapter 13 with eight CEE countries. It "provisionally closed" the chapter with Bulgaria and Romania at that time, and determined that it was "definitely closed" in December 2004. However, that did not mean that all provisions within the chapter were successfully addressed. The 2002 Regular Report for Bulgaria, for example, stated that "no progress has been made in the field of adoption of framework legislation on equal treatment for men and women" (European Commission 2002, 80). It recommended that "Bulgaria should focus further efforts on continuing transposition, particularly in the areas of anti-discrimination, equal opportunities, labour law and occupational safety and health where considerable work remains with regard to transposition of the *acquis*" (European Commission 2002, 81). By 2004, the Regular Report noted that "important progress has been made" (European Commission 2002, 83) in the field of equal treatment through the implementation of key directives on equal pay, equal treatment in employment, and burden of proof through the Law on Protection against Discrimination. In addition, amendments to the Labor Code introduced requirements regarding parental leave as well as protection of pregnant workers, while the Ministry of Labor and Social Policy developed a sector focused on "Equal Opportunities for Women and Men." While implementing legislation on antidiscrimination was introduced, the report noted that the Commission for the Prevention of Discrimination still needed to be established. The report concluded that "in order to complete preparations for membership, Bulgaria's efforts should now focus on effectively implementing the *acquis* and establishing the necessary implementing structures in the areas of labor law, anti-discrimination, equal opportunities for women and men and public health" (87). While the EU offered technical and financial assistance to candidate countries (through programs such as PHARE), it has fairly limited resources to monitor and ensure compliance in all areas. In this case, the failure to implement fully and enforce gender equality provisions did not prevent the European Commission from closing that chapter of accession negotiations with Bulgaria.

Maternity Leave and Burden of Proof in Sex Discrimination

As the EU was established first and foremost as an economic union, the requirement for candidate countries to meet accession requirements focuses primarily on the need to ensure a sustainable market economy and fair competition. This was clearly stated by the European Council in Copenhagen whose declaration of preaccession requirements "underlined the importance of approximation of laws in the associated countries to those applicable in the Community, in the first instance with regard to distortion of competition and, in addition—in the perspective of accession—to protection of workers, the environment and consumers" (European Council 1993, 15). The requirement to implement the EU's equality *acquis* contains a normative assumption that such laws will improve the position of women in CEE, protecting their status as workers as well as ensuring fair competition across the region. This section examines the implementation of two directives, maternity leave and the burden of proof in sex discrimination cases, to assess the effect of EU legislation on post-Communist gender equality. The former provision existed under state socialism, while the latter is a novel concept introduced to CEE countries by the EU. Although the legal framework is in place for greater equality and nondiscrimination, research has found that many CEE countries are failing to enforce the legislation or pay sufficient attention to the impact of unequal treatment of women in the private sphere. While legislative initiatives are a useful first step, it seems that a change in social attitudes is also necessary to ensure true gender equality.

PRE-1989

All CEE countries had legislation that safeguarded the work of the pregnant woman: no employment could be denied because of pregnancy, while no pregnant woman could be dismissed or have her work conditions altered. Companies were required to transfer expectant mothers to less burdensome work and ensure that nursing mothers could breastfeed. If a woman returned to her job after finishing maternity leave, the employer was required to reassign her to her original work and workplace; if this was impossible because the work was made redundant or the workplace had closed, the organization had to provide other work according to her contract. Maternity provisions during state socialism were intended to support the state's pronatalist policies: through attractive benefits, the state tried to encourage and influence women to bear children in circumstances in which many mothers were unwilling or unable to give up their job for the sake of raising their children. The assistance provided for women during the first years of motherhood was part of an affirmative policy that was wrongly understood as promoting women's interests. Many parents disliked the family policies, which allowed limited time for child care without the mother breaking her service record and losing her job.

POST-1989

The EU required the implementation of legislation on the "protection of pregnant women, women who have recently given birth and women who are breastfeeding" (92/85/EEC). The directive takes minimum measures to protect the health and safety of women who fall within this specific risk group. It requires employers to protect such workers from harmful chemical and physical agents, and to exempt them from performing night work during their pregnancy and for a period following childbirth. Maternity leave must be for an uninterrupted period of at least fourteen weeks before and/or after delivery, two of which must occur before the delivery. Women may not be dismissed for reasons related to their condition during the period from the beginning of their pregnancy to the end of the period of leave from work.

While accession countries were required to ensure that the general provisions of the law were met, they were allowed to implement the legislation as they wished. Bulgaria is still relying on pre-89 legislation, which provides de jure if not de facto protection. The Czech Republic and Slovakia are the only two CEE countries that have constitutional provisions on maternity protection rights. For example, Article 28 of the Slovak constitution entitles women, young people, and people with disabilities to special health protection and working conditions.

Article 41 gives pregnant women the right to special treatment, legal protection in working relations, and adequate working conditions. Half the CEE countries that joined the EU (the Czech Republic, Hungary, Latvia, Poland, Slovakia) used existing or new labor laws to implement the provisions of the maternity leave directive. In Slovakia, the Labor Code includes regulations on dismissing pregnant women and women on maternity leave (part of pre-89 legislation); it also includes a new legislative feature that prohibits the employer from asking for any information related to a woman's pregnancy. It defines the terms "pregnant employee" and "breastfeeding mother" for the first time, while still entitling breastfeeding mothers to take breaks for feeding as pre-89. Other countries introduced new legislation. For example, Estonia's Parental Benefit Act (2004) regulates the conditions and procedures for the payment of parental benefit and seeks to compensate for the loss of income arising from rearing a child and to support the combination of work and family life.

Generally speaking, newly implemented and revised legislation created an even more favorable maternity situation for women in CEE.[2] In the Czech Republic, small modifications occurred systematically, such as the replacement of the prohibition on sending pregnant women and women caring for children under one year of age on business trips with the necessary approval of the woman being sent on such trips. Romanian legislation contained more precise provisions and more detailed statements, particularly in regard to the obligations of the employer and to women's ability to defend their rights with the support of trade unions. Many rights were extended in terms of the period of leave and monetary benefit: the maximum length of parental leave for infant care was extended from twelve to twenty-four months; such leave is now paid, unlike pre-89; and the maternal leave for pregnancy and nursing was also extended by 14 days, currently totaling 126 days. However, these provisions also have a double-edged effect: on the one hand, they improve women's maternity and maternity-related leave entitlements; on the other hand, they can act as a means of keeping women out of the workforce for an extended period of time. It could be argued that this is the case in Slovenia, where the Parental Protection and Family Benefit Act (2001) provides maternity leave of 105 days—one week longer than prescribed by the European directive. It also requires the mother to begin maternity leave 28 days prior to the expected date of birth, as opposed to the European requirement of taking leave two weeks prior to the birth.

Burden of Proof in Sex Discrimination

PRE-1989

Under state socialism, there were no specific regulations for or any concept related to the reversal of the burden of proof in sex discrimination cases. Legal regulations offered only basic protection, as exemplified by Article 7 of the Czechoslovakian Labor Code, which simply stated that women had the same standing at work as men and that working conditions had to enable women's participation. Similarly, Article 20 of the constitution established equal opportunities for all citizens and equal rights for men and women regarding the family, workplace, and public life. The lack of case law tradition on sex discrimination across the region further hindered efforts to secure legal remedy in such situations. Incidents of indirect discrimination, usually latent but occasionally explicit in job advertisements (and always directed against women), were sometimes brought to the attention of the public and criticized by women's organizations, the women's sections of trade unions, and women sociologists interested in women's issues, but to little effect.

POST-1989

The EU directive on the "burden of proof in sex discrimination cases" (97/80/EC) requires member states to take such measures in accordance with their national judicial systems to ensure that, where the plaintiff establishes before a court or other competent authority facts from which discrimination may be presumed to exist, the defendant must prove that there has been no contravention of the principle of equality. The concept of requiring an employer to prove that she or he did not act in a discriminatory way is a novelty for most CEE countries, as neither the law nor the concept existed during state socialism. Just over half of the CEE countries (the Czech Republic, Hungary, Latvia, Poland, Romania, Slovakia) introduced new or amended labor laws to implement this directive. The Czech Republic, for example, transposed the directive mainly through the Civil Code, Labor Code, and civil judicial regulation in order to facilitate the legal standing of victims of sex-based discrimination by defining direct and indirect discrimination and by requiring the burden of proof to be borne by the one who allegedly carried out the discriminatory conduct. This so-called reverse burden of proof—which applies to discrimination on the basis of sex, racial or ethnic origins, religion, creed, worldview, disabilities, age, or sexual orientation—is laid down in the Czech Civil Judiciary Code.

Several countries utilized alternative legislative measures. Bulgaria used the overarching Anti-Discrimination Act (2003) to implement about half of the directives within the equality *acquis*. In Slovenia, Article 6 of the Employment Relationship Act (2002) provided a general definition of indirect discrimination relating to gender, race, age, religious belief, nationality, and other personal circumstances. The act places the burden of proof on the employer in cases where different treatment must be justified by the type and nature of the work (Article 6) and in the event of an accusation of sexual harassment (Article 45). Article 5 of the Equal Opportunities Act (2002) focuses on indirect and direct sex discrimination, and provides a method for dealing with cases of suspected unequal treatment of the sexes through the Equal Opportunities Office.

The main weakness in the handling of this directive in most CEE countries is its narrow focus on employment-related discrimination. This is the case in Poland, where the Labor Code reverses the burden of proof in discrimination cases before labor courts when it orders

> the employer to prove that it was guided by considerations other than sex in the refusal to initiate or terminate an employment relationship with a given person or detrimental formation of his/her remuneration for work or other employment conditions or upon overlooking such person during promotions or awarding other benefits associated with the employment, or overlooking such person when designating participation in instruction courses to raise job qualifications. (Fuszara 2004, 15)

While the formulation of the principle meets and even exceeds the requirements of the directive, its work-based application excludes the possibility of its extension to sex discrimination in other contexts, such as the provision of goods and services.

Although the EU directive expands women's legal protection and rights in theory, evidence from across CEE suggests that it is not being adequately enforced—particularly as victims of sex discrimination have not been educated or empowered to use laws that protect against discriminatory behavior. This is clearly demonstrated by the lack of case law on the subject across CEE. For example, only seven cases have been brought to the Estonian Supreme Court since 2000 where the word "discrimination" was mentioned; none was connected with gender discrimination (Laas 2004). In the Czech Republic, there have been no recorded disputes since 1999 in labor-management relations with the motive of discrimination on the basis of sex (Hašková et al. 2004). Latvian women have initiated and won only two legal actions related to discrimination since the early 1990s: one on equal pay and one following a refusal to hire a woman for a job at a men's prison (Cimdina 2004). The first discrimination suit in Slovakia was brought in 2004 by two female employees of Volkswagen—Electrical Systems who were fired after being employed on nine short-term contracts for over two years; they took the employer to court and won the case (Filipko 2004). There have been an increasing number of sexual harassment lawsuits in Poland, though most were drastic incidents (for example, an employer forcing a woman into sexual intercourse by abusing the superiority relationship) that were brought first to the criminal courts.

Several explanations have been given for the small number of discrimination-based lawsuits that have been brought in CEE courts. In Hungary, legal proceedings cannot provide sufficient compensation, be used as a preventive power, or protect against unlawful dismissal (Eberhardt 2004). In the Czech Republic, explanations include the lack of legal awareness regarding discrimination on the basis of sex, the pressure of unemployment, and the lengthy adjudication process (Hašková et al. 2004). As labor management disputes in the Czech Republic last on average 693 days from the day they are submitted to the day they are decided, women who are dependent on daily wages are reluctant to subject their families to such economic risk. Many Slovakian women are reluctant to take legal action in cases of gender discrimination because they do not know their rights and were never empowered by any women's movement or awareness-raising exercises like their Western European counterparts (Bitusikova 2004). Similarly, many Romanian women remain unaware that legal recourse exists. A study by the Partnership for Equality Centre (PEC 2003) on violence at the workplace found that 45% of the population was unaware of juridical instruments against sexual harassment. In sum, the introduction of a novel piece of protective legislation is virtually worthless if it is not implemented fully, if women lack knowledge about its existence, and if there is limited judicial enforcements of its provisions.

The EU's Impact on Gender Equality in CEE

While having equal opportunity laws on the statute books is a necessary require-ment for EU membership and a helpful step in the quest for gender equality, it is important to ensure that such laws provide a meaningful framework for the delivery of equal opportunities and that women understand and protect their rights. This chapter has considered the question of whether EU accession has improved women's equality in CEE by using the lens of legislative initiatives. A Hungarian researcher determined that in her country:

the twin factors of the unsophisticated legal culture and the dominant traditional perceptions of gender relations are militating against making those policies a reality. The accession process was accompanied by mostly hollow disputes, reflecting the predictable conflicts of national politics instead of calling attention to the significance of becoming a member state. The fact that the government's actions were determined by the exterior requirements of the EU, rather than demands and expectations at home, resulted in empty rhetoric echoing certain fashionable Euro-centric phrases without meaning to attribute any significance to them. (Eberhardt 2004, 25)

The remainder of this chapter analyzes the lessons of the case studies across the region, assessing the mixed impact of the introduction of EU legislation on shaping both attitudes and practices in CEE.

CHANGE IN ATTITUDES

Following the 1989 transition, most people's perception of social change was the burden of economic restructuring (in which women were particularly vulnerable), while democracy and civic freedom were seen as secondary. Many people began to value job security as one of the key aspects of a good job, which partly explains why so few women have been willing to risk unemployment by taking employers to court on discrimination charges. Reinvigorated conservatism abolished many social measures that used to protect and promote women, while campaigns for gender equality were seen as unnecessary because the Communist agenda had damaged awareness of women's rights by emphasizing women's (supposed) liberation. Perceptions of gender equality in CEE remain heavily influenced by the legacy of Communism, particularly as "the countries themselves inherited a 'social *acquis*' from decades of communist rule" (Matyja 2002, 2). Thus, the introduction of some EU polices such as maternity leave were not generally seen as a radical departure from the equality measures put in place by socialist governments.

The culture of CEE countries has not yet institutionalized gender equality as a political norm, as legislation introduced under socialism "often had the reverse effect of actually reinforcing stereotypical roles and unequally distributing men and women's family responsibilities" (OSI 2002, 13). In Hungary, for example, the concepts of "antidiscrimination" and "equal opportunities" do not have the expected impact, partly because the nature and extent of gender discrimination are not socially recognized. Because many Hungarians do not consider gender inequality as a problem, equal pay and equal treatment are not widely recognized social goals since the unequal status of women in the labor market and at home is considered a normal state of affairs. When comparing the pre- and post-89 gender equality culture, Eberhardt (2004, 4) concludes that

> both are ruled by a patriarchal structure of ideas and values that were supported and legitimated by the state itself. This legitimacy primarily springs from legislation that, while asserting equal rights for all citizens, also includes provisions putting women at a relative disadvantage as compared to men. Many of the measures originating under the previous state socialist political regime survived almost unchanged because of the underlying norms remained the same to date.

Furthermore, efforts to introduce feminism and the importance of equal opportunities for men and women have often been regarded negatively as an import from Western Europe that is completely unrelated to the daily reality of women in CEE. Many CEE women dislike feminism's perceived linkages to antimale attitudes and stereotyped Western feminism, while others prioritize economic development over the achievement of equality (Fábián 2002). Some women continue to associate "feminism" with state intervention and discredited "isms" of the past (Einhorn 1996; Goldman 1996; Gal and Kligman 2000): because the Communist regimes considered emancipation a state ideology and emphasized women's liberation under Communism, many believed the women's movement was humiliated and consequently unnecessary post-89. This view is perpetuated by some political leaders who argue that the "equal rights" granted to women have not been abolished, so therefore discrimination based on one's gender cannot be a current problem (Taljunaite 2004). This intellectual and ideological construct has hindered the development of a Europe-wide debate about the achievement of gender equality and the importance of addressing the inherent sexism of CEE societies, as well as complicated efforts to introduce and gain acceptance of equality initiatives.

That said, the requirement to implement the EU equality *acquis* has raised awareness within CEE governments and societies In Poland, for example, equality regulations were commonly associated in the early 1990s with the former political system and considered to be a "thing of the past" that was incompatible with a free market economy. EU accession legitimized equality concerns and increased public awareness of European regulations regarding equality between women and men (Fuszara 2004). Slovenia has one of the region's strongest equal opportunity programs with well-informed civil servants; governmental bodies, aware that equality of women and men cannot be achieved solely by legislation, have developed action plans and educational activities (Bahovec 2004a). Slovakian institutions responsible for gender equality have begun demonstrating a more positive approach, though they cite the need for more experts in their departments to monitor and enforce the new legislation (Bitusikova 2004). Officials working on gender equality in the Czech Republic also appear to have developed a greater sensitivity toward its importance. While they frequently lack knowledge of the reasons for the EU equality *acquis,* there has been a positive change in the attitudes of some officials who have been explicitly appointed to implement equal opportunity policies (Hašková et al. 2004).

The major impact of the introduction of European equality legislation has been providing social actors with a more precise definition of equal opportunity provisions, as the EU forced the creation of nondiscrimination frameworks that predominantly male governments might otherwise have neglected—particularly given religious opposition in some countries and the post-89 prioritization of economic development. The preaccession requirement to adopt gender-sensitive legislation and establish institutions to implement these policies legitimated the efforts of civic actors and enabled them to penetrate decision-making structures. The EU also imparted crucial knowledge, financial support for the development of equality institutions, and a model for sensitivity to gender issues. These developments have been particularly appreciated by the few women's NGOs in CEE that are directly advocating gender equality and gender-sensitive legislation. For example, the cofounder of a Slovenian women's NGO observed:

> If I look at the foundations of my work, the EU has certainly promoted equality between the sexes; at least, we often used the EU as a kind of argument, a standard, in the sense, "The EU recommends, the EU requires." It's difficult to say whether we would in any case, even without joining the EU, have reached the same conditions that exist today in the area of sexual equality; I think it would have taken significantly longer and herein, too, lies the question as to whether we have always been moving in the same direction. (in Bahovec 2004b, 26)

CHANGE IN PRACTICE

Reports from across CEE suggest that legislative harmonization has made only a marginal change in practice, as women generally hold less favorable positions and remain numerically weaker than men. In Slovenia, the Bureau for Equal Opportunities phone line reports many cases where women have been discriminated against (for example, after a woman goes on maternity leave her job is suddenly "closed"; when a woman gets pregnant her work is suddenly "no longer necessary";

women are sexually harassed and because of social perception leave their jobs; and incoming male colleagues get promoted over long-serving women) (Bahovec 2004a). The case study on the burden of proof in sex discrimination highlights continuing challenges in the implementation and enforcement of EU equality legislation. Despite new guarantees of nondiscrimination, women do not feel empowered to claim such rights and to take cases to court (Marcher 2001). As Jivka Marinova from the Bulgarian Gender Research Foundation aptly concludes: "Real equality of opportunities increasingly requires not just the elimination of discrimination, but the active promotion of equality through monitoring, planning, training and improving skills, developing wider social networks and encouraging adaptability" (in Videva 2004, 15).

Part of the problem stems from the decision of the European Commission to allow CEE governments to "consolidate" EU policies by grouping together differ-ent categories of socially disadvantaged individuals (women, ethnic minorities, people with disabilities) into a single legislative act. Many countries chose to issue a single detailed plan in order to simplify and streamline the body of EU law, cut red tape, and make the *acquis* more understandable and user-friendly to EU citizens (Uniting Europe 2003; Eberhardt 2004). In reality, this has meant that less time and money have been spent on gender issues, as the other groups are seen to be a greater priority (for example, the Roma in Slovakia and Bulgaria). This approach also fails to recognize and address adequately the nature of discrimination suffered by CEE women.

The lack of public awareness of equality legislation is also to blame. Greater education would be beneficial for state bureaucrats at every institutional and political level, as well as for the general public. Educational programs must begin by reshaping the way in which gender equality issues are understood, as women's issues have traditionally been connected to demographic concerns (that is, reproduction). "Gender politics" in the official sense is still effectively the equivalent of "strategic family policies" intended to deal with family crises, housing policies, tax benefits, and other provisions for families with children (Eberhardt 2004). Given the dominant conservative values regarding the role of women and sexual politics that are adhered to by the majority of the population and backed by some demographic data (*Család és munka* 2000), the proposals for measures helping housewives to stay at home are still considered to be at the heart of such policy making. Social norms in most countries still regard women as bearing primary responsibility for managing domestic life, while limited and expensive child care hinders the ability of some women to seek outside employ-ment. For example, a Gender Barometer survey in Romania (OSF 2000, 5) found that 63% of the interviewees believe that it is women's duty more than men's to do household chores; 70% believe that it is more men's duty to bring money to the house; and only 26% believe that men can raise children just as well as women can. Gender equality will never be fully achieved as long as home and family remain seen as primarily women's domain.

In conclusion, the introduction of the EU equality *acquis* has achieved some success in improving women's standing in employment by developing a legal framework for the protection of women's rights, beginning to raise social awareness, and providing a set of principles through which women can begin to articulate and claim their rights. However, it has failed to address women's discrimination in the private sphere—including the disproportionate burden of domestic responsibilities and the effect of domestic violence. Recognizing this gap, the European Women's Lobby has called for the broadening of EU standards beyond labor and for the introduction of a specific directive on gender discrimination as a means of addressing these wider challenges (OSI 2002, 54). Furthermore, there has not been enough action at the EU level to ensure that gender equality provisions are fully implemented and enforced by the new member states. Increasing women's political participation and economic involvement requires more than new legislation; it also necessitates a shift in social attitudes to enable women's self-realization. Such a change will take time and cannot be accomplished by legislation alone; rather, it will require increased awareness by politicians and officials of the importance of ensuring that gender equality and antidiscrimination rights are fully implemented and enforced, continued dialogue among women across Europe about the nature and effect of equal opportunities, and concerted action by CEE women to claim their rights.

NOTES

1. This chapter draws from a research project entitled "Enlargement, Gender and Governance: The Civic and Political Participation and Representation of Women in EU Candidate Countries" (EGG). The three-year (December 2002–November 2005) study was funded by the EU Fifth Framework Programme (HPSE-CT2002-00115). Project participants are from the three Baltic countries (Latvia, Lithuania, Estonia), Central Europe (Hungary, Poland, Czech Republic, Slovakia), Eastern Europe (Romania, Bulgaria), and the former Yugoslavia (Slovenia). The chapter uses Central and Eastern Europe (CEE) as shorthand for all ten countries. For more information, see the project's Web site at www.qub.ac.uk/egg.

2. There are some exceptions to the generosity of maternity regulations. In Lithuania, the system retains its Soviet-era features while reducing some pre-89 provisions. Some Hungarian laws—especially in respect to relieving pregnant women from work duties—seemed more favorable during state socialism.

WORKS CITED

Bahovec, Eva. 2004a. Implementing the Equality *Acquis:* Slovenia. Unpublished report prepared for the European Commission during the EGG research project.

———. 2004b. Mapping Women's Campaign for Change: Slovenia. Unpublished report prepared for the European Commission during the EGG research project.

Bitusikova, Alexandra. 2004. Implementing the Equality *Acquis:* Slovakia. Unpublished report prepared for the European Commission during the EGG research project.

Cimdina, Ausma. 2004. Implementing the Equality *Acquis:* Latvia. Unpublished report prepared for the European Commission during the EGG research project.

Család és munka—értékek és aggodalmak a rendszerváltozás után (Family and work—values and worries after the regime change). 2000. Budapest: Central Statistical Office, Population Research Institute.

Eberhardt, Eva. 2004. Implementing the Equality *Acquis:* Hungary. Unpublished report prepared for the European Commission during the EGG research project.

Einhorn, Barbara. 1996. "Gender and Citizenship in East Central Europe after the End of State Socialist Policies for Women's 'Emancipation.'" In *Citizenship and Democratic Control in Contemporary Europe,* ed. Barbara Einhorn, Mary Kaldor, and Zdenek Kavan, 69–86. Cheltenham, UK: Edward Elgar.

European Commission. 2002. *2002 Regular Report on Bulgaria's Progress toward Accession.* COM (2002) 700 Final, SEC (2002) 1400, 9/10/2002.

———. 2004. *2004 Regular Report on Bulgaria's Progress toward Accession.* COM (2004) 657 Final, SEC (2004) 1199, 6/10/2004.

European Council. 1993. Conclusions of the Presidency. June 20–21. SN 180/1/93, REV 1.

Fábián, Katalin. 2002. "Cacophony of Voices: Interpretations of Feminism and Its Consequences for Political Action among Hungarian Women's Groups." *European Journal of Women's Studies* 9(3): 269–290.

Filipko, Richard. 2004. "Zamestnavatel prehral spor so zamestnankynami" (An employer lost court case with the female employees). *SME,* March 26.

Fuszara, Malgorzata. 2004. Implementing the Equality *Acquis:* Poland. Unpublished report prepared for the European Commission during the EGG research project.

Gal, Susan, and Gail Kligman. 2000. *The Politics of Gender after Socialism: A Comparative-Historical Essay.* Princeton, N.J.: Princeton University Press.

Goldman, Lenore. 1996. "To Act without 'Isms': Women in East Central Europe and Russia." In *The Gendered New World Order: Militarism, Development, and the Environment,* ed. Jennifer Turpin and Lois Lorentzen, 35–50. New York: Routledge.

Hašková, Hana, Gabriela Koláŕová, and Jana Pomahačová. 2004. Implementing the Equality *Acquis:* Czech Republic. Unpublished report prepared for the European Commission during the EGG research project.

Laas, Anu. 2004. Implementing the Equality *Acquis:* Estonia. Unpublished report prepared for the European Commission during the EGG research project.

Marcher, Brigitte. 2001. Gender Orientation of the EU-Enlargement Policy. Written version of an intervention made during a panel discussion at a conference organized by WIDE Austria, "EU-Eastern Enlargement: Empowerment of Marginalisation," Renner Institute, Vienna.

Matyja, Miroslaw. 2002. "Gender Equality in the European Union after the Eastern Enlargement—Aspects of Subsidiarity." Paper presented at the conference "Alva Myrdal's Questions to Our Time," Uppsala University, March 6–8.

OSF (Open Society Foundation). 2000. Barometrul de Gen (The gender barometer). A poll by the Gallup Institute (Gallup Organization Romania). Bucharest: Open Society Foundation.

OSI (Open Society Institute). 2002. *Monitoring the EU Accession Process: Equal Opportunities for Women and Men in the European Accession Programme.* Budapest: OSI.

PEC (Partnership for Equality Centre) (Centrul Parteneriat pentru Egalitate). 2003. *Cercetarea naţională privind violenţa în familie şi la locul de muncă* (National research regarding domestic violence and violence at the workplace). Bucharest: PEC.

Taljunaite, Meilute. 2004. Implementing the Equality *Acquis:* Lithuania. Unpublished report prepared for the European Commission during the EGG research project.

Uniting Europe. 2003. "EU Set to Simplify EU Body of Law." *Acquis,* no. 219, February 17.

Videva, Nelly. 2004. Implementing the Equality *Acquis:* Bulgaria. Unpublished report prepared for the European Commission during the EGG research project.

Zielińska, Elenora. 2002. "Sytuacja kobiet w Polsce w świetle zmian legislacyjnych okresu transformacji" (Women's legal situation during the transformation period). In *Kobiety w Polsce na przełomie wieków. Nowy kontrakt płci?* (Women in Poland at the turn of the century: New gender contract?), ed. Malgorzata Fuszara. Warsaw: Instytut Spraw Publicznych.

3

Public Policies as Vehicles of Social Exclusion: The Case of Romani Women's Access to Reproductive Health in Romania

Enikö Magyari-Vincze

This chapter addresses the issue of how Romani women's access to reproductive health in Romania has been shaped by public policies both because such an analysis can provide real insight into the dynamics of gender politics in post-Communist Romania and because it can illuminate more generally how politically and ideologically driven policies function in a postsocialist context.[1] In particular, it highlights how these policies—by not being able to diminish the effects of the patterns of social exclusion produced as a result of economic, social, and cultural forces—are maintaining and reinforcing inequalities created at the intersection of ethnicity, gender, and class. Moreover, this chapter also contributes to theorizing how gender, ethnicity, and class are intertwined within systems of power (Moore 1994, 2000; Bradley 1992), on the ways cultural forms and political-economic processes shape one another (Ortner 1999), and on how an individual is at once a social person and an individual agent (Strathern 1992) when making decisions under the constraints of material conditions, social expectations, and cultural conceptions. These contributions are developed in the conclusion, together with some final remarks about Romani women's access to reproductive health as a policy issue.

In this chapter, I rely on Marxist approaches that treat reproductive issues as embedded in the context of explicit and variable material conditions and broader economic relations, class divisions, the nature of health care and access to it, and the types of birth control that are available (see Ginsburg and Rapp 1995). I also draw from analyses that focus attention on women's moral claims (entitlements) in the area of reproduction, and emphasize that such claims are articulated in relation to social expectations about fertility, sexuality, and motherhood (see, for example, Unnithan-Kumar, 2003).

Recognizing that public policies are "action-oriented instruments, which decision-makers use to solve problems" (Titmuss 1974, 23), my analysis will not concentrate on the orientation of the policy makers themselves. Rather, my goal is to analyze policies for Roma and policies of reproductive health as cultural texts: written documents and discursive formations that empower some people while silencing others (in this case, Romani women), and as having "material outcomes that impinge on people's lives" (Seidel and Vidal 1997, 59). Therefore, policies are treated here as cultural texts that talk about the dominant conceptions and about the power relations in society, which transform Romani women into one of the most underserved categories. At the same time, in observing how these policies have been put into practice by the health care providers, this chapter considers these policies as forms of power, which—together with other forces such as economic conditions, social expectancies, and cultural conceptions— "organize society and structure the ways people perceive themselves and their opportunities" (Shore and Write 1997, 7). This means I will explore how public policies in action shape the way a Romani woman living in poverty may think about her access to reproductive health and may make her reproductive decisions as a member of a particular group exposed to the institutional racism of the majority society, and as an individual evaluated through strict community norms regarding maternity, fertility, and sexuality. Thus, the chapter contributes to efforts to explain how the practices that implement certain policies and the underlying conceptions of the main actors within the (reproductive) health care public system together reproduce social inequalities along the axis of gender, ethnicity, and class. Taken as a whole, then, this chapter aims to contribute to the anthropology of policy conducted as critical applied research that can provide input into public discussions of social issues in Romanian society (Shore and Wright 1997). Accordingly, I also formulate some recommendations regarding policies for Roma and policies of reproductive health that the research suggests will increase Romani women's de facto access to resources in this domain.

The research on which the analysis of this chapter is based involved a multisite ethnography, including participant observation, interviewing and filming in the Boyash Gypsy community from the city of Orăştie and within different sites of local health care providers[2]; an examination of the Romanian policies of reproduction and policies for Roma; and an investigation of Romani women's organizations. Through these multiple approaches, I analyze "connections between levels and forms of social process and action," explore "how those processes work in different sites," and trace connections "between different organizational and everyday worlds" (Shore and Write 1997, 14). As a result, I could understand the multidimensional processes of social exclusion, which—through the interplay of their ethnicity, gender, and class—place Romani women in a multiply disadvantaged position, from where—while making their decisions about reproduction—they negotiate and resist the forces that shape their lives.

The International Significance of Addressing Romani Women's Reproductive Health

Statistics and estimates suggest that Romania has the highest number of Roma in Europe. In the 1992 census, 401,087 people (1.8%) of a total population of approximately 22.6 million identified themselves as Roma; by the 2002 census, the number of those self-identifying as Roma increased to 535,250 (2.5%). Unofficial estimates of the actual figure of Roma in Romania range between 1.8 and 2.5 million. In 2002, among the 21,213 inhabitants of Orăştie, 865 persons (4.07%) declared themselves Roma, and 156 stated that they spoke Romanes. The research rooted partially in this local setting has relevance beyond Orăştie, for, as we will see, it is related, on the one hand, to Roma's condition in Europe and, on the other hand, to reproductive health, issues that are being addressed more and more both in the social sciences and European politics.

The concept of Roma/Gypsy as a "European issue" was formally acknowledged in 1993, when a Resolution of the Council of Europe declared Gypsies to be "a true European minority," insofar as they were identified in almost every European country, totaling a population of 7 to 9 million, or even 12 million according to other estimates. In 1996, the European Roma Rights Centre was created to monitor the situation of Roma across Europe, and its findings have documented that anti-Gypsy racism is flourishing not only in the Central and Eastern European candidate countries but also in the old European Union member states. Human rights violations and the deteriorating socioeconomic conditions of Roma led the European Community in 2000 to enact the so-called Racial Equality Directive. At the same time that the human rights of Roma have attracted the attention of European policy makers, international organizations have begun to recognize reproductive health and reproductive control as issues of human rights central to women's well-being and crucial for achieving gender equity and social justice. The declaration of the International Conference on Population and Development held in Cairo in 1994, and a year later the Fourth World Conference on Women in Beijing stressed that it is women's right to have control over and decide freely about matters related to their sexual and reproductive health, including decisions on the number of children, on the time and spacing of birth, and on the contraceptive method used in order to avoid unwanted pregnancies.

Linking the issue of Roma's general condition to that of Romani women's access to reproductive health should reveal the complex processes of social exclusion and the ways in which ethnicity, gender, and class intertwine while producing and maintaining social hierarchies. The phenomenon of reproductive health might be analyzed as a "small problem" that allows us to look at the dynamics of a "large issue." In particular, it affords an opportunity to see how different resources are unequally distributed by these systems of classification, as people within certain social categories are excluded from access to employment, proper housing, education, health care, or services of a good quality. Briefly put, my ethnographic case study aims to contribute to the understanding of the social and cultural processes of exclusion that produce marginalization and inequality in a postsocialist context. In particular, I focus on the impact of public policies on this phenomenon.

In what follows, I analyze how policies for Roma and policies of reproductive health fail to consider the particular needs and reproductive entitlements of Romani women and how, as a result, these policies are responsible for the marginalization, discrimination, and exclusion of Romani women from vital resources, including good quality (reproductive) health services.

Policies for Roma in Romania: From Gender Blindness to Pronatalist Concerns

Due to the large Romani population in Romania and the extreme deprivation of Roma there, many international organizations have been focusing attention on their situation in this country. For example, the European Roma Rights Centre has made Romania a priority country since beginning activity in 1996, and the EU has been strongly critical of Romania's treatment of its Romani population. In its Regular Report on Romania's Progress towards Accession of November 8, 2000, for example, the European Commission stated that "Roma remain subject to widespread discrimination throughout Romanian society. However, the government's commitment to addressing this situation remains low and there has been little substantial progress in this area since the last regular report."

The current situation of Romani communities should be viewed in the context of the legacy of both the presocialist and the socialist eras. Roma were enslaved for a long period of time (the first records of their enslavement in the provinces of Wallachia and Moldavia date from the mid-fourteenth century, and they were liberated only by the second half of the nineteenth century). After emancipation, they continued to live on the margins of rural and urban communities. The Communist regime did not recognize Romani as national minorities, and during this period half of the Romani workers were employed in rural areas; their traditional jobs were on the margins of legality. Indeed, a state decree in 1970 identified Romani with the dangers of social parasitism, anarchism and deviant behavior and followed with measures aiming to eliminate nomadism. All these transformed Romani people (living in approximately forty "nations," some of them keeping old cultural traditions and speaking Romany) into a culturally undervalued and socially excluded category whose "problems" were identified as a consequence of social underdevelopment and a "culture of poverty" and not as issues resulting from forced de-ethnicization and related structural racism and discrimination.

Strategy of the Government of Romania for Improving the Condition of the Roma

As many reports document, anti-Romani sentiment broke out in a wave of collective violence against Roma after the collapse of the Nicolae Ceauşescu regime in December 1989. Under the pressure from international organizations and internal activism, the Ministry of Public Information issued the *Strategy of the Government of Romania for Improving the Condition of the Roma* on April 25, 2001. Since then, the *Strategy* has been through monitoring processes, both at the central and local levels, and reports from 2002 and 2004 appraised the government strategy.

The government document included a commitment to ensuring the conditions necessary for Roma to have equal opportunities in obtaining a decent standard of living, as well as a commitment to the prevention of institutional and societal discrimination against Roma. The *Strategy* included as "sectorial fields" of action "community development and administration," "housing," "social security," "health care," "economics," "justice and public order," "child welfare," "education," "culture and denominations," and "communication and civic involvement." The overall time frame of the *Strategy* was to be ten years (2001–2010), with the medium-term plan of action having a target of four years. While the *Strategy*'s general aims were for the most part noble in sentiment, there was a considerable lack of detail in the plans. For example, the goal of "including the Roma community leaders in the local administrative decision-making which affects the Roma" is to be welcomed, but the means of realizing this aim are not stated. The sections of the program on "Justice and Public Order" and "Education" are particularly weak. Revealed is the image of a passive state, viewing discrimination as solely the effect of laws, unwilling to act to address discriminatory acts, and content to "observe" human rights without acting to guarantee that they are respected by all. Other measures implicitly rehash the prevailing view that Roma are to blame for the unsatisfactory human rights situation in Romania. Provisions on education are basically flawed. Similarly, the development of a family planning and contraceptive program within the set of targets to be achieved in health care suggests a lack of sensitivity in approaching the issue of Romani women and health care. Another fundamental question raised by the *Strategy* in its present form is the question of resources. Nowhere in the *Strategy* document is the issue of funding addressed.

Decade for Ethnic Roma Inclusion

Under the joint support of the World Bank and the Open Society Institute, eight governments in Central and Southeast Europe sponsored the "Decade for Ethnic Roma Inclusion." This initiative was launched in Romania in February 2005. Its activities focus on increasing access to education at all levels and to basic medical services, on supporting the Roma cultural heritage, and on improving the living conditions in areas populated mainly by ethnic Roma. Beginning in July 2005, Romania held the first Presidency of the Decade. Obviously, the National Agency for the Ethnic Roma of the Romanian Government has played a major role in this. Its aim is to give substance to the concept of Roma inclusion and, among other things, to coordinate the process of sharing the best practices in terms of Roma policies. At this point, Romania has been presented as a model for its program on Roma health mediators (Schaaf 2005). But debates about its efficiency, results, and limitations have escalated, and these are related to a broader controversy about the advantages and disadvantages of affirmative action (in Romania, called "positive discrimination").

In light of the many difficulties encountered in the implementation of the *Strategy*, the National Agency for the Ethnic Roma has adopted the view that policy should emphasize mainstreaming of Roma as the best approach to ending their isolation. From this perspective, policy makers believe that Roma do not need special treatment, that targeting and special treatment reinforce dependency and isolation and reproduce the prejudice according to which Romani issues are seen as a distinctive set of problems unrelated to and separated from the rest of the society. The National Agency endorses a policy of mainstreaming, according to which all state authorities share the role of promoting inclusion and the National Agency for Ethnic Roma plays a coordinating role, making sure that Roma are taken into account in each area of public policy.

Conference on Roma Health

At a conference on Roma health held in Bucharest in December 2005, it became clear that the central Romani agencies do not want to concentrate as much on the issue of women's reproductive health as do international agencies. Forced sterilization cases in Slovakia have made Romani agencies particularly sensitive about an overemphasis on reproductive health, given that reproductive rights are a highly sensitive issue within the Romani communities and Roma movement. However, this is not only because such policies might be deployed to take actions against Roma reproduction and transformed into an alibi for fertility control. This sensitivity is also due to the fact that some Roma leaders interpret reproductive policies as an attack against Romani traditions regarding the "proper" number of children or cultural values regarding women's role and sexuality, or even as an assault against the unity of the movement. The fears regarding the assimilation of reproductive rights norms with fertility control policies are compounded by the suspicions that treating family planning (alongside with sexual disease) as a Romani issue will reproduce negative prejudices about Roma. My observation of the different positions taken at this conference suggest something of the complex ethnic and gender politics that are entailed in this issue.

During the conference, a Romani leader affirmed: "It is not acceptable that if Roma families are having four children, the latter are considered being unwanted ones. We should not forget that infant mortality within Roma communities is of 16 percent and Roma could maintain itself due to the fact that we dared to make five or six children, or more" (quote from field)[3] Basically, no discussions ensued around the issue of family size at the conference, as it became clear to everybody, Roma and non-Roma alike, that this was too sensitive to be discussed. Similar suspicions were evident regarding disaggregating statistics along lines of ethnicity and gender within ethnic groups.

The international organizations at the conference formulated a different perspective, which claimed that the political reaction was a problem of the timing and framing of the issues: "the reaction to the so-called overemphasis of women's reproductive health was probably due to the fact that in the first part of the day, the participants discussed this issue. It is not that reproductive health would not be important because, for example, maternal mortality in the case of Romani women is 28%. The problem is that this is discussed in wrong terms, due to which reproductive health is associated with family planning, and with forced sterilization and fertility control. We should define reproductive rights more broadly and consider them alongside the right to work, the right to nondiscrimination, and the right to have decent living conditions" (quotes from the field). Again, there was no serious discussion about this at the conference, especially because it seemed that two "camps" were formed, and there was no third position from where to talk, or there was no one who had the courage of talking from this position: on the one hand, there were the non-Roma international representatives talking about women's reproductive health and rights, and, on the other hand, the (mostly male) Roma representatives stressing the traditional family values and warning about the inappropriateness of this issue altogether.

Even if there are initiatives by Romani women that activate for women's rights in Romania, their voices were not heard at this meeting. The issue of reproductive health as a reproductive right was formulated as such only by representatives of international organizations. It was spokespersons from international organizations who also emphasized that Roma health mediators are a way to empower women. But seemingly there was no consensus on this among the participants at the conference. However, initially, when the Institute of Health Mediator was established, the decision was made that women should serve as Roma health mediators on the basis of the following arguments:

- a woman is the one who maintains contacts with the gadje world (city hall, school, doctors); she takes the children to doctors and sends her husband as well, even if she is not taking care of herself; and when she would think about buying contraceptives, she would better think about using that money for the sake of her children;
- in terms of health issues, one may enter most successfully into the community through women, because they take care of their families; due to the fact that health mediators are supposed to inform individuals about their rights and their access to medical information and services, it is good if health mediators are women, because in this way they may contact women easier;

- through health mediators, it is possible to identify women's needs and also to promote women in public roles, while recognizing their role in the family, in the community, and in the broader Roma movement.

Although many sensitive issues were not talked about at the conference, the debate about Roma health mediators was important because at least potentially it might be linked to a series of other issues, such as women's role in Romani communities, women's presence in the Roma movement, advantages and disadvantages of affirmative action, negotiations between and within governmental agencies and Roma nongovernmental organizations (NGOs), and the governmental involvement in solving the problems of Romani communities. That is why this topic should continue to be the focus of policies regarding Romani women's reproductive rights.

Reproductive Health Policies: From Ethnic Blindness to Racism

The abolition of the Ceausescu era anti-abortion law (a law that conferred, among other things, the specificity of Romania among the by-then socialist states) was among the very first issues on which the new political leaders focused their attention in December 1989. Abortion became legal if performed by a medical doctor upon a woman's request up to fourteen weeks from the date of conception; no spousal consent, no mandatory counseling, no waiting period was required. One could suppose that, through this, "women's issues" were to be included among the priorities of the new regime. But this was not going to happen.

It is true that through this change women gained the formal right to control their bodies and reproduction. The fact that women really used this right is reflected by the following figures. In 1990, the number of registered abortions increased to 992,300 (from 193,100 in 1989), but the number of maternal deaths as a result of abortion decreased to 181 (from 545 in 1989). But it was also true that for many years to come, the medical system did not improve to increase access to modern contraceptive methods that might have reduced the demand for abortions and assured women's reproductive health. In 1993, when the first Reproductive Health Survey was made in Romania, only 57% of the married women were using contraceptive methods; 43% were using traditional methods (coitus interruptus, calendar); and only 14% used modern methods. Repeated in 1997, the survey showed a moderate change, with the percentage of women using modern contraceptive methods increasing to almost 30%.

A real concern with women's interests would not have turned the respect for women's right to control their bodies into a celebration of abortion as the gift of democracy. Instead, it should have meant the development of an entire health care and educational system within which women—as responsible and accountable individuals—could decide on the most proper contraceptive method that might assure their own well-being. So the very first change in this domain (which wanted to be recuperative) was actually a sign of the exclusion of women as reproducers from those priorities of the new regime and of the view that women's rights had been solved in a way that was concerned with the real interests of the involved individuals. Viewed from this point of view, too, the social order of the postsocialist Romanian "transition" was revealing a tendency toward exclusionary practices on the base of gender, which were also observable in other arenas (such as women's presence in the labor market and politics, for example). Eventually, international pressure (ranging from the loan agreement between the World Bank and Romanian government in 1991, to the leverage based on financial support coming from the United Nation's Population Fund in 1997 to the need to harmonize the national legislation with the European one) and the local civic initiatives structured around these international pressure forced the Romanian national government to include the issue of reproductive health on its agenda. As a result, some formal structures were constituted across the health care system, and family planning was integrated into the basic package of services provided to the population (but only in 1999). The Strategy of the Ministry of Health on the domain of reproduction and sexuality (developed with the technical assistance of the World Health Organization and supported by the United Nations Fund for Population) was launched in 2003, as a result of which courses on family planning for family doctors and the distribution of free contraceptives started. The strategy provided the framework within which the related legislation could have been developed. An important role in this process was and still is played by the Society for Sexual and Contraceptive Education (SECS), an NGO with a center in Bucharest and with several focal points across the country. such as that from Cluj covering many Transylvanian counties. The SECS is currently involved in training the medical staff at the primary health care level to become family planning providers, and it provides technical assistance for Local Health Authorities to implement the national family planning program. This program aims to create an expending network of medical providers in order to ensure access to free contraceptives for a large segment of the population. The SECS recognizes that the use of contraceptives among the population living in smaller towns and rural areas continues to be low, abortion remaining the main method of fertility regulation for this population segment.

The SECS was involved in 1996 in the creation of the Coalition for Reproductive Health, which, as part of its POLICY project, published a booklet entitled "*Sănătatea Femeii—sănătatea naţiunii* (The health of woman—the health of the nation), a title that suggests that public talk in today's Romania on women's (reproductive) health is not treated explicitly in (feminist) terms of women's rights but in the context of well-established national discourse. The latest booklet published by the SECS, entitled *Fiecare mamă şi copil contează* (Each mother and child counts), aims to make available information about contraceptive methods for a large segment of the population, but—at least according to its title—is not addressing (and empowering) women as autonomous subjects located in particular social conditions, but as human bodies centering on their reproductive function.

Ultimately, in 2004 a law regarding reproductive health and medically assisted human reproduction, which defines the issue of reproductive health and health of sexuality as a priority of the public health system, and discusses these issues in terms of rights, was proposed in Romania; but its discourse was mostly couples-based (family) rather than women-centered. As stated, the proposed regulations sought to reduce the number of unwanted pregnancies, illegal abortions, maternal mortality, and abandoned children. In the spirit of this proposal, each woman who decides to have an abortion would have to be informed appropriately to make a decision, doctors would have to prove that they provided this information, women would have to express their decision in a written form, and free provision of postabortion contraception should also be provided. This part of the proposed law would restrict women's free decision on abortion by trying to convince them that abortion is wrong and giving birth to their children could have many benefits; but mostly the articles referring to the medically assisted human reproduction were highly contested by many civic organizations. Although it was passed by the lower house, the proposal did not pass in the senate.

The liberalization of abortion, the establishment of the family planning network, the provision of free contraceptives through the family doctor's system, the above-mentioned strategy and law proposal, and the law on violence against women reflect the progress achieved since 1990 in Romania. But much remains to be done until these formal provisions would function in reality and make a change in the reproductive health situation of women. Furthermore, none of the mentioned documents and underlying policies consider the particular situation of Romani women, so one may conclude that they are not aware of (or do not care about) the existing ethnic inequalities, and about the social and cultural factors that transform Romni into an underserved category regarding access to reproductive health.

However, the problem of access of Roma to health care was addressed in a broader context. In 2004, the counselor of the Ministry of Health and a representative of the Roma non-governmental organization for human rights, Romani Criss presented a strategy entitled National Health Policies Relevant to Minority Inclusion. This program aimed to develop and strengthen a network of community nurses and Roma health mediators in order to improve Roma's health condition and to involve different Roma representatives in finding solutions for these issues. Its goals were "to implement the National Health Programs in 100 percent of the Roma communities, with special focus on preventive programs, health promotion, and health of child and family"; "to guarantee the access of 100 percent of the Roma communities to the primary medical and pharmaceutical services, corresponding to the EU standards"; "to promote intercultural education among all categories of medical personnel nationwide"; and "to facilitate the including in the health insurance system of the Roma not meeting the current legislative criteria due to objective reasons (lack of ID, poverty)" (Dobronanteanu and Buceanu, 2004). The rules regarding the sex of the health mediator are promoting Romni, but no emphasis is put on Romani women's specific health problems—in particular, on the obstacles of their access to health services, however they are recognized on the international scene. For example, the Organization for Security and Co-operation in Europe, the European Monitoring Centre on Racism and Xenophobia, and the Council of Europe were coordinating a joint project in 2003 that was arguing for the need of involving Romani women in developing policies specifically for women and to build better access to health care for Romni and their communities alongside the principles of equality, nondiscrimination, and participation.[4]

Scholars and activists addressing the access to health care of Roma emphasize the high rates of illness, lower life expectancy, and higher infant mortality. They also underscore that Romani women begin childbearing at a young age and have less access to preventive sexual and reproductive health information and care, including gynecological care, family planning, and natal care (Packer 2003). They stress the following reasons for this situation: Romni tend to postpone attention to personal well-being in the interest of attending to family care and the home (so obtaining contraception for themselves is among the last on their list of medical priorities); they are dominated by a feeling of shame when seeking help, especially if this requires a break in social codes of modesty; there are Romani customs that prevent women from seeking care during or after pregnancy; under the circumstances of unequal gender relations, women feel little power to choose when, with whom, and with what form of protection, if any, to have sex; women are reluctant to seek medical care because they fear that they will face violence, abandonment, or ostracism from their partner, family, and community; and last but not least, gender and ethnic stereotypes such as the stereotypical view that Romani women do not think of the future may lead health care workers not to offer family planning information and services or to provide information only on certain types of contraception.

Recognizing that the effects of discriminatory health care are felt disproportionately by women (because women typically bear principal responsibility for family health care and maintain the contact between Romani communities and public health services), Romani women's perspectives and experiences urgently need to be included in policies devised on the behalf of Roma and in policies devised on the behalf of women.

In order to comprehend how policies function as forms of power that organize societies and shape an individual's perception of self (for example, Romani women's understandings of their opportunities in the domain of reproduction and reproductive health), one needs to observe how they are put into practice by health care providers. In what follows, I focus on this aspect using the empirical materials resulting from the fieldwork I conducted in the city of Orăştie.

Health Care Providers' Attitudes toward Romani Women

As part of my research, I conducted individual and group interviews, but I also held informal discussions with those local health care providers who dealt with women's reproductive health: family doctors, gynecologists, their medical assistants, and staff of the County Health Directorate, including the community medical nurses. Below, I summarize those results and my analysis for each of the different types of health care providers.

MEDICAL COMMUNITY NURSES

In the city of Orăştie, there was no Roma health mediator and no center for family planning. The role of the Roma health mediator was filled by a community medical nurse. Although a Roma health mediator should be a community member, this nurse did not belong to the community. There were few Roma among the large number of patients (almost 2,000) whom she had under her supervision, and she did not have much authority either in the eyes of the community or in the eyes of the family doctors and gynecologists. She was directly subordinate to the County Health Directorate, possessed an office belonging to the city hall, and had positive cooperative relations with the Department of Social Work. When I met the (female) director of this public service, she became very excited about the fact that my research was linked to the issue of reproduction and the use of contraception. In our discussion, she quickly revealed her belief—otherwise shared with the mentioned community nurse—about the need for a "campaign of fertility control" among Romani women (*campanie de injectare*) using inject-able contraceptives; she expressed her conviction that the main causes of Roma poverty (and of the troubles that both city hall and she have to face day-by-day due to such poverty) were rooted in Roma "overpopulation." During the formal interviews, however, neither she nor the community nurse mentioned this idea, suggesting that they understood it was not politically correct to express this kind of language. Indeed, this view of Roma "overpopulation" is not an "officially sustained" position, so I can not assume that no such a campaign will be explicitly adopted. Nevertheless, these hidden opinions can be very harmful and dangerous, as far as they are held by persons who are in a position from where they might manipulate Romani women and might not serve their reproductive health but some other causes.

The lack of real communication between health care providers and Romni symbolically is well illustrated by the following story. When the Society for Sexual and Contraceptive Education planned to publish some advertising materials regarding contraceptives, whose information might have been understood also by Romani women, the latter were asked by the community nurse about the photo that they would like to see on the cover page of such a booklet. The Romni with whom I talked remembered that they expressed their desire to have both a Romani and a non-Romani woman depicted on the cover. Eventually, the local organizers opted for a picture of a middle-class blond woman.

FAMILY DOCTORS

Of the thirteen family doctors of the city of Orăştie in 2004, four were part of the network through which free contraceptives were distributed. The Romani families were allocated to those family doctors who did belong to this network. But the huge number of patients, the administrative work related to the distribu-tion of free contraceptives, and the fact that these four doctors do all this work on a voluntary basis have meant that these doctors do not really have time to offer a serious consultation in family planning. On the basis of discussions with them and their patients, I have concluded that there are many cultural beliefs and attitudes (in addition to the material conditions under which they live) that prevent women from the use of contraceptives. These include fear of becoming fat (resulting in the rejection of pills); fear of cancer (resulting in the rejection of intrauterine devices); fear of the deregulation of menstruation (resulting in the rejection of injectables); sexual taboos within the community (and the resulting fear of family and community control); shyness in front of medical doctors as strangers; a lack of confidence toward the health care system because it is part of what is viewed as unfriendly state authority; the disregard of health under the harsh conditions of poverty; dominant religious beliefs; the passive role of women in sexual relations (as a result of which men are supposed "to take care," but if they fail to do so, women are supposed to find a solution).

Among the family doctors, I encountered attitudes that suggested racist orientations, such as the following examples: "I am having too many Roma patients, and this happened because I was a newcomer in this city, so I had to take what was left by my colleagues"; "They do come very often to my office and are always claiming something"; "It is very hard to work with them because they do not listen to you"; "They do make too many children" (quotes from the field). But there were also opinions that emphasized what they perceived to be the positive characteristics of their Roma patients: "Romani women do take good care of their children, they bring them in for shots"; "Roma children are healthier because their mothers breastfeed them for a long period of time" (quotes from the field).

GYNECOLOGISTS

The three gynecologists of the city were working both at the public hospital and at their own private clinics. Their prestige within the former location was quite reduced both materially and symbolically. Their private enterprises went pretty well, but obviously Romani women—due to their financial conditions—could not benefit from the better services offered by this sector. At the public hospital, the gynecology section was downsized to a compartment (the number of beds was drastically reduced due to the reduced number of births after 1990), and its material infrastructure was very old. As one gynecologist put it, "Here we are the loser in the transformation process, totally devalued and mistreated, even if, theoretically, for example the Ministry of Health talks about the need to take care of maternities." Due to the marketization of public health care, gynecologists were paid according to a strict set of procedures. Their salaries did not include, for example, family planning consultation, the administration of intrauterine devices, or the provision of abortion on the patient's request. All these were done on a voluntary basis, and there was a lot of such "voluntary" work during the 1990s. As Romni wanted to benefit from abortion services at the state clinic (because these were more expensive in the private sector), among these physicians one could encounter even an anti-Roma attitude based on cultural prejudices about their "dirtiness," "excessive fertility," and "stupidity": "They cannot do anything but children, they do not have the will and the intelligence and the education for using properly the pills" (quotes from the field). These were the reasons why a decision was made in 2004 about the relocation of the abortion-on-request-service, whose site was moved from the hospital to the public medical center and practically became the responsibility of one of the three gynecologists. The price of this intervention increased, and the free access to abortion in the case of women having four children or in the case of minor girls was eliminated. The move took three months, and meanwhile no abortions were performed at women's request; those who could afford to do so approached the private offices; others probably gave birth to the unwanted child, but fortunately no cases of complications related to induced abortions were reported during this period of time.

In the attitudes of doctors toward Romani women, I discovered a double talk. Their gestures, the words used for characterizing these women (as those quoted above), and their informal confessions (about the "fact" that mainly Romani women are requesting abortion at the state clinics, or about the "need" to segregate them in order "to protect our Romanian patients," or about the "immorality of abortions") revealed the existence of mechanisms that aimed to exclude Romni on the basis of their ethnicity from particular locations, but also from certain rights, such as the right to request an abortion at a state clinic under safe conditions. Complaints about the "fact" that "mainly Romani women do give birth nowadays" were maintained even if they ran counter to the figures used to sustain this opinion: "Last year 17 percent of the births were given by Romani women, and this year is even more, around 26 percent." These statements prove to be more biased and prejudiced than they seem if we put them together with the complaints of having "too many" Romani women demanding abortions at the public hospital. There are no figures on this, as no statistics are permitted to be compiled in these terms. But in the realm of feelings about and fears from "Roma overpopulation," these affirmations clearly express a deep aversion against Roma, suggesting that even if Romani women have more abortions, they still bear more children, but anyway, they are disturbing altogether, they are "too many everywhere."

Insofar as my study aims to be a kind of anthropology of policy that is critical toward how policy functions as a form of power that silences and marginalizes certain social groups (like Romani women) and how it tries to empower Romani women, it has to take a step beyond analysis and make some policy recommendations regarding the improvement of the real access of Romani women to reproductive health.

Policy Recommendations: Mainstreaming Gender and Ethnicity into Public Policies

My policy recommendations might be subsumed under a larger heading, which refers to the need of mainstreaming ethnicity and gender into Romanian public policies. This idea reflects the recognition of the fact that Romani women's issues (among them, their reproductive health understood as a reproductive right) are an integral part, on the one hand, of the broader problems faced by Roma and, on the other hand, of the larger issues faced by women from Romania. Romani women's issues should be treated as such because otherwise their solutions would be only partial and not efficient enough. That is why there is a need for mainstreaming ethnicity into public policies, which means the need to analyze each public policy (including reproductive health policy) from the point of view of its impact on different ethnic groups living under different social conditions. At the same time, there is a need for mainstreaming gender, meaning that public policies (among them, policies for Roma) should be gendered, or, put differently, should be assessed from the perspective of their impact on both women and men.

The ethnicization of reproductive health policy and the gendering of Romani policy refer to the importance of raising awareness about how ethnicity and gender are understood and treated in a social context and that they do have an impact on people's everyday life—for example, by excluding them from vital resources. Mainstreaming ethnicity into the public health policy and mainstreaming gender into policy for Roma could overcome the effects of ethnic and gender discrimination in relation to reproductive rights and Romnis' access to health care.

Subsumed under these broader aims, I have formulated the following policy recommendations related to Romani women's reproductive health understood as a human right.

GENERAL RECOMMENDATIONS

FOR GOVERNMENTAL AGENCIES, FOR NGOS WORKING ON THE DOMAIN OF ROMA RIGHTS
AND REPRODUCTION/SEXUAL EDUCATION/CONTRACEPTION, AND FOR DONORS

- The reproductive health policy should be aware of ethnic differences and of the inequalities between women of different ethnicity, in particular of the social and cultural factors that turn Romani women into underserved categories. This links the issue of Romni reproductive health to rights regarding proper housing (including satisfactory sanitation infrastructure), education, employment, living in dignity, and not being exposed to different forms of cultural devaluation and social exclusion.

- The reproductive health policy should include mechanisms of self-control in order to eliminate those factors that expose Romani women to the risk of becoming the subject of racist manipulations, and in order to avoid the transformation of the free distribution of contraceptives among Romani women into an instrument of institutionalized Roma fertility control governed by the "fear of Roma overpopulation." A clear and explicit distinction should be made each time between fertility control and reproductive rights.

- The policies responding to the health needs of Roma should be mainstreamed into national health strategies and services, which in turn should be gender sensitive.

- The policies responding to the needs of Romani women should be mainstreamed into the national strategies of promoting Roma rights and women's rights, including reproductive rights. These rights should also be respected by Roma organizations, and women's perspectives should be introduced into the discussions concerned with demographic issues.

- A balance between policies of mainstreaming and targeting should be assured in order to guarantee equal opportunities for Roma (women). For this, there is a need to integrate the special measures intended to provide equal access to health care (and reproductive rights) of the underserved categories into the policies, which generally aim to ensure equal access to well-being on each domain of life.

- The position of Roma mediators, including health mediators (who should be sensitive toward the particular needs of Romni), needs to be strengthened within the institutions of local authorities (including medical institutions) in order to not be used only as sources of information about the community but also to act as empowered individuals able to make decisions and control the available human and financial resources needed for the community development projects.

- More primary research (both quantitative and qualitative) should be done on Roma (women), with the involvement of Roma (women), in order to produce more data on which effective policy making should be based. The advantages and risks of the disaggregated statistics by ethnicity, sex, and rural/urban residential status should be considered from this point of view as well.

SPECIAL RECOMMENDATIONS FOR GOVERNMENTAL AGENCIES

FOR THE COMMITTEE OF ANTI-DISCRIMINATION AND COMMITTEE FOR EQUAL OPPORTUNITIES BETWEEN WOMEN AND MEN

- They should enforce the application of the Law of Equal Opportunities and of the Law of Anti-Discrimination in the domain of health care and in particular in the domain of reproductive rights.
- They should give attention to the field of health care for Roma in their monitoring and recommendations.
- They should consider how discrimination works at the crossroads of ethnicity and gender—in particular, how Romani women, for example, are prevented from access to (reproductive) health care of a good quality and how they might become victims of racist fertility control.
- The implementation of complaint mechanisms and the provision of legal assistance to those in economic need should be assured.

FOR THE NATIONAL AGENCY FOR ROMA OF THE ROMANIAN GOVERNMENT

- More attention should be paid to permanent contact and communication with Roma NGOs at local levels, in order to assure that they really have access to information, services, and funds needed for different community development projects.
- Stronger support should be given to Romani women's organizations and initiatives, which would be the sign of recognizing de facto the role of women in the community and within the Roma movement.
- The participation of Romani women in the decision-making processes regarding Romni's rights (including the right to reproductive health) should be increased, and the needs of Romani women should be included in the mainstream Roma policies.
- There is a need for recognizing Romani women's reproductive rights within the strategies regarding Roma rights and for revisiting the pronatalist concerns from the perspective of women who are morally entitled to choose the number of children they desire to have.

FOR THE MINISTRY OF HEALTH AND PUBLIC HEALTH CARE PROVIDERS

- A culturally sensitive and antiracist curriculum should be introduced into the education of physicians, including knowledge about taboos within Romani communities regarding women's bodies and sexuality.
- A greater emphasis should be placed on the permanent education of health care providers in the domain of contraceptives.
- Material and symbolic support should be given to physicians involved in family planning counseling.
- Mechanisms that would enforce cooperation within the community of health care providers (among family physicians, gynecologists, medical assistants, health mediators) should be implemented.
- A stronger commitment of physicians toward patient's rights should be assured, in particular toward the rights of vulnerable and underserved groups, including Roma and, of course, Romani women—for example, related to their right to choose the contraceptive method most appropriate for their medical condition.
- Efforts should be made to train medical professionals belonging to Romani communities, an objective that links the issue of reproductive health of Romni to the issue of access to education at all levels (including medical high schools and universities).
- Besides the ethnic perspective, the gender perspective should be also introduced into the development and implementation of national health strategies.

SPECIAL RECOMMENDATIONS FOR NGOS

- Cooperation between Romani and non-Romani women's organizations, local Roma experts and mediators, and NGOs working on sexual/contraceptive education should be strengthened. Together, they should coordinate at local levels several programs, aiming to break the barriers between Romani women and health care providers, while considering the particular social and cultural background of the communities within which they work. Their aim should be the empowerment of Romani women, both as caregivers and as patients. They could provide, for example, the following services:
  - health and sexual education for both women and men within Romani communities, in a way that respects women's moral entitlements and rights to decide on reproduction-related issues;
  - information on patients' rights and reproductive rights;
  - culturally sensitive education of health care providers and authorities.

Conclusion

THE ACCESS OF ROMANI WOMEN TO REPRODUCTIVE HEALTH
AS A POLICY MATTER

My initial project defined the policy problem as Romani women's lack of real access to reproductive health, asking how a gender-conscious policy for Roma and an ethnic-aware reproductive policy might better serve women's reproductive health. But in the light of my fieldwork experiences, I would like to emphasize another aspect of this issue. Since 2004, when I visited the same settlement, the access of Romni to free contraceptives increased, and injectables became the most widespread fertility control method "suggested" and administered to Romani women by family doctors.

I am observing here the risk of turning the women-centered reproduction policy (which aims to assure that women, including Romani women, are really using their reproductive rights as a right to control their own lives and bodies, including the right to decide on the contraceptive method that is the most proper for their health and lifestyle) into an instrument of structural (and hidden) racism by which one may "prevent Roma overpopulation."

In my original research proposal, I emphasized that the policy recommendations to be made would contribute to the development of a (reproductive) health policy aware of ethnic differences and inequalities as produced by the social and cultural system, and able to overcome the effects of discrimination in relation to access to health care for Roma. I would like to add that this policy would need to function in a way that excludes the risk of becoming a mechanism that reproduces racism by practicing and hiding it under the surface of a "humanitarian aid" (claiming that it provides Romani women with reproductive control methods while it actually is concerned with "preventing Roma overpopulation").

As my research demonstrated, the context of the real access of Romni to reproductive health is composed by several social, economic, and cultural factors, among them the ones related to policies:

- The general life conditions of Roma (including a whole set of social and economic problems, ranging from the lack of proper housing, to the lack of access to education, to unemployment). Under these conditions, the concern for Romani women's reproductive health is defined as a luxury and an unimportant issue even by women themselves, and under these circumstances even Romni internalize the "explanation" according to which population growth is the causal determinant of poverty.

- The mistreatment of Romani communities as a cultural group by the majority population, using "culture" and "cultural difference" to legitimate discrimination and negative prejudices against Roma (women), as if these would be the "natural" consequences and not the structural causes of Roma's life circumstances.

- The gender regime's dominance within Romani communities, including power relations between women and men, and cultural conceptions about Romani women's role in the family and larger community, women's bodies, sexuality, childbearing, abortion, contraception, and so on.

- The ethnic-blind reproductive health policy (including the National Strategy of Reproductive Health and Sexuality adopted by the Ministry of Health in 2004) and the actual functioning of the medical health care system, which turns Romani women into an underserved social category and/or exposes them to the risk of being treated as instruments for a racist "Roma fertility control."

- The actual functioning of the gender-blind governmental strategy for the improvement of the situation of Roma from Romania (adopted in 2001), which, generally speaking, has many insufficiencies and which, in particular, neglects Romani women's needs and interests, reproducing their status of a minority within a minority group, and related to this, the pronatalist concerns of Romani communities and their leaders, which prevent considering women's reproductive health and rights as a priority.

- The malfunctions of communication and cooperation between central and local Romani organizations and experts, as a result of which local people might not be supported properly in their efforts to get information and resources for their activities on behalf of their immediate communities.

- The marginalization of Romani women's activists within the larger movement for Roma rights, and the lack of authority and prestige of women's issues, including women's reproductive rights within the mainstream policies for Roma.

SOCIAL EXCLUSION AT THE INTERSECTION OF ETHNICITY, GENDER, AND CLASS

After Hall et al. (1992), Moore (2000), and Woodward (1999), I consider that the identities (including cultural representations and social positions) of women and men of different ethnicities are constituted at the crossroads of the subject positions prescribed for them by ideologies, policies, and institutions, and of their subjectivities (everyday experiences and meanings through which they perceive themselves within their significant social relations). I am not treating ethnicity/"race" and gender as naturally given internal essences that shape one's destiny, but as socially and culturally constructed subject positions that are constituted by cultural representations and social locations where people are situated also due to the ways in which society builds up hierarchies according to the social expectations and cultural prejudices regarding ethnic and gender differences.

The ethnicized/racialized and gendered construction of the order within which a person's life is embedded is a cultural and social process. Through this, on the one hand, women and men are defined and classified on the basis of some characteristics supposedly determined by their ethnicity and sex, as if these were their natural and inborn essences. On the other hand, through this mechanism women and men are located in certain social and economic positions (and consequently have access to or are excluded from specific material and symbolic resources) according to the hegemonic representations of their ethnic and sexual belongings. These processes might be observed inside different institutions and in the context of their complex relationships, including different sites of everyday life.

This chapter describes and understands the construction of the social order at the crossroads of several systems of classification (ethnicity, gender, and class) as performed by concrete people in their everyday lives and lived through their personal experiences. More precisely, the chapter views this process as mediated by access to reproductive health. It deals with the relationship between ethnicity, gender, and class as systems of classification and as social organizations of cultural differences. This relation—among other mechanisms not addressed here—structures the social order in a particular spatio-temporal location, and, as such, defines and positions women and men within private and public hierarchies, which in turn are under the impact of broader economic and political changes. But this regime could not function if it were not sustained from below. People not only adjust their expectations and performances to its norms—they do not automatically take up certain roles—but they also interpret, negotiate, and act them out within their personal relations with "significant others."

On the basis of the conceptual framework described above, I address the formation of the postsocialist order (in Romania) as consisting of the processes of social differentiation and the underlying cultural mechanisms that produce and legitimize the newly constituted hierarchies. Above the individual's will and control, the former shape his or her chances of participating with success in the (classificatory) struggles around positions and resources, which in turn include ideologies and practices of inclusion and exclusion. Obviously, this whole system functions with the complicity of the individuals, but one should note that, most important, out of these processes some gain privileges, and others get blocked in disadvantaged positions. On this stage, gender, ethnicity, and class—besides being prescribed subject positions and lived experiences—function as intertwined classificatory tools, markers of differences, and (after Barth 1969) as processes of socially organizing cultural differences. Otherwise, the gendered and ethnicized/ racialized social differentiation is nothing else than the hierarchical distribution by gender, ethnicity, and class of society's economic and social resources. My research views these processes in the context of Romania and through the issue of reproduction and reproductive health.

PUBLIC POLICIES AS FORMS OF POWER MEDIATED BY STRUCTURAL FACTORS, CULTURAL CONCEPTIONS, AND AGENCY

This chapter treats the access of Romani women to reproductive health as a socially, economically, culturally, and politically determined phenomenon, observing that policies—even if presented as neutral technologies—are making a contribution "to empower some people and silence others" (Shore and Wright 1997, 7). It approaches reproductive health as a "small problem" through which one may understand the broader issue of social exclusion as it functions under the circumstances of postsocialist transformations. As such, the chapter shows how exclusion works at the crossroads of ethnicity, gender, and class while (re) producing inequalities, and how Romani women's multiple discriminations function, turning Romani women into one of the most underserved categories of Romanian society. These processes are mediated by structural factors, cultural conceptions, and agency, which are working through each other while shaping women's everyday desires, claims, and practices related to reproduction and reproductive health.

The chapter focuses on the role of policies for Roma and policies of reproductive health—as discursive formations and as practices—that embody certain cultural conceptions about Romani women, and are developed and put into practice within the existing system of power structured by economic, political, and social forces. The policies under scrutiny function within a postsocialist environment where Roma are facing structural unemployment, improper housing, school segregation, ghettoization, lack of sanitation, and many other social and economic problems. In addition to this, these policies are mediated by anti-Roma racist attitudes and behaviors embedded in the public (including health care) institutions and are having their impact on the underserved people who develop their own reactions to marginalization and encapsulation (including the culture of living in the present). Besides, the policies themselves embody certain cultural conceptions about public priorities, women's role in society, cultural differences, and, of course, Romani women, while their prescriptions are implemented within particular social relations saturated with power inequalities between women and men, health care providers and patients, Roma and non-Roma, and so on.

The circumstances where the targeted individuals of the policies under scrutiny live include not only material conditions but also social expectancies and cultural conceptions regarding maternity, sexuality, fertility, and, more broadly, gender relations. While addressing why policies for Roma and policies of reproduction in their present form do not meet Romani women's particular needs, besides the already mentioned factors, one has to also consider how Romani women perceive themselves as individuals and as members of their community. Only in this way may one understand their reproductive desires and practices (like the number of children they bear, or the recourse to abortion, or the use of contraceptives that are for free even if they have side effects). Romani women, like other people, act both as social persons and as individual agents. They are situated at the crossroads of contradictory subject positions, basically "between two fires." On the one hand, since December 1989, as Romanian citizens, they are formally entitled to make use of their reproductive rights; but being culturally devalued and socially excluded, they are subjected to racial discrimination, which obstructs them from really using these rights. As a result, they are transformed into underserved social categories, or even exposed to racist fertility control that aims to make them have fewer children than they possibly may desire, and all this in order to not "threaten" the majority. On the other hand, the patriarchal Roma movement views Romani women as life-givers and caretakers who are obliged to carry the burden of the biological and cultural reproduction of Roma. This position prescribed to them may also become an obstacle to their de facto access to reproductive rights as far as it culturally imposes on them to give birth to more children than they would like, and all this in order to ensure the preservation of their community. However, while Romani women are enduring these contradictory regulations, they express a powerful desire toward taking their destiny in their own hands (or acting as agents). On the basis of what they consider to be a right decision in the context of their given material conditions and social relations, they feel morally entitled to decide, for example, on the number of their children or on having an abortion or on using contraceptives. Of course, this decision making is limited by structural factors, social expectations, and cultural conceptions that women cannot control; however, the regulative rules (of reproduction) do not simply and totally subjugate them, because they manage to transform this domain into an area of subversive practices. Nonetheless, their insubordination is restrained, among other things, by their desire of being accepted and respected persons within their community. At this stage, Romani women eventually face a problem known by any other human being, even if they experience and express it differently than others living in different social and cultural contexts. This is the problem of being at once a social person and an individual agent, or, paraphrasing Strathern (1992), of being constructed by one's social relations while trying not to preclude one's sense of autonomy or self-control.

Altogether, my research identified the obstacles of the reproductive health services usage both from the perspective of Romani women's life conditions and from the point of view of the health care system. In this way, I was able to show that the Romanian reproductive health policies and the existing Roma policies were failing to respond to the interests and particular conditions of Romni, and willingly or not transformed them into an underserved and multiply discriminated against social category.

NOTES

My research on this issue was made possible by the International Policy Fellowships Program of the Open Society Institute due the policy research grant offered to me between April 2005 and March 2006. In 2004, I had my first contact with the Roma communities under scrutiny in the framework of empirical research conducted in the city of Orăştie with the support and on the behalf of the Society of Sexual and Contraceptive Education from Romania. Eventually, the Andrew Mellon fellowship of the Institut für die Wissenschaften vom Menchen from Vienna gave me the opportunity between April and June 2006 to write up my research results and to produce the first draft of this chapter, together with a broader research report on social exclusion at the intersection of gender, ethnicity, and class (Magyari-Vincze 2006).

1. Throughout the chapter, from time to time, instead of the term "Romani women," I use "Romni" (referring to the feminine singular). "Roma" is used in the case of plural and "Rom" as masculine singular, while the form "Romani" is mostly used as an adjective.

2. When I first approached the city of Orăştie from the southern part of Transylvania in 2004, I was following the choice of the Society of Sexual and Contraceptive Education, which aimed to identify the reasons why the number of abortions continued to be

high there despite the contraceptive programs implemented by that organization in that location. One year later I returned to this town and in particular to its Roma communities in order to understand better Romani women's reproductive practices in the context of a system of power that constrains them to make more or to have fewer children than they would possibly desire according to their material conditions, social relations, and emotional ties. Elsewhere (Magyari-Vincze 2006), I have described in detail their living conditions in this postindustrial city. There are many similarities in the effects of encapsulation and marginalization of Roma observed: improper housing, structural unemployment, school segregation, nonaccess to health care of a good quality, racist attitudes, and different forms of discrimination. Eventually, the analysis of the ways in which local everyday practices and organizational processes are linked will take the relevance of this investigation beyond the local setting.

3. As a comparative report on Roma in Central and Eastern Europe shows, the health status of Roma populations is another area that is negatively impacted by the lack of statistical data, which are disaggregated by ethnicity. Still, the report suggests that "there is much evidence that life expectancy, infant mortality, morbidity, and other major health indicators are substantially worse for Roma than for majority populations in CEE countries." Making a reference to the Romanian Reproductive Health Survey from 1999 regarding children born between July 1994 and June 1999, the report observes that the infant mortality rate in the case of Romani children is 80.0 per 1,000 live births, being three to four times higher than those for the Romanian or Hungarian population (*Roma in Central and Eastern Europe*).

4. The results of this research were published under the title *Breaking the Barriers—Report on Romani Women and Access to Public Health Care.* The project was administered by the Council of Europe and overseen by an advisory group consisting of representatives of the Council of Europe, OSCE High Commissioner on National Minorities (HCNM), OSCE Office for Democratic Institutions and Human Rights ODIHR), the European Union's European Monitoring Centre on Racism and Xenophobia (EUMC), and the World Health Organization Regional Office for Europe. In the course of this study, two independent experts were engaged to conduct country visits and individual interviews, Anna Pomykala assisted by Mariana Buceanu.

WORKS CITED

Barth, Fredrick, ed. 1969. *Ethnic Groups and Boundaries: The Social Organization of Cultural Difference.* Boston: Little, Brown.

Bradley, Harriet. 1992. "Changing Social Divisions: Class, Gender and Race." In *Social and Cultural Forms of Modernity,* ed. Robert Bocock and Kenneth Thompson, 11–69. Cambridge: Polity Press in Association with Open University.

Chiriac, Marian. 2004. "O necesară schimbare de strategie: Raport privind stadiul de aplicare a Strategiei guvernamentale de îmbunătățire a situației Romilor din Rom?nia" (A necessary change of strategy: report on the implementation stage of the Romanian government's strategy for the improvement of the Roma situation). In *The Challenges of Diversity: Public Policies Regarding the National and Religious Minorities in Romania,* by Marian Chiriac. Cluj Napoca: Ethno-Cultural Diversity Resource Center (ERDC). Http://www.edrc.ro/docs/docs/Report%20on%20Roma%20Strategy_2004.pdf.

Dobronanteanu, Hanna, and Mariana Buceanu. 2004 *National Health Policies Relevant to Minority Inclusion.* Ministry of Health and Romani Criss.

EU Accession Monitoring Program. 2002. *Report on the Implementation of the Strategy for the Improvement of the Situation of Roma Community from Romania.* Http://www. eumap.org/topics/minority/reports/minority01-02/minority02/international/sections/ romania/2002_m_romania.pdf.

European Commission. 2000 *Romania: Regular Report from the Commission on the Progress towards Accession.* November 8. Http://ec.europa.eu/enlargement/archives/pdf/key_ documents/2002/ro_en.pdf.

Fourth World Conference on Women. 1995 *Beijing Declaration.* Http://www.un.org/women-watch/daw/beijing/platform/declar.htm.

Ginsburg, Faye, and Rayna Rapp, eds. 1995. *Conceiving the New World Order: The Global Politics of Reproduction.* Berkeley: University of California Press.

Government of Romania. 2001. *Strategy for Improving the Condition of the Roma.* Bucharest: Ministry of Public Information. Http://unpan1.un.org/intradoc/groups/public/docu-ments/UNTC/UNPAN016040.pdf.

Hall, Stuart, David Held, and Tony McGrew, eds. 1992. *Modernity and Its Futures.* Cambridge: Polity Press.

Magyari-Vincze, Eniko˝. 2006. *Social Exclusion at the Crossroads of Gender, Ethnicity and Class: A View through Romani Women's Reproductive Health.* A Research Report with Recommendations. Cluj: EFES.

Moore, Henrietta. 1994. *A Passion for Difference: Essays in Anthropology and Gender.* Cambridge: Polity Press.

———. 2000. *Feminism and Anthropology.* Cambridge: Polity Press.

Network Women's Program. 2003. *A Place at the Policy Table. Report on the Roma Women's Forum, Budapest, June 29* Budapest: Open Society Institute. Http://www.soros.org/ initiatives/women/articles_publications/publications/romawomensforum_20030923/ roma_womens_finalreport.pdf.

Okely, Judith. 1983. *The Traveller-Gypsies.* Cambridge: Cambridge University Press.

Open Society Institute and Resource Center for Roma Communities. 2004. *Monitorizarea implementării la nivel local a Strategiei pentru Îmbunătățirea Situației Romilor din Rom?nia* (Monitoring the local implementation of the government strategy for improving the condition of the Roma). Http://www.soros.org/initiatives/roma/articles_publications/publications/romap_20040927.

Ortner, Sherry B. 1999. *The Fate of "Culture": Geertz and Beyond.* Berkeley: University of California Press.

OSCE (Organization for Security and Cooperation in Europe), the European Monitoring Centre on Racism and Xenophobia, and Council of Europe. 2003. *Breaking the Barriers—Report on Romani Women and Access to Public Health Care.* Http://fra.europa.eu/fra/material/pub/ROMA/rapport-en.pdf.

Packer, Corinne. 2003. "Roma Women and Public Health Care." *Entre Nous: The European Magazine for Sexual and Reproductive Health* [special issue on Sexual and Reproductive Health in a Multicultural Europe] 20–22, no. 55. Http://eumap.org/journal/features/2002/sep02/romwomenprior.

Romania Ministry of Health. 2005. *Reproductive Health Survey Romania 2004.Summary Report* (May). Romania Ministry of Health, World Bank, UNFPA, USAID, UNICEF. Http://siteresources.worldbank.org/INTROMANIA/Resources/study.pdf.

Schaaf, Marta. 2005. *Mediating Romani Health. Policy and Program Opportunities, Network Public Health Program.* New York: Open Society Institute.

Seidel, Gill, and Laurent Vidal. 1997. "The Implications of 'Medical,' 'Gender in Development' and 'Culturalist' Discourses for HIV/AIDS policy in Africa." In *Anthropology of Policy: Critical Perspectives on Governance and Power,* ed. Cris Shore and Susan Wright, 59–88. New York: Routledge.

Shore, Cris, and Susan Wright. 1997. "Policy: A New Field of Anthropology." In *Anthropology of Policy: Critical Perspectives on Governance and Power,* ed. Cris Shore and Susan Wright, 3–43. New York: Routledge.

Stewart, Michael. *The Time of the Gypsies.* Boulder, Colo.: Westview Press, 1997.

Strathern, Marylin. 1992. *Reproducing the Future: Essays on Anthropology, Kinship and the New Reproductive Technologies.* Manchester: Manchester University Press.

Surdu, Laura, and Mihai Surdu, coordinators. 2006. *Broadening the Agenda: The Status of Romani Women in Romania.* New York: Open Society Institute.

Titmuss, Richard M. 1974. *Social Policy: An Introduction.* New York: Pantheon Books.

UNDP (United Nations Development Program). 2002. *Roma in Central and Eastern Europe: Avoiding the Dependency Trap. A Regional Human Development Report.* Http://roma.undp.sk/online.php.

UNFPA (United Nations Population Fund). 2003. *Country Profiles for Population and Reproductive Health.* Http://www.unfpa.org/worldwide/.

Unnithan-Kumar, Maya. 2003. "Reproduction, Health, Rights. Connections and Disconnections." In *Human Rights in Global Perspective: Anthropological Studies of Rights, Claims and Entitlements*, ed. Richard Ashby Wilson and Jon P. Mitchell, 183–208. New York: Routledge.

Woodward, Kathryn. 1997. "Concepts of Identity and Difference." In *Identity and Difference*, ed. Kathryn. Woodward, 7–62. London: Open University and Sage.

PART 2

Gender Politics in Russia, Central Asia, and the Caucasus

4

Human Trafficking in the Twenty-first Century: Implications for Russia, Europe, and the World

Mary Buckley

I n the globalized post-Soviet world of the twenty-first century in which the Communist experiment has been severely discredited, leaders across states are beginning to work together to tackle a growing international problem— that of human trafficking. This is being done very much at the instigation of the United States and guided by its spearheading world leadership on this particular issue.

Thus, there are currently two global "wars" being fought by the United States, to which President George W. Bush referred in his rhetoric. The first is the war on terror, which has received a mixed reception elsewhere since it is often interpreted as a guise for extending U.S. dominance, particularly control over oil and furtherance of U.S. business interests (Chomsky 2005; Buckley and Singh 2006). Recent exposés of corruption in war-torn Iraq by U.S. companies, with lucrative contracts for so-called reconstruction, has reinforced this negative perception, as has torture of prisoners in Guantanamo Bay for flouting of the Geneva Convention (Dispatches 2006).[1] By contrast, and viewed as a far more moral war in its execution, is the war against human traffickers, even if many still cynically claim that this war is self-interested, too, on the grounds that it is a way of cleaning up the flow of prostitutes into the United States, which has increased since the collapse of the state socialist systems. This U.S. battle, however, is appreciated by feminists and women's groups in Russia in a way and to an extent that the first war is not, since they believe that without U.S. action and pressure on the governments of the world, anti-trafficking legislation would have been far slower to reach the statute books. This is unquestionably the case in Russia.

A broad spectrum of political actors has come together to wage this second global war—groups that are not always united in their views, namely, the Religious Right; a wide span of church groups; international organizations such as the International Organization for Migration (IOM), the Organization for Security and Cooperation in Europe (OSCE), and the United Nations (UN); women's groups; non-governmental organizations (NGOs); and human rights groups, such as Amnesty International. They all draw on information provided by the U.S. State Department's annual Trafficking in Persons (TIP) Reports.

Thanks to the passage by the U.S. Congress in 2000 of the Victims of Trafficking and Violence Protection Act, with renewed commitment of high priority in December 2005 in the Trafficking Victims Protection Reauthorization Act, the State Department was required to produce annual reports on the extent and nature of trafficking in different states of the world and to document what governments were doing about it. The resulting TIP reports categorized states in Tiers 1 to 3 according to their efficiency in passing anti-trafficking legislation and their effectiveness on the ground in tackling the problem.

In 2002, the U.S. State Department concluded that Russia had failed to meet minimum standards as it was doing nothing to address human trafficking; thus it was allocated to Tier 3, along with Afghanistan, Armenia, Bahrain, Belarus, Bosnia-Herzegovina, Burma, Cambodia, Greece, Kyrgyzstan, Tajikistan, Turkey, Indonesia, Iran, Qatar, Saudi Arabia, and the Sudan (U.S. State Department 2002). Due to some progress subsequently, in 2003 Russia was moved up to Tier 2, but was kept on the State Department's "watch list" in 2004, 2005, and 2006 (U.S. State Department 2002, 2003, 2004, 2005, 2006).

The object of this chapter is to examine the growing global scope of human trafficking, paying attention to its significance for Russia in some detail and to assess its wider ramifications for Europe and the world. The issue possesses economic, social, psychological, and political dimensions and carries serious implications for equality, security, and human rights. Thus, interdisciplinary understandings are essential.

The Scale of the Problem

The TIP Report released in mid-2006 revealed that, according to U.S. government estimates of 2004, between 600,000 and 800,000 women, men, and children are trafficked across international borders each year. Of these, around 80% are women and girls, and up to 50% are minors, the majority of whom are trafficked into commercial sexual exploitation, although there is also a flow into domestic, building, agricultural, and manufacturing work. In addition to trafficking across state borders, often to far-flung countries, there is a problem of trafficking within states, often harder to identify, which means that the figures of those in bonded labor globally are considerably higher. As the report acknowledges, there are also competing estimates from other organizations, which suggest a bigger problem. According to the International Labor Organization, there are 12.3 million people across the world trapped in forced labor and sexual servitude, and "other estimates range from 4 million to 27 million" (U.S. State Department 2006). The hidden nature of much bondage makes precise statistics hard to collate.

The Russian example neatly illustrates the very wide reach of contemporary global patterns of trafficking from a given state and shows how governments can be slow to recognize, name, and address the problem, and how NGOs, international organizations, and the press can play crucial roles in putting pressure on the state to take action. In 2006, a fresh wave of press articles in Russia regretted that estimates now suggested that every year in Russia, from 20,000 to 60,000 become trapped by traffickers and that so far no fewer than 500,000 had endured this fate (Danilkin 2006). The Russian Assembly of NGOs reiterated in 2006 its concerns about the scale of human trafficking and stressed the threat posed by human trafficking both to national security and to the Russian gene pool, especially since 90% of trafficked women are thought to be under twenty-five years old (*Pravda* 2006).

Citizens from Russia and other newly independent states that emerged out of the Soviet Union are trafficked in all directions where there are borders leading to other states. From the Far East, they are trafficked to China, Japan, and Thailand. From Azerbaijan and Armenia, common routes are to the United Arab Emirates, Saudi Arabia, Turkey, and Israel. From all areas of Russia there are routes to Turkey, the Czech Republic, Bosnia-Herzegovina, Croatia, Hungary, Poland, Israel, Germany, Holland, Greece, Italy, France, the United Kingdom, the United States, and Canada. There is both internal trafficking within the post-Soviet space, such as Ukrainians and Central Asians being sent to Moscow, and trafficking out of it, either to transit states from which the women are sold again or directly to destination states. The span of trafficked space is global, but denser where the demand for prostitutes is high and where Slavic women are prized as exotic and beautiful. Some researchers, such as Donna M. Hughes, argue that where prostitution has been legalized, high demand for women has led to increased levels of trafficking, and its legalized status makes it easier for traffickers to evade prosecution. Germany and Holland are cited as prime examples (Hughes 2001, 2002).

Bonded labor is not a historically new phenomenon, but the nature of the globalized world means that several developments taken together are conducive to it. These include the migration of workers to labor-deficit markets in an attempt to overcome unemployment and/or poverty at home; the international political economy of sex, which encompasses demands not just from a given state's residents but also from sex tourism and military postings; the failure or unwillingness of many states to tackle the insufficient protection and regulation of contract workers; patriarchal norms and values about gendered labor and also discriminatory attitudes concerning ethnicity; the role of organized crime, particularly since the collapse of the state socialist systems; and corruption within police forces, among border guards, and in judiciaries, amounting to collusion with traffickers. The result is widespread slavery in the twenty-first century. States that are especially poor, such as Moldova, suffer badly. Up to 1 million of its 4.3 million population work outside its borders. High levels of domestic violence obtain here, and it is estimated that 80% of the women who have been trafficked were victims of domestic violence beforehand. Flows of the trafficked, however, are not restricted to the post-Soviet states and Eastern Europe. According to Hughes, they constitute the "fourth wave" of trafficked women after the first of Thai and Filipino women, the second of Dominicans and Colombians, and the third of Ghanaians and Nigerians.

It should be stressed, however, that not all migrants end up among the thousands of trafficked. Much labor mobility across Europe and worldwide is free from trafficking. Indeed, although human trafficking can be subsumed under "migration," most migrants are not trafficked, although many may endure various hardships. Moreover, among the trafficked, not all end up in the sex industry; some find themselves in private homes, in factories and sweat shops, on building sites, in window cleaning, or in child begging rings.

Slavery Old and New

Human slavery has a long history, having existed across the centuries and across continents. Moreover, although the writing of history has focused dispropor-tionately on ancient Greece, the Roman Empire, and the southern United States, slavery has not been restricted to these examples (Genovese 1967, 1973, 1974,

1979; Miller 1996). William D. Phillips has underscored that slavery has "appeared in nearly every part of the world," traced back to "the earliest civilizations of Mesopotamia and Egypt" and has also been found in "more recent societies at various levels of development" (1985, 3; Archer 1988; Conrad 1986; Klein 1986; Reid 1983; Miers and Kopytoff 1977). Slavery has characterized both urban and rural settings and been evident in both Christian and Muslim societies. In short, slavery can take root in various contexts and carry various dimensions, shaped by socio-economic and historical backdrop.[2]

The important point for this analysis is that the nature of slavery, whenever and wherever it exists in time and space, is itself framed and shaped by the prevailing nature of international and domestic systems. At the end of the twentieth century and into the new millennium, human slavery is situated in a far more "global" world than witnessed in the times of Thucydides, Plato, Aristotle, and, more recently, even Hobbes and Locke. New technologies and global financial markets mean that "known" worlds have hugely expanded, as news flashes across continents in seconds and as some citizens even aspire to space travel. Although there is very lively debate about quite how "new" globalization is due to its evident economic roots in the nineteenth century, today's forms of slavery are nonetheless located in a faster world with a high degree of mobility and interconnectedness and one in which immense disparities obtain between rich and poor states.[3] Kevin Bales has dubbed this a "new" slavery since it is not about "owning people in the traditional sense of the old slavery" but about controlling them completely, then disposing of them when they are spent. The drive is to make "big profits" out of cheap and disposable lives without legal ownership (Bales 2004, 4–33).[4] It must be highlighted, however, that various patterns of slavery do still obtain, and the so-called old slavery does in places persist. Moreover, the core of slavery is about exploitation, control, and abuse, whether it is legal or illegal.

Migration

Like slavery, patterns of migration have long histories on all continents and have been shaped by other complex conjunctures (Castles and Miller 1988). Relevant independent and intervening variables include famine, climate, war, conflict, fear, unemployment, the search for a better life, and available modes of transport. Added to these must be human needs, wants, hopes, and aspirations, variously defined across time and space.

In the case of the Russian Federation in the late twentieth and early twenty-first centuries, the factor of system collapse is crucial. The demise of the Soviet empire in 1989 in Eastern Europe and then the protracted implosion of the Soviet Union, which formally ended in December 1991, had huge implications for the nature of economic systems, investment and employment patterns, opportunities for movement and criminality, and, with them all, new possibilities for exploitation, particularly of the economically marginalized. That trafficking became a sexualized phenomenon is not especially surprising in hindsight given the broader context of what Jan Pettman dubs "an international political economy of sex" (1996, 157–207). Sheila L. Croucher sums up the situation, which is facilitated by today's technologies, as one of "the transnational marketing, export, exchange and exploitation of women" through use of the Internet, fax machines, cell phones, and jet planes (2004, 166). The result in Sally Stoecker's estimation is quite simply a "commodification of persons" (Stoecker 2000, 129–144; Stoecker and Shelley 2005). Easier travel across borders, expanding opportunities for crime through fake passports, and corrupt border guards and militias together make for a relatively easy and low risk exploitation of women. The international political economy of sex is stimulated by demand from clients, which appears high and growing. Arguably, clients, as ready consumers, fuel trafficking, guaranteeing a ready market for victims. If they were more ready to blow the whistle on brothels where crying prostitutes were obviously coerced, more convictions might result—depending upon the state.

Liberal democracies and ongoing processes of democratization may have brought many rights and freedoms to citizens, but they do not guarantee an absence of exploitation or an end to hackneyed gender stereotypes and patriarchal practices that degrade and disrespect. Indeed, despite the many legal advances for women throughout the twentieth century in liberal democracies concerning property ownership, voting, and equal opportunities, the sad reality remains that patriarchal attitudes, male domination, and mechanisms that demean and exploit women have been far from eradicated. Although many kind and loving "new" men do indeed exist, the opposite persists. The beauty industry, sex shops, pornographic films and magazines, popular culture, and female collusion in their own sites of subordination complicate matters, often working against women's emancipation from gender stereotypes.

The Russian Case Study

The Soviet state officially supported the emancipation of women in law and in ideology and held that female "factual equality" in life (*fakticheskoe ravenstvo*) could only be attained through participation in social production and through political mobilization. Although the "woman question" (*zhenskii vopros*) was declared "solved" in the 1930s, a recognition of the social sciences under Nikita Khrushchev and more so under Leonid Brezhnev enabled critical sociologists such as Zoiia Iankova, Maia Pankratova, and Elena Gruzdeva in the late 1960s to point out that the *zhenskii vopros* was not, in fact, solved (Buckley 1986, 1989). The "double burden" of housework, caring for children and possibly other family members, and paid work gave rise to "non-antagonistic contradictions" in women's lives.

Although in the Soviet state patriarchal attitudes persisted, and notwithstanding the fact that prostitution did exist despite denials from the state until glasnost under Gorbachev exposed it and discussed its significance, human trafficking as we know it today did not obtain (Buckley 1993). That developed very much in the 1990s and after laissez-faire economics had brought laissez-faire sexual exploitation of women, girls, men, and boys, including pedophilia.

In the new millennium, newspaper articles in Russia exposing the dangers and results of human trafficking have been more visible than they were in the 1990s. How different newspapers treat the topic, however, varies according to their style of reporting and whether the newspaper's main aim is to inform or to sensationalize, shock, or titillate. Arguably, all revelations inform readers in some way, but do not necessarily deter or educate in the way intended. Some newspapers addressed the topic sooner than others, and some with greater seriousness. A trawl across papers finds articles in the main newspapers, including *Izvestiia*, *Nezavisimaia gazeta*, *Rossiiskaia gazeta*, *Argumenty i Fakty*, *Komsomol'skaia Pravda*, *Pravda*, *Moskovskie Komsomolets*, and *Moskovskie Novosti*. Coverage in states of the former Soviet Union has also been increasing (Buckley 2007). For example, articles on Central Asia can be found in *Vechernii Bishkek*, *Ekspress K*, and *Kazakhstanskaia Pravda*.

Notwithstanding variations in details or the extent of violence used, the stories are by now familiar and follow a pattern. In 2004, Ekaterina Karacheva reported in *Argumenty i Fakty* that in recent years, around four million young women between the ages of eighteen and twenty-five had left Russia. Having responded to advertisements promising well-paid jobs, many found themselves forced into prostitution. Under the heading "Beautiful Slaves," Karacheva told the tragic story of Oksana, whose classmate offered her a couple of months of highly paid work in Cyprus as a dancer. Assured that the work was safe and not in prostitution, Oksana signed a work contract. Once there, however, Oksana was initially asked to perform striptease but after a week was forced into prostitution, servicing thirty clients a day. When her boss took her to a private flat and locked her up, Oksana decided to make a run for it as soon as she could. She tore up a sheet, secured it, threw it through the railings of a seventh-floor balcony, and started carefully to climb down. The attachment broke, and her body was found the next morning. *Argumenty i Fakty* commented that the Angel Coalition estimated that 2,000 women a year were lured into Cyprus (Karacheva 2004).

Less sensational in its coverage, *Izvestiia* more dryly told the tale of a twenty-eight-year-old Muscovite, Pavel Golenko, who organized a flow of young women to the United Arab Emirates (UAE). Elena Vlasova reported that since March 1998, the UAE would not admit unmarried women under the age of thirty into the country, or married women under the age of thirty not accompanied by their husbands, so Golenko provided the women with fake passports that adjusted their ages. The young women were initially found by P. Khisametdinova in Tashkent and promised high-paid work as waitresses. Khisametdinova targeted women with unhappy family situations and no paid work, offering them a "happy ticket." The future "waitresses" were then flown to Moscow and met by Golenko and then later flown on to Dubai, where V. Gnedin took charge of them. Their documents were taken away, allegedly to "register" them, but in fact in order to control them. Gnedin informed the women that he did not mind if they wanted to return home, but first they had to earn the passage and food already given to them. Prostitution was the work (Vlasova 2006).

This flow of women via Golenko lasted for four months, but stopped in December 2004. Inadvertently, Golenko let slip to five women in his care from Tashkent what sort of work awaited them in Dubai. They were in shock, but frightened, so agreed to continue. The next day before departure at Moscow's Sheremetyevo-2 airport, the young women managed to inform the airline management of internal affairs what was happening, and Golenko was apprehended. The investigation of his case lasted almost a year. Vlasova reported that he was found guilty of setting up a criminal group, of trafficking in persons, and of illegal deprivation of freedom and of falsifying documents. The other members of the group at the time of reporting had not been found (Vlasova 2006).

These two different stories illustrate the span of possible results for the women themselves. In the first example, Oksana became a prostitute against her will and endured physical and mental assaults and had a fatal and tragic end. In the second, the women luckily avoided ever working as prostitutes in Dubai and blew the whistle on Golenko to their advantage and his conviction. Both cases illustrate women fighting to triumph, to escape, and not to suffer in victimhood. Not all trafficked persons, however, can easily contest their lot. Many are too afraid to attempt to break out, deterred by threats from pimps and brothel owners to themselves and to their families and children back home. Some fear rushing to the local militia for help since they do not trust them and cannot speak the local language anyway; and many lack ready opportunities to leave due to the level at which they are guarded.

Tales like those illustrated here, and many that fall in between this broad span of results, can occur across the wide geographic stretch already described. Problems persist for many if they manage to return to Russia. They can be shunned by their community on the grounds that they have "lowered" themselves and brought "shame." Myths surround them. One is that they were prostitutes anyway and surely knew what would be expected of them. Another is that they brought it on themselves and should shoulder the blame, not deserving help. They now suffer both stigma and discrimination (Hughes 2000, 2001, 2006).

The naming of human trafficking (*torgovlia liud'mi*) inside Russia came in the late 1990s, initially from women's groups, NGOs, and academics. A key conference in this early process was held in 1997, part of a project of the Global Survival Network (Global Survival Network 1997). The first response from the Russian government and politicians, however, was that human trafficking did not exist. Denial indicated a lack of willingness either to investigate or act. This was followed by the charge that women who found themselves in this position were themselves to blame either for their stupidity for being duped by traffickers or for the fact that they were really prostitutes. Denial was thus followed by denigration. Accompanying these negative responses was the suggestion that since the trafficked were now in other states such as Germany or Israel, it was an issue "*tam*," or "there," rather than "here." Thus, ran the argument, Russia had no responsibility for the women (Buckley 2004, 2006).

Pressure from the United States was productive in Russia in the long run, but not instantly. Indeed, those attempting to point out to politicians and the government that human trafficking existed and required action either were ignored or their arguments were contested and dismissed. Key among the most knowledgeable in the Russian academic community were Elena Tiuriukanova, based in Moscow at the Institute for Socio-Economic Studies of the Population of the Russian Academy of Sciences as a specialist on forced labor (*prinuditel'nyi trud*), and psychologist Natalia Khodyreva of St. Petersburg University and a Petersburg crisis center (Tiuriukanova et al. 2004; Tiuriukanova and Erokhina 2002; Khodyreva and Tsvetkova 2000; Khodyreva 2004). The women's groups interested in seeing anti-trafficking legislation debated and adopted in the State Duma included the crisis center Sestry (sisters). Its hotline to answer calls about violence against women had picked up several stories about trafficking, even though trafficking per se was not its main concern, which fell more broadly on violence against women in general. Nonetheless, in 2001 and 2002, organizations like Sestry and its energetic director Mariia Mokhova were invited to participate in the Duma working group on trafficking, through which the People's Deputy Elena Mizulina, a lawyer, was attempting to spearhead draft legislation on human trafficking. Not all Russian researchers in the field, however, were consulted. Moreover, the NGO community in Moscow was not devoid of mutual criticisms and different views about the legalization of prostitution, which clouded their common goal of getting recognition of the existence of a growing problem of human trafficking and of seeing anti-trafficking legislation passed. For example, as an "outsider" from the United States, Dr. Juliette Engel and her organization, Miramed, were praised by some activists and criticized by others. Engel is an American medical doctor who went to Russia to tackle the fate of orphans and health issues concerning mother and child. She subsequently became committed to setting up an umbrella organization, the Angel Coalition, which initially drew together forty-three NGOs with a view to coordinating anti-trafficking action. Miramed was viewed with some suspicion and skepticism. Its presence was resented by those who thought its members to be interfering in issues best dealt with by locals. Dr. Engel, however, appeared genuinely keen to help with a high level of commitment and commented to me in an interview in 2004 that "nothing is easy in Russia." She had made links with NGOs outside Moscow, set up education campaigns, and attempted to discuss matters with the Russian presidential administration and several Western embassies in Moscow. As outsiders ready to try to influence the legislative process of the Duma, Engel and her coworker, Robert Aronson, were criticized by some Russian activists for trying to play a part in a political system that was not their own.

Tensions were aggravated because the Angel Coalition condemned prostitution as immoral, in disagreement with other groups who argued that sex work should be given a legitimate status, and was probably most likely to be legalized sooner or later. Some women held less fixed views, either changing their minds about it or being less condemnatory than others. Thus, under the surface of the anti-trafficking initiatives were quite heated differences, which occasionally boiled into accusations, criticisms, and a lack of trust. This particular controversy has fueled a lot of disagreement and dislikes, all part of the process of lobbying for legislation from slightly different positions. One researcher whom I interviewed pointed out that, as she perceived the situation—whether rightly or wrongly—for a while Mizulina had been pro-prostitution and that the Angel Coalition mistrusted her for having once held that view. Cooperation and coordination across NGOs suffered not only over differences about prostitution but also since they competed for Western funding.

Despite tensions and arguments amid political actors, quite usual in all political systems over most issues, lobbying from the United States and from women's groups in Russia finally resulted in the bill that was discussed in the Legislation Committee in February 2002, but which failed to be passed by the Duma. Its existence, however, was sufficient to push Russia up the State Department's rankings into Tier 2 on a provisional basis to be monitored closely. Natalia Khodyreva suggested to me in an interview in St. Petersburg in 2004 that "without Western influence nothing would have happened." As well as the Americans, Germany's Gerhardt Schroeder had played a constructive role. The IOM, the Association of American Lawyers, and the United Nations Children's Fund (UNICEF) were also involved in the process. The U.S. embassy in Moscow played an educational role by inviting foreign experts and in facilitating productive seminars.

Why did this first draft bill fail to pass into law? Key factors include low perceived salience of the issue among politicians, lack of time, and the prohibitive cost of the package suggested. First, reception in the Duma was, in fact, poor. It was not a high-profile issue, even though three Duma committees were relevant to it, namely the Legislation Committee, the Security Committee, and the Committee for Family and Children. In a telephone interview in 2005, Tat'iana Kholshevnikova, administrator of the Duma Legislation Committee, confirmed that "not more than ten deputies turned up for the first reading of the bill." This was at a time when many dismissed the existence of the problem or the need to help prostitutes.

Second, according to Elena Tiuriukanova in an interview in Moscow in 2004, the first draft law had insufficient time in the Duma to make much headway, but is best seen as a vital preparatory "first step," necessary for something to happen later. The advantage of tabling the draft law and of having it discussed in the Legislation Committee was that it put the topic on the agenda and enabled others to prepare the climate for later legislation. Third, passage of the entire package was most unlikely due to the cost, which prompted huge budgetary concerns. Witness protection was part of the initial draft and is highly expensive.

Slowly, attitudes about the need for anti-trafficking legislation altered as awareness of the problem's dimensions grew and as Vladimir Putin gave it firm backing. By December 2003, there was a readiness to follow his lead and vote to amend the Criminal Code. This was not the massive legislative package that women's groups and the U.S. State Department had wanted, but it did change the law. Article 127.1 declared that trafficking in persons is punishable by a term in jail of up to five years. The same act with regard to two or more persons, or to a minor, committed through false documents, through the use or threat of force, or for the purpose of removing organs or tissues from the victim is punishable by a prison term of three to ten years. If committed by an organized group, or a threat to lives and health, punishment of eight to fifteen years is possible. Here, trafficking in persons is defined as "the buying-selling of a person or other actions committed for the purpose of such person's exploitation in the form of recruitment, transportation, transfer, harboring, or receipt of such person" (State Duma 2003).

The U.S. State Department kept up pressure for more legislation. At a conference on trafficking in January 2004 in Moscow, U.S. Secretary of State Colin Powell stressed that new norms resulted only from enforcement and that "good intention is not enough." The message to Putin's administration was that it should ensure that the law was enforced and the traffickers be apprehended and convicted. Powell also called for more legislation, particularly on witness protection and a national referral system. For its part, Powell declared, the United States "is with you in spirit, but also in practical terms." They were states "working together" in a manner comparable to the war on terrorism in order defeat traffickers and "to rescue, save and rehabilitate the victims" (U.S. Embassy, Moscow 2004). In his statement to the conference, which was attended by representatives of NGOs as well as executive government officials, Putin said that he hoped the event would "unite the efforts of government bodies and non-governmental organizations and will help solve this problem" (Putin 2004).

By 2004, human trafficking was defined as a threat to Russia's national security by the Ministry of the Interior, with some recognition that work by the militia in anti-trafficking was often inadequate. This work was not helped by the fact that victims' families hesitated to come forward and give information out of fear of blackmail and threats, making human trafficking what Mizulina dubbed "a very safe business for criminals" precisely because of fear of testifying (Yablokova 2004). Hence, there was a pressing need for special witness protection for the trafficked and their families. Huge costs, however, militated against this, just as they worked against setting up an interagency commission favored by women's groups. Different state bodies were reluctant to take on the responsibility of dealing with human trafficking given the attendant drain on their budgets. Additional funds would be imperative for such an initiative. Indeed, women's groups suspected that many politicians might say that they were committed to tackling trafficking, but were more concerned about the cost. As a consequence, the U.S. State Department's 2004 TIP Report declared that "trafficking victims had no specially defined status under Russian law, nor specific mechanisms to assist or protect them" (U.S. State Department, 2004).

One solution has been to proceed by adopting parts of the package in piecemeal fashion. For example, in the summer of 2004 a law on witness protection was finally passed, but this was not specifically "trafficking victim protection legislation." Nonetheless, in 2004 fresh draft legislation circulated in the Duma, and the process continued of aiming for protection and assistance to victims of trafficking, including shelters and support centers. The June 2006 U.S. State Department TIP Report, however, rebuked Russia for its "uneven progress" and regretted that the "comprehensive legislation on victim assistance" that had been "anticipated for three years" had not yet materialized. Rather, protection remained ad hoc and was "highly dependent upon local and regional authorities." Moreover, local government support was "not formalized" but "dependent upon relationships between NGOs and local government officials" (U.S. State Department 2006).

To What Extent Are Russia, Europe, and the World Fighting Back?

In some respects, good progress has been made since the mid-1990s concerning the naming, researching, and recognition of human trafficking. In 1996, the issue was first discussed in the OSCE at a time when few participating governments helped victims. In 1998, President Bill Clinton issued a directive that put in place a U.S. anti-trafficking strategy of prevention, protection of victims, and prosecution of traffickers. In 1999, the UN Office on Drugs and Crime (UNODC), working with the UN Interregional Crime and Justice Research Institute (UNICRI), set up the Global Program against Trafficking in Human Beings (GPAT) (Miko 2006). Since these starting European, U.S., and UN initiatives, academics, the OSCE, the IOM, UN agencies, the U.S. State Department, and Amnesty International have produced a mountain of research findings. In the new millennium, however, although 150 states have known trafficking problems, "all but 14" have recently made "significant efforts" to address them (U.S. Mission to the OSCE 2005). In

2004 and 2005, twenty of the OSCE countries had adopted new legislation or amended old laws to combat trafficking.

In all aspects of life, however, legislation is an insufficient protector. It is a necessary first step in the defense of rights and equalities, but is not necessarily implemented. Equality on paper has never, in any state of the world, guaranteed equality in life, or what Soviet sociologists used to call "factual equality," as distinct from "legal equality" or "formal equality." It is here that action is required and positive results needed. As the Council of Europe Convention against Human Trafficking puts it, governments need to ensure that not only are sanctions imposed, but that they be "effective, proportionate and dissuasive" (U.S. Mission to the OSCE 2005). The general view is that the "risk/reward equation" needs to be rebalanced.

Evidence shows that in states of the OSCE, notably Armenia, Azerbaijan, Bosnia, the Czech Republic, Estonia, Kazakhstan, Latvia, and Ukraine, "courts have been imposing suspended or conditional sentences for serious trafficking crimes" (U.S. Mission to the OSCE 2005). If convicted traffickers spend little or no time behind bars, deterrence is inevitably wanting. This problem is exacerbated by the reluctance of some judiciaries to give firm sentences for first offenses, preferring instead "the use of low sentences." Moreover, sometimes the law can backfire on victims. Amnesty International reported the case of a woman in Albania who withdrew her testimony after being confronted by the defendant at the trial and after having suffered previous threats. As a consequence, she was arrested and charged with perjury (Amnesty International 2005). In the case of Ukraine, although in 2005 it stepped up investigations into trafficking, two-thirds of convicted traffickers were given probation, not prison sentences. Of 115 of those convicted, 47 were given sentences ranging from three to eight years, and the remainder were given probation (U.S. State Department 2006). By contrast, Romania has been praised for its network of "specially trained judges" for human trafficking, aware of the "heinous nature" of the crime and concerned to deliver "real punishments" (U.S. Mission to the OSCE 2005). In 2005, Romania convicted 235 traffickers. Of these, 137 received prison sentences. Sixty-four were jailed for between one and five years, and 64 were sentenced to from five to ten years (U.S. State Department 2006). The message to the OSCE from the United States is to keep human trafficking high on its agenda (U.S. Mission to the OSCE 2005).

In December 2005, a two-day OSCE Ministerial Council meeting in Slovenia called upon all participating states "to prevent sexual exploitation and abuse by its civilian and military personnel or incidents of forced labor" and also "investigate and punish any such cases" (reported in U.S. Mission to NATO 2005). This was integral to its decision on "Ensuring the Highest Standards of Conduct and Accountability of Persons Serving on International Missions and Forces." This was warmly welcomed by the Commission on Security and Cooperation in Europe, also known as the Helsinki Commission, which is a U.S. government human rights watchdog group that monitors the implementation of the 1975 Helsinki Accords concerning the implementation of basic human rights (reported in the U.S. Mission to NATO 2005).[5] The commission praised the OSCE for this "important step in establishing an internationally recognized standard of behavior of military and civilian personnel serving in peacekeeping and related roles around the world" (reported in UN Mission to NATO 2005).

In fact, the OSCE was following the lead of the United States in this regard. In 2002, a scandal had broken in U.S. news, which suggested that in Korea's red-light districts, the U.S. Army was protecting businesses in which trafficked women had been forced to work. The U.S. Congress reacted swiftly to the implication that the U.S. Army was enabling and condoning human trafficking by organizing an investigation into the link between U.S. armed forces and both prostitution and trafficking. The situations in Korea and the Balkans were analyzed, with the conclusion that U.S. troops did not facilitate human trafficking, but that their relationship with brothels was "overly familiar" (Allred 2005, 63–79).[6] As a consequence, the U.S. Defense Department adopted a "zero-tolerance" policy, according to which U.S. troops and contractors were prohibited from being "complicit in any way in trafficking in persons" (Allred 2005, 65–66). In addition, areas where trafficking was suspected were defined as "off-limits" for military personnel, who now had to undergo "counter-trafficking training"—effectively an education program designed to alert, inform, and pass on the punishments for violations.

Following on from these developments, in 2004 proposals were put forward to amend the Uniform Code of Military Justice, which is a federal criminal code applicable to U.S. military personnel. "Patronizing a prostitute" was to become, in July 2005, a criminal offense for all military personnel, even in instances where sex took place in a country in which prostitution was legal and if it was also consensual (Allred 2005, 67). Law professor Michael Noone, who is also a former judge advocate in the U.S. Air Force, has posed the inevitable question: Will the law be obeyed? He cites an online reader survey done between September 30 and October 5, 2004, by the *Air Force Times* in which 74% of the 2,856 readers who responded declared the patronage proposal "a waste of time." A smaller 22% thought that "the change is long overdue," and only 4% did not know. Noone doubts whether the commanders who are meant to initiate disciplinary action, or the subordinates who are the potential targets of disciplinary action, expect any radical changes in behavior on the ground. He questions whether the U.S. military, or any military, possesses "an enforcement mechanism capable" of both identifying offenders and bringing them to trial (Noone 2005, 81–89).

Moving in the same direction, the North Atlantic Treaty Organization (NATO), at its Istanbul summit in June 2004, endorsed a common policy on human trafficking. This prohibits NATO staff from engaging in trafficking or from facilitating it. They are also required to report known or suspected incidences of it. Here "NATO staff" includes those participating in military and civilian operations, as well as those who are non-NATO troops and subcontractors (NATO Seminar 2005). This development was triggered by the knowledge that international troops, particularly in the Balkans, were known to be "a driving force behind the flourishing sex market" (NATO Seminar 2005).[7] The problem here, as Norway's state secretary Kjetil Skogrand noted at a seminar held in Sweden in November 2005 on how to implement NATO policy on human trafficking, is that policy effectiveness "depends upon the support and commitment of national authorities." He recognized that this is complex since legislation on trafficking varies across states and that "some nations simply do not see prostitution as part of this problem. Some do not see the problem at all." He deemed predeployment education vital, not least because "the great majority of personnel operating in NATO theatres of operation are still not aware of what human trafficking is about" (Skogrand 2005). As in all organizations and states, policies, regulations, and legislation are first-step keys to changing behavior. The latter, however, is never automatic, and new rules are not necessarily easily implemented, respected, or followed. Skogrand called for close dialogue across NATO, the OSCE, and the EU.

The UN in April 2006 issued a sober assessment of the global picture. The UNODC, in a report entitled "Trafficking in Persons: Global Patterns," pointed out that no country is unaffected by human trafficking for sexual exploitation or forced labor (UNODC 2006). It named 137 countries of destination, 98 of transit, and 127 of origin. Analysis and action, it regretted, were seriously hampered by the absence of reliable information since some states were better at data gathering than others. In part this was accounted for by the reluctance of some governments to acknowledge the problem, as had been the case in Russia until recently. But it is not just countries of origin that shirk from admitting the scale of trafficking. The UNODC's executive director, Antonio Maria Costa, pointed out that many countries of destination "have great difficulty in acknowledging the level of trafficking within and across their borders" (UNODC 2006). This makes fighting trafficking more difficult than it otherwise might be, as it fuels the problem of uncoordinated and inefficient efforts. European and global coordination is difficult enough without a lack of reliable comparative data. As a consequence, traffickers were able "to capitalise on weak law enforcement and poor international cooperation," not deterred in any way by low conviction rates (UNODC 2006). The UNODC defined the pressing tasks of governments as follows: first, to reduce demand both for the services of "sex slaves" and for cheap goods produced in sweatshops; second, to target the criminals involved; and third, to protect the victims of trafficking, especially women and children. One serious problem was that the victims themselves were often treated like criminals, frequently facing charges for flouting immigration rules or anti-prostitution laws, depending upon the state in which they found themselves.

Efforts in individual states vary according to the nature of the legislation passed, the scale and sort of policing devoted to tracking down and apprehending traffickers, and the level of resources given to protecting the trafficked. One advance in the United States occurred in January 2002 when the attorney general announced a special new "T" visa. This enabled victims of trafficking to stay in the United States if they cooperated with law enforcement against traffickers, especially if they might suffer harm if they returned home. After three years on a "T" visa, they could apply for permanent residence (Miko 2006). New endeavors of a different kind are being pursued elsewhere. In 2006 in Britain, the Labour government under Tony Blair, for instance, set up the Serious Organized Crime Agency (SOCA), a new Federal Bureau of Investigation–style organization, which breaks the pattern of traditional British policing. In April, the prime minister declared that it was designed to fight twenty-first-century crime with "modern methods" and would make "life hell" for the "Mr. Bigs" of organized crime. A former head of MI5, Sir Stephen Lander, chairs its staff, who number over 4,000 and include members of the intelligence and security services. The annual budget was initially £400 million, and a central aim is to prosecute criminals and to track down their assets. SOCA can require crime bosses who are released from prison to show their bank statements for twenty years afterwards to demonstrate that they have not returned to crime (Guardian Unlimited 2006). It is too soon to assess its performance, but tracking down human traffickers and drug traffickers is an overriding goal. This initiative was followed in October 2006 by the setting up of the UK Human Trafficking Center in Sheffield, designed to carry on the work of the UK's first national campaign to target human trafficking, known as "Operation Pentameter," which took place earlier in 2006 and resulted in hundreds of arrests, raids on brothels, and the rescue of eighty-four people.

Limits to Success?

Corruption beyond criminal gangs inhibits the implementation of sound legislation, regulations, and initiatives. Police behavior often militates against progress over the entire post-Soviet space. In Serbia, for example, off-duty police officers have been spotted providing security to establishments where trafficked women were working. Yet only one of them was charged (Amnesty International 2005, 6). Conviction rates across Eastern Europe vary, depending upon the year and the state. Until recently, there has been widespread evidence of a reluctance to prosecute or to convict. For example, in Montenegro, since 2002 fifteen cases were submitted for prosecution, but by the end of 2004 there had been no convictions at all (Amnesty International 2005, 6). Russia's conviction record to date cannot be described as "enthusiastic," but it is improving. As the 2006 U.S. State Department TIP Report noted, police investigations of trafficking went up from twenty-six in 2004 to eighty in 2005. Sixty of the latter concerned sexual exploitation, and twenty were cases of forced labor. Prosecutions did increase fivefold, from eleven in 2004 to fifty-three in 2005. "At least" nine traffickers were convicted and six sent to prison, but sentences ranged from only three-and-a-half to eight years (U.S. State Department 2006). Given the scale of human trafficking from and within Russia, this number of convictions is pitifully low.

Despite huge problems in Central Asia stemming from poverty, polygamy, and traditional attitudes, by February 2004 in Uzbekistan, there were eighty convictions out of 101 prosecutions, resulting in five to eight years' imprisonment. However, Uzbek girls and women who end up in Bangkok come up against the belief that the abused are to blame, not the abusers (Tursunova 2004). Complicity with crime or the practice of accepting bribes also deters the meting out of justice and due punishment, although attempts to bribe are not always successful. An Israeli who was known in Ukraine as a "respectable" businessman in the property market illegally tricked thirty-five Ukrainian girls and women to work abroad. When he was apprehended, he tried unsuccessfully to bribe his way out of the situation for $150,000. *Pravda* reported that he would be extradited to Israel (*Pravda* 2005).

Similarly, the reluctance of the trafficked to blow the whistle out of fear of reprisals for themselves and their families means that most traffickers remain untouched. A report in *Pravda* pointed out that despite more than a decade of trafficking girls and women from the Krasnodar region of Russia, the Interior Ministry's Central Department of the region revealed in 2005 that "not a single victim of sex trafficking has appealed to the police within the past several years."

Moreover, an opinion poll in the city of Krasnodar had shown that when they finished studying, two-thirds of schoolgirls and students were planning to go abroad "for any employment," even if it was "dangerous for health and life." The potential number of young women ripe for abuse in the Krasnodar region is estimated at 800,000, unless education programs make them change their minds (*Pravda* 2005).

More vigilant policing of brothel areas and whistle-blowing help from clients who see that girls and women are in the sex trade unhappily and coerced would help enormously, especially in states where the prostitute is not automatically imprisoned but counseled and protected. Indeed, a global debate about the role and significance of clients would be timely, following Sweden's lead. Without clients' demand for prostitutes, the business could not sustain itself, although realistically demand is unlikely to plummet. Nonetheless, clients are complicit in trafficking in the sense that they consume the trafficked.

There are also other sorts of mechanisms already in place that can be used to help the trafficked out of their plight and to challenge the limits of success. The Angel Coalition has set up international and national toll-free helplines to Russia, direct to Russian speakers, for women stranded in Russia, Europe, or the United States and able to reach a telephone. They provide information for those intending to work abroad as well as a lifeline to the trafficked. The trafficked who call for advice and rescue can be found by the hotline establishing contact with government agencies, domestic and international law enforcement, and Interpol (Angel Coalition 2004). The IOM has also launched a campaign in Turkey to save trafficked women with the free telephone number 157 ("V Turtsii spasaiut" 2006).

Finally, one controversial area that needs further thought is that of huge events that attract large numbers of males into city areas. The 2006 World Cup held in Germany saw much advance publicity in Britain about whether Wayne Rooney's injury would be healed in time for him to play and whether English football hooligans would disgrace themselves yet again with violence. Absent from the front pages of newspapers discussing the World Cup were fears as expressed by Donna M. Hughes, Juliette Engel, the European Parliament, the IOM, Swedish officials, and Russia's newspapers such as *Trud* and many others, that thousands of women and children were about to be trafficked from Eastern Europe and sold into Germany's legal sex industry for the sexual servicing of football fans in twelve cities (Hughes 2006; Engel 2006; Kolchanov 2006). It was estimated that around three million fans were about to arrive, and the German Women's Council thought that as many as 40,000 additional women were expected to be added to the approximately 400,000 women in Germany's sex industry. Hughes and others accused German officials of virtual partnership with the brothel owners, pimps, and traffickers since megabrothels and "sex-huts" were being constructed. Since Angela Merkel was not speaking out, Hughes dubbed this "a disgraceful distinction for Germany's first woman chancellor." The president of the German Police Union, however, did join the "Red Card for Forced Prostitution" campaign (Hughes 2006).

In cases such as the German one, the interconnections between the "legal" and the "illegal" are vivid, with the latter feeding the former. The result is that because the practice of prostitution is legal in the destination state, the origins of the unwilling and coerced prostitute are not sufficiently queried, nor are the consequences for her security or well-being even considered. Both the state and the client, in such instances, can be deemed culpable of collusion with traffickers, putting their own gain and pleasure ahead of the security and safety of the young women. As Engel put it, the German government was acting as "official pimp" for the 2006 World Cup, "anticipating millions of dollars in revenues" (2006). Since Germany retained its position in Tier 1 in the U.S. State Department's TIP Report, released early in June just before the games, some greeted its results with outcries (U.S. State Department 2006).

It has not, however, been substantiated whether such huge numbers of trafficked women did in fact arrive ahead of the World Cup, and one cannot easily gather precise statistics. Nonetheless, the event did trigger some debate about what large sports gatherings of males can mean for the process of trafficking in states where prostitution is legal. Immediately some, such as the NGO Doctors for Life, began to wonder about the implications for the 2010 World Cup in South Africa and called for "tougher laws" there. Doctors for Life was keen to stress that "prostitution is inherently harmful," likely to result in post-traumatic stress syndrome and other mental and physical conditions (De Capua 2006).

Conclusion

Human trafficking is now one of the most serious social and security problems in Russia, Europe, and the world. Its existence threatens the safety, dignity, and rights of the individual and challenges assumptions about automatic "progress" with the spread of democracy. Notions of an ongoing "civilizing process" as humankind develops are also questionable in some dimensions of life. Moreover, human trafficking undermines the physical and mental health of the trafficked and shows in many traffickers the worst characteristics that humankind, both male and female, can display: brutality, sadism, sexism, disrespect, psychological terror, and greed. Integral to the process are dishonesty, deception, and a lack of kindness or altruism. The morality of the twenty-first century on the ground in some sections of society is highly questionable. Furthermore, human trafficking's globalized nature means that easy linkages and connections foster quick opportunities for traffickers to plug into organized crime networks. Corruption within police forces, among border guards, and in some legal systems also means that deterrence is often weak. Lack of punishment, or weak punishment, in some states makes the job of trafficker alluring for those so inclined—hence its growth due to factors of huge profit and low risk.

Thus, the way forward in the twenty-first century includes the following for all states of the world: more education programs for potential trafficked persons to deter duping; economic and investment initiatives for job creation and training schemes; the provision of crisis centers and psychological counseling; increased conviction rates and sentences for the traffickers; witness protection for informers; a tackling of corruption in police forces and among border guards; and a reduction in demand by clients. Together, these require a commitment not only of higher levels of resources and more services that compete with other government programs but also changes in the attitudes and behavior of corrupt police and clients. The overturning of corruption is a vast challenge since it is embedded in practices and informal procedures. The behavior of clients is similarly hard to alter in a world in which patriarchal attitudes persist and sexualized recreation of an anonymous kind is increasing. Perhaps even more deeply entrenched and hard to erode are the attitudes of parents who sell their daughters into prostitution for their own economic betterment and who instil in their daughters the notion that they are taking on responsibility for the family by complying. This is the case in northern Thailand, where parents send daughters to brothels in the south of the country (Bales 2004, 39–64).[8] The tasks are immense, but that should not deter attempts to tackle them, piece by piece, with the initial realistic goals of preventing instances of trafficking, reducing the flows, and convicting more traffickers than hitherto.

On a positive note, it is inevitable that with improved policing and effective judicial processes, conviction rates will increase, as they already have in some states. What is imperative for wider success is for convictions to deter trafficking by increasing the risk factor and thereby radically altering the risk/reward balance. Improved judicial systems, however, will not solve the problems of poverty and patriarchal attitudes, which require much broader and wide-ranging initiatives.

Solutions to both of the United States' global wars demand an understanding of their sources and the reasons that spur them on. Poverty and income disparities across the globalized world are common to both. Although each war carries its own specifics and the two are quite different in nature and meaning and have their own complexities, the United States government must pay serious attention to alleviating global poverty and to listening to what those affected have to say about their plight. In the war on terror, far more listening needs to take place. In the war on human trafficking, the TIP reports have proved vital in providing pictures as comprehensive as possible of the issues concerned, given the inadequacies of data collection, and constitute a necessary first step to legal and police actions. The next step in this war will be for states to tackle patterns of their own domestic trafficking, often patterns that leaders and police forces do not want to curb, and patterns in which international businesses in a "disinterested capitalism" have a stake for the cheap labor that they reap, often without themselves knowing it to be in conditions of slavery (Bales 2004, 237).

NOTES

I should like to record my thanks to the Centre for Research in the Arts, Social Sciences and Humanities (CRASSH) at the University of Cambridge for one of its nine-week Visiting Fellowships in 2004 under its "Migration" theme. Gratitude is also due to the British Academy and the Russian Academy of Sciences for a research visit to Moscow and Petersburg in September 2004 and to the British Academy for research support from its Elisabeth Barker Fund. I am grateful to Linda Racioppi and Katherine O'Sullivan See for their editorial comments and to participants at the conference in Istanbul for their feedback on the earlier paper. The final draft was completed two years before publication and therefore cites data up to 2006.

1. This was explored in depth by excellent investigative reporting into "Iraq's missing billions" on one the UK's most probing documentary news programs.
2. These points are explored more fully elsewhere (Buckley 2006).
3. For interpretations of globalization, consult Giddens 1999; Halliday 1994; Gray 1998; Hirst and Thompson 1999; Strange 1996; French 2000.
4. How best to define slavery has always been controversial, revolving around the role of the master, the slave's powerlessness, property, relations of production, outsider status, kinship ties, legal rights, and physical movement. See Archer 1988; Conrad 1986; Klein 1986; Reid 1983; Miers and Kopytoff 1977.

5. The Helsinki Commission is composed of nine members from the U.S. Senate, nine from the House of Representatives, and one from each of the Departments of State, Defense, and Commerce.

6. For fuller discussion, see Allred 2005, 63–79.

7. Allred points out that incidents of sexual assault by UN peacekeepers have been documented in Angola, Cambodia, East Timor, Liberia, Mozambique, Kosovo, Sierra Leone, and Somalia (2005, 68–69).

8. Bales adds that Thai girls are socialized to be obedient and retiring, and their Buddhist religion instructs that suffering in this life amounts to paying the "karmic debt" accrued in past lives. This reinforces the belief that they must accept their role as prostitutes for the good of their families (Bales 2004, 62).

WORKS CITED

Allred, Keith J. 2005. "Human Trafficking: Breaking the Military Link." *Connections: The Quarterly Journal* 4(4): 63–79.

Amnesty International. 2005. Excerpts from Amnesty International Annual Report on Trafficking in Persons, released May 25, 2005 (about the year 2004).

Angel Coalition. 2004. International and National Toll-Free Helplines to Russia. Http://www.angelcoalition.org/hotlines.html.

Archer, Leonie J., ed. 1988. *Slavery and Other Forms of Unfree Labour.* London: Routledge.

Bales, Kevin, 2004. *Disposable People: New Slavery in the Global Economy.* Rev. ed. *Berkeley: University of California Press.*

Buckley, Mary. 1986. *Soviet Social Scientists Talking: An Official Debate About Women.* London: Macmillan.

———. 1989. *Women and Ideology in the Soviet Union.* Hemel Hempstead, Hertfordshire: Harvester Wheatsheaf; Ann Arbor, Mich.: University of Michigan Press.

———. 1993. *Redefining Russian Society and Polity.* Boulder, Colo.: Westview Press.

———. 2004. Trafficking in People. *World Today* (August/September): 30–32.

———. 2006. *Menschenhandel als Politikum: Gesetzgebung und Problembewusstsein in Russland* (Human trafficking as politics: Legislation and problem-awareness in Russia). *Osteuropa* 56(6): 195–212.

———. 2007. "Press Images of Human Trafficking from Russia: Myths and Interpretations." In *Equal or Different? Gender, Equality and Ideology under State Socialism and After,* ed. Rebecca Kay, 211–229. London: Macmillan.

Buckley, Mary, and Robert Singh, eds. 2006. *The Bush Doctrine: Global Responses, Global Consequences.* London: Routledge.

Castles, Stephen, and Mark J. Miller. 1988. *The Age of Migration: International Population Movements in the Modern World.* 2nd ed. London: Palgrave.

Chomsky, Noam. 2005. *Imperial Ambitions: Conversations on the Post-9/11 World.* New York: Metropolitan Books.

Conrad, Robert Edgar. 1986. *World of Sorrow: The African Slave Trade to Brazil.* Baton Rouge: Louisiana State University Press.

Croucher, Sheila L. 2004. *Globalization and Belonging: The Politics of Identity in a Changing World.* Lanham, MD: Rowman and Littlefield.

Danilkin, Aleksandr. 2006. *Zhenu otdai diade* (Give your wife to uncle). *Trud,* March 21.

De Capua, Joe. 2006. 2010 World Cup Lure for Human Traffickers. *Voice of America.* Http://www.voanews.com/english/Africa/2006-08-09-voa37.cfm.

Dispatches, Channel 4. 2006. "Iraq's Missing Billions." March 20.

Engel, Juliette M. 2006. Statement to House Committee on International Relations. May 4. Http://wwwa.house.gov/international_relations/109/eng050406.pdf.

French, Hilary. 2000. *Vanishing Borders: Protecting the Planet in the Age of Globalization.* New York: W. W. Norton.

Genovese, Eugene D. 1967. *The Political Economy of Slavery: Studies in the Economy and Society of the Slave South.* New York: Vintage.

———, ed. 1973. *The Slave Economies.* New York: John Wiley.

———. 1974. *Roll Jordan Roll: The World Slaves Made.* New York: Vintage Books.

———. 1979. *From Rebellion to Revolution: Afro-American Slave Revolts in the Making of the Modern World.* Baton Rouge: Louisiana State University Press.

Giddens, Anthony. 1999. *The Third Way: The Renewal of Social Democracy.* Cambridge: Polity Press.

Global Survival Network. 1997. "The Trafficking of NIS Women Abroad." November. Http://www.globalsurvival.net/femaletrade/9711conferenceresolutions.html.

Gray, John. 1988. *False Dawn: The Delusions of Global Capitalism.* London: Granta.

Guardian Unlimited. 2006. "Blair Launches FBI-Style Crime Squad." April 3. Http://www.guardian.co.uk.

Halliday, Fred. 1994. *Rethinking International Relations.* London: Macmillan.

Hirst, Paul Q., and Grahame Thompson. 1999. *Globalization in Question: The International Economy and the Possibilities of Governance.* Cambridge: Polity.

Hughes, Donna M. 2000. "The 'Natasha' Trade: The Transnational Shadow Market of Trafficking in Women." *Journal of International Affairs* 53(2): 455–481.

———. 2001. "The 'Natasha' Trade: Transnational Sex Trafficking." *National Institute of Justice Journal* 246 (January): 8–15.

———. 2002. "The Corruption of Civil Society: Maintaining the Flow of Women to the Sex Industries." Paper delivered at the Andalusian Women's Institute, Malaga, Spain,

September 23.

———. 2006. "Chancellor Missing Her Chance: Angela Merkel's World Cup Trafficking Silence." National Review Online. Http://author.nationalreview.com/latest/?q=MjY1NA==.

Karacheva, Ekaterina. 2004. *Krasavitsy-rabyni* (Beautiful ones—slaves). *Argumenty i Fakty*. May 5.

Khodyreva, Natalia. 2004. "Sexuality for Whom? Paid Sex and Patriarchy in Russia." In *Sexuality and Gender in Postcommunist Eastern Europe and Russia*, ed. Aleksandr Stulhoger and Theo Sandfort, 243–259. New York: Haworth Press.

Khodyreva, Natalia V., and Mariia G. Tsvetkova. 2000. *Rossiianki i iavlenie treffika* (Russian women and the phenomenon of trafficking). *Sotsiologicheskie Issledovanniia*, no. 11: 141–144.

Klein, Herbert S. 1986. *African Slavery in Latin America and the Caribbean*. New York: Oxford University Press.

Kolchanov, Rudol'f. 2006. *Futbol seksu ne pomekha* (Football does not stand in the way of sex). *Trud*, February 22.

Miers, Suzanne, and Igor Kopytopp, eds. 1977. *Slavery in Africa: Historical and Anthropological Perspectives*. Madison: University of Wisconsin Press.

Miller, William Lee. 1966. *Arguing About Slavery: The Great Battle in the United States Congress*. New York: Alfred A. Knopf.

Miko, Francis T. 2006. *Trafficking in Persons: The U.S. and International Response*. Washington, D.C.: Congressional Research Service, Library of Congress.

NATO Policy Document. 2004. *NATO Policy on Combating Trafficking in Human Beings*. Http://www.nato.int/docu/comm/2004/06-istanbul/docu-traffic.htm.

NATO Seminar. 2005. *On Implementing the NATO Policy on Combatting Trafficking in Human Beings*. Http://www.norway-nato.org/misc/print.aspx?article={d691a6e0-39de-4b35-91fa-60b.

Noone, Michael. 2005. "The U.S. Approach to Combating Trafficking in Women: Prosecuting Military Customers. Could It Be Expected?" *Connections: The Quarterly Journal* 4(4): 81–90.

Pettman, Jan Jindy. 1996. *Worlding Women: A Feminist International Politics*. London: Routledge.

Phillips, William D., Jr. 1985. *Slavery from Roman Times to the Early Transatlantic Trade*. Manchester: Manchester University Press.

Pravda. 2005. Russian Girls Eager to Work Abroad, Despite Danger of Sex Trafficking. March 31. Http://english.pravda.ru/society/stories/7977-slaves-0.

———. 2006. "Thousands of Russian Women Sold to Slavery Abroad." March 22. Http://english.pravda.ru/russia/politics/77696-trafficking-0.

Putin, Vladimir. 2004. "Remarks to Russian Trafficking in Persons Conference in Moscow."

St. Petersburg Times, February 3.

Reid, Anthony, ed. 1983. *Slavery, Bondage and Dependency in Southeast Asia.* St. Lucia: University of Queensland Press.

Skogrand, Kjetil. 2005. "Keynote Address at NATO/EAPC Seminar on Implementing the NATO Policy on Combating Trafficking in Human Beings." November 24. Http://www. dep.no/ud/english/news/speeches/political_staff/032191-090020/dok-bu.h.

State Duma. 2003. Federal'yni zakon: O dolpolnenii stat'ei 126-1 Ugolovnogo kodeksa Rossiiskoi Federatsii (Federal law: Concerning supplementary Article 126-1 in the Criminal Code of the Russian Federation). Http://asozd.duma.gov.ru/komi . . . /282E7 51623E0352FC3256E2B00488702?OpenDocument; see also http://legislationonline. org/view.php?document=58712.

Stoecker, Sally. 2000. "The Rise of Human Trafficking and the Role of Organized Crime." *Demokratizatsiia* 8(1) (Winter): 129–144.

Stoecker, Sally, and Louise Shelley, eds. 2005. *Human Traffic and Transnational Crime.* Lanham, Md.: Rowman and Littlefield.

Strange, Susan. 1996. *The Retreat of the State.* Cambridge: Cambridge University Press.

Tiuriukanova, Elena V., Vera Anishina, Dmitrii Poletaev, and Stanislav Shamkov. 2004. *Prinuditel'nyi Trud v Sovrememmoi Rossii* (Forced labor in contemporary Russia). Moscow: Mezhdunarodnaia Organizatsiia Truda.

Tiuriukanova, Elena V., and Ludmila D. Erokhina. 2002. *Torgovlia Liud'mi* (Trafficking in persons). Moscow: Izdatel'stvo Academia.

Tursunova, Zulfiya. 2004. *Preventing Human Trafficking: The Case of Uzbekistan.* Http://www. transcend.org/t_database/articles.php?ida=531.

UNODC (United Nations Office on Drugs and Crime). 2006. "Trafficking in Persons: Global Patterns."

U.S. Embassy, Moscow. 2004. "Remarks by Secretary of State Colin L. Powell at Russian Trafficking in Persons Conference." January 27. Http://moscow.usembassy.gov/bilateral/ transcript.php?record_id=5.

U.S. Mission to NATO. 2005. Http://nato.usmission.gov/Article.asp?ID=3CABE5ED-8F82- 44E1-80EC->7C9AEBA5.

U.S. Mission to the OSCE. 2005. Statement on Trafficking in Human Beings[1]. Http://www. humantrafficking.org/updates/282.

U.S. State Department. 2002. *Trafficking in Persons Report.* Http://www.state.gov/g/tip/rls/ tiprpt/2002/10682.htm.

———. 2003. *Trafficking in Persons Report.* Http://www.state.gov/g/tip/rls/tiprpt/2003/.

———. 2004. *Trafficking in Persons Report.* Http://www.state.gov/g/tip/rls/tiprpt/2004/33192. htm.

———. 2005. *Trafficking in Persons Report.* Http://www.state.gov/g/tip/rls/tiprpt/2005/.

————. 2006. *Trafficking in Persons Report.* Http://www.state.gov/g/tip/rls/tiprpt/2006/65990. htm.

Vlasova, Elena. 2006. *Devushkam dobavliali vozrast, chtoby prodat' v pritony Dubaia* (They increased the girls' ages in order to sell them into Dubai's dens). *Izvestiia.* Http:// www.izvestia.ru/investigation/article3027606.

"V Turtsii spasiut zhenshchin iz seksual'nogo rabstva" (In Turkey they are saving women from sexual slavery). 2006. *Trud,* February 8.

Yablokova, Oksana. 2004. "New Russian Law is One of Country's First Steps Against Human Slavery." *St. Petersburg Times,* February 3.

5

Gender Politics in Russia

Nadezda Shvedova

his chapter addresses gender equality in Russia through the lens of the international development agenda of the twenty-first century, a perspective that posits that policies which will improve women's capacity to exercise their rights, increase their freedom, and participate actively in the collective process of change are key to successful development. An international consensus regarding the importance of gender equality has been developing over many years. At its inception, the United Nations (UN) proclaimed the equal rights of men and women, through its Charter. The equal participation of women and men in public life is one of the cornerstones of the UN Convention on the Elimination of All Forms of Discrimination against Women (CEDAW), which is recognized as an international "Bill of Rights" for women. Covering the full range of civil, political, economic, social, and cultural rights, CEDAW creates legal obligations for states to ensure the protection, promotion, and fulfillment of the rights of women. States are supposed to consider legislative, regulatory, and other appropriate means of enacting economic and social policies to secure equality between women and men. Similarly, under UN auspices, the Fourth World Conference on Women (1995) defined the strategic objectives of women's full participation in power structures and decision making and of their increased capacity so that they could participate in decision making. More recently, in 2000 a new UN initiative, the Millennium Declaration, signaled a renewed international effort to promote gender equality and the empowerment of women as basic human rights and as key to effectively combating poverty, hunger, and disease and stimulating sustainable development. This initiative has emphasized the ways gendered inequities in education, health, and poverty continue to undermine global socioeconomic development.

In this chapter, I examine women's empowerment in Russia in light of the international agenda of gender equity and development. I begin with a review of the goals of the Millennium Declaration for equitable human development. I then trace the major problems that women in Russia face in achieving these goals, despite legal equality. In addition, I explore the ways in which the Russian government has responded or failed to respond to these problems, paying particular attention to the Gender Strategy developed in 2002. Throughout the chapter, I argue that discrimination against women in practice is complex and often invisible. Policies and programs that are developed without attention to gender-based differences and disadvantages may not violate antidiscrimination laws, but they often discriminate against women. I particularly emphasize the stereotypes about gendered roles, responsibilities, and expectations that further promote a climate for social discrimination against women and pose a critical obstacle to gender equality. The chapter concludes with a discussion of the policy recommendations that follow from this analysis of international norms and Russian realities.

The Millennium Development Goals and Women's Representation in Government

At the UN Millennium Summit in 2000, 147 member states participated in the creation of a set of Millennium Development Goals (MDGs), signaling international cooperation in addressing the problems of poverty, hunger, disease, illiteracy, environmental degradation, and discrimination against women, which the UN had identified as crucial limitations on global development. Within each of the MDGs, specific measures were adopted to assess states' progress in addressing the particular problem areas. The third among the eight MDGs called explicitly for "empowering women and promoting gender equality, specifically setting targets to eliminate gender disparity at all levels of education by 2015, with additional indicators on women's employment and the proportion of women in parliaments" (UN Press Release 2003). The measures for progress in this goal include increases in the proportion of women as members of national legislatures; in the share of women employed in nonagricultural sectors of the economy; in the percentage of girls in primary, secondary, and high schools; and in the literacy rates for young women aged eighteen to twenty-four. Thus, the MDGs recognize that women's fundamental right to participate in political life as equals with men is at the core of both gender equality and equitable socioeconomic development.

At the same time, the summit addressed the significance of including women as key, active participants in determining development agendas. These commitments were reaffirmed at the Summit Outcome session in September 2005 in the following statement: "We reaffirm that gender equality and the promotion and protection of the full enjoyment of all human rights and fundamental freedoms for all, in particular for women and children, are essential to advance development, peace and security" (UNPGA 2005).

Following the Summit Outcome, activists pressed for increased public attention to the need for women's full political participation and to the extent of underrepresentation in decision making. At a roundtable of nongovernmental organizations (NGOs) on the progress made on women's equality, Rachel Mayanja, a UN Special Adviser on Gender Issues and Advancement of Women, issued a strong statement at which she underscored "the barriers that exist to women's opportunities to shape a world based on gender equality" (2006). She pointed out that "the issue of gender equality in decision making has emerged as an international priority" and stressed the multiple forces that make such equality so difficult:

> Ten years after Beijing, women and men enjoy equal rights with regard to franchise in almost every country in the world. In most countries, also, de jure equality exists between women and men in the area of political participation. Yet, critical barriers to women's equal participation in politics persist. They are deeply rooted in feminization of poverty, in violence against women, illiteracy, and attitudes resulting in women's exclusion from political systems. Entrenched stereotypical ideas regarding the role of women in the family and their participation in public life, in a pervasive climate of discrimination, discourage women from entering public life. They are thus unable to influence key decisions that affect their lives and the future of society. (Mayanja 2006)

Data from the Inter-Parliamentary Union highlight the extent of women's limited political representation across the globe. These indicate that the number and proportion of women participating in legislatures have increased only incrementally over the last decade. For example, in 1997 women constituted on average 12% of members in lower and upper houses of parliaments. As of March 2008, this percentage had increased to only 17.7%. Of course, these percentages mask substantial regional variance. The Nordic European counties have a combined rate of 41.4% female representation; the American region has 21.3%; the sub-Saharan African region has 17.6%; and the figures are lower for women in the regions of Asia (16.3%), the Pacific (15%), and the Arab states (9.%) (Inter-Parliamentary Union 2008). Describing this slow progress in achieving equal participation in legislatures, Mayanja argued, "If current incremental rates continue, it will not be until 2025 that an average of 30 per cent women in parliament would be reached, and not until 2040 would parity be achieved" (2006).

The trends are similar in the executive branches of government. Of the 192 member states of the UN, only 5.7% have women heads of states.[1] And the numbers of women in high-level cabinet positions are equally limited. Globally, only 14% of ministers in the executive branch are women. As Mayanja also noted, these figures include only "23 Foreign Ministers, 12 Defense Ministers of Finance. In 2006, only in two countries (Chile and Spain) women reached parity with men in Cabinet level positions" (2006). And the UN, which should be a model for the promotion of gender equity, is also culpable. In 2005, women made up only 27% of those who had staff appointments at the D-1 level or above (UN Woman Watch 2006).

These data on political representation underscore that all countries face gender inequality in political power, regardless of the level of development. A similar investigation would document gender asymmetry across the globe in the many areas of life targeted by the MDGs—for example, labor market, access to resources, and education. I address these in the following section, through an explicit focus on gender politics in post-Soviet Russia.

The Russian Context

During the last decade and a half, Russia has turned from an isolated, closed society into one of the world's largest centers of modernization. The more open society that has developed has been a valuable achievement for democracy. At the same time, the transition from Communism has brought new social problems, challenges, and hazards for democracy and gender equality. It would be a mistake to address these problems of development and gender equity as if Russia were interchangeable with other societies even in the former Soviet Union. Indeed, as a report on implementing the Millennium Development Goals in Russia summarizes, a number of factors distinguish the gendered development context of Russia from that in many developing countries, suggesting that Russia needs distinctive strategies for achieving gender equity (Roschin and Zubarevitch 2005). Most obviously, Russia is highly industrialized and is moving toward a postindustrial economy. Thus, in contrast to many developing societies where the populace is primarily agrarian, the bulk of men and women in the Russian labor force are employed in the manufacturing and service sectors. Similarly, the majority of the economically active population in Russia, both male and female, is comprised of wage laborers (92.3% and 93.4%, respectively, in 2002) (Roschin and Zubarevitch 2005). And the proportion of Russian women working outside the home is high. Indeed, the extremely high level of women's employment, which Russia inherited from the Communist period, is equivalent only to that of the Scandinavian countries. Increasingly in Russia, social well-being depends on the extent of support derived from employment and wages. Thus, the relative status of men and women in the labor market is a critical factor for gender equity. In contrast to much of the developing world (but like much of post-Communist Eurasia), men and women in Russia have had equal access to education for many years, and women's educational levels today are somewhat higher than those of men (which might suggest that women should have a relatively strong position in the market). During the Soviet era, norms and social benefits to support women's reproductive rights were quite generous compared with other countries. One would expect such normative and social support to continue, as Russia has adopted laws endorsing equal rights of men and women, including the Russian Federation Constitution of 1993. Finally, unlike some other countries, Russia signed practically all major international documents promoting gender equality (Roschin and Zubarevitch 2005; Roschin 2003a).

At the same time that Russia occupies a distinctive position in relation to the MDGs, as in other countries, the gender structures in politics, society, and the economy hinder gender equality. For example, like women across the globe, women in Russia carry a disproportionate share of the domestic work, combining their jobs with family responsibilities. And in Russia as elsewhere, this view that women should assume the bulk of family care results in all kinds of hidden discrimination. Women tend to be concentrated in lower-paid occupations, and the so-called prestigious high-salaried professions are often not for women. As in other transition states, the citizens of Russia have endured a number of very stressful experiences since the end of the Soviet Union, including unemployment and high rates of poverty. As a rule, these have had a female face because women were pushed out of the process of sharing property and state power; there are few women at the decision-making levels in the government or the economy. Some of the stressful experiences during the transition have been particular to men: their life expectancies have declined and are much lower than women's, and they have higher rates of alcohol dependency, suicide, and criminality. The dichotomized gender norms in Russia have produced a social devaluation of fatherhood and limited men's paternal rights in situations of divorce. Russian government policies on these and other issues have had important impacts on gender politics across the federation. In order to understand the changes to date, as well as the prospects for further changes in gender relations, an examination of those policies and the changing legal environment in Russia is necessary.

The Legal and Policy Environment for Gender Equity in Russia

Russia has a history of adopting domestic legislation and of participating in international agreements that purport to advance women's equality. The Soviet Union was one of the early signatories to the Convention on the Elimination of All Forms of Discrimination against Women in 1981, as well as to many other international documents promoting human and women's rights. The Constitution of the Russian Federation, adopted in 1993, states that the "principles and norms . . . of international agreements of the Russian Federation are an integral part of its legal system" and, further, that human rights will be guaranteed according to both the constitution and to "universally recognized principles and norms of international law" (Article 17, part 1). This language means that CEDAW and other international agreements have the force of law in Russia.

The Russian Federation has adopted an approach to gender inequality that affirms the formal legal equality of men and women, as evidenced in the Constitution. Article 19, part 2, for example, stipulates "The State guarantees the equality of human and civil rights and freedoms regardless of sex, race, nationality, language, origin, material and official status, place of residence, attitude to religion, convictions, membership in public organizations, or of other circumstances." Part 3 of the same article continues: "Men and women shall enjoy equal rights and freedoms and equal opportunities to exercise them." In addition to these constitutional guarantees, other legal documents developed in the 1990s reaffirmed governmental support of formal gender equality and equal opportunity. These included official decrees by the Russian Federation president, government statements supporting a national plan of action to improve women's status, endorsement of a Family Code and of a new Labor Code to address gender inequality, and a draft federal law, On State Guarantees of Equal Rights and Freedoms for Men and Women and Equal Opportunities for Their Realization.[2]

In March 2006, a roundtable was held to discuss possible amendments to this proposed law on equal rights and to prepare for the second hearings (in April) in the State Duma of the Russian Federation.[3] However, the law has not yet been passed. In addition to laws and decrees, special commissions and councils were created within the structure of the federal government and at the regional level. Generally, these were part of the National Machinery established to implement CEDAW, but these commissions and councils had no power to initiate legislation or influence the formation of policies.

Among the most important policy initiatives was the Gender Strategy of the Russian Federation elaborated in 2002 by the Ministry for Labor and Social Development.[4] The Strategy defined three areas in which gender policies needed to be developed to realize gender equality and sustainable development: economics-environmental, political-organizational, and socio-cultural. It outlined ways to ensure that a gender dimension would be included in the implementation of all policies, and it included a broad range of policy proposals, including the development of comprehensive gender statistics and the monitoring of gendered effects of policies, policies to combat feminized poverty and unemployment, initiatives to promote education and training, and ways to address gendered stereotypes and to promote women's representation in public bodies and legislatures from the local to the regional to the federal level. It proposed a national action plan that would structure the implementation of policy at all of these levels. The Gender Strategy thus viewed the realization of the equality objectives of the Russian Federation Constitution from within the international framework of both CEDAW and the MDGs. But mechanisms were not determined for the implementation of the objectives of the Strategy, and resources were not provided to support it. Indeed, the Strategy was not widely disseminated, and it was never passed into law.

As limited as these initiatives have been for realizing women's rights, the Russian government, as part of its reorganization under President Vladimir Putin, dissolved a number of ministries and agencies at the federal level that had been oriented toward women's rights. These included the elimination of the Commission for Women, Family and Demography in the Office of the President (in 2000) and of the Commission on the Status of Women; the Department of Women, Family and Children; and the Permanent Round Table of Women's Nongovernmental Organizations in the Government of the Russian Federation (all in 2004). In their stead, a Coordinating Council on Gender Issues and a Department on Medico-Social Issues of the Family, Maternity and Childhood were established under the new Ministry of Health and Social Development (ABA/CEELI 2006,

125–126). It is too early to tell if these will address issues of gender equality in any substantive way; but there is a good sign insofar as an intergovernmental Commission on Men and Women's Equality in the Russian Federation has been developed, and at its first meeting in September 2006, it explicitly addressed Russia's compliance with CEDAW, the need to approve the Gender Strategy and to develop a plan of action for its implementation, and the need for a gender approach in health care. Throughout the discussions, participants stressed that any gender strategy must be based on the norms and principles of international agreements and conventions and on the Constitution of the Russian Federation and other official documents (OWL 2006a).

Despite this hopeful sign, it is important to identify the major problems in Russia's legal and policy environment that underscore the need for the Gender Strategy but suggest the challenges entailed in its adoption or realization. First, no laws in Russia have the scope or substance of CEDAW's concept of gender discrimination, which encompasses any acts that distinguish the populace in ways that limit women's equal exercise of rights in political, economic, social, cultural, and civil arenas. A review by the American Bar Association and Central European and Eurasian Law Institute (ABA/CEELI) of Russia's compliance with CEDAW concluded that the Russian government "has not taken measures to harmonize Russian law with the Convention's definition of discrimination." There seemed to be no understanding on the part of the government that actions may not be based on intentional discrimination but nonetheless have discriminatory effects . Indeed, acceptance of CEDAW's expansive meaning of discrimination has been very limited in Russia among both legal professionals and the general public—and among both men and women (ABA/CEELI 2006, 21). If the general public of the Russian Federation does not have a general awareness of or feel for the meaning of gender equality as something more substantial than formal equal rights, then it should not be surprising that in the last few years, "women's rights have been disappearing from the political agenda" (ABA/CEELI 2006, 16.) The consequences of that disappearance are evident in the many measures of women's political and socioeconomic status in the Russian Federation.

Status of Russian Women

Despite the constitutional embrace of the principle of gender equality, women's status has declined across the Russian polity, economy, and society during the last decade. This decline is most acutely evident in the reduced capacity for women's participation in formal decision making and politics, the ways in which gender stereotypes and familial responsibilities have undermined women's economic position and fostered a feminization of poverty, and in the failure of the government to address issues of violence against women. And recent limitations on civil society, especially in working with international NGOs may make it more difficult for women activists to counter that decline.

POLITICAL PARTICIPATION

As the previous discussion of Russia's legal and policy environment suggests, the low proportion of women in decision making is among the most important indicators of gender inequality in the Russian Federation. Gendered vertical disparity in political power is characteristic of all branches of power. Government institutions at the federal level have remained largely male since the end of the Soviet Union (Shvedova 1998). In the lower chamber of the legislature, women made up 13.5% of the legislators during the first State Duma (1993–1995); this declined to 9.7% in the second State Duma (1996–1999) and even further to 7.6% in the Third State Duma (1999–2003). A slight increase in the fourth State Duma (2003–2007) brought women up to only 9.84% of the lower house, and women made up 14% of the legislators in the latest fifth State Duma (2007–2011) (Inter-Parliamentary Union 2008). The situation at the federal level is replicated at the regional level. Women have made up no more than 10% of the total number of deputies in the regional legislative bodies for many years. Across the entire Russian Federation, only one woman serves as a governor (Valentina Matvienko in St. Petersburg), and only one woman is mayor of a large city—in Kostroma. This low level of representation of women is replicated throughout the administrative and judicial branches of government at every level. It was not until 2007 that women were appointed as ministers at the federal level (two of the twenty-one in 2008; Russia is ranked 70th place among 185 countries in the proportion of women in ministerial positions); and in 2005, women made up only 17.6% of the justices on the Supreme Court and 16% on the Constitutional Court (ABA/CEELI 2006, 58–59). And, as pointed out earlier, the administrative reforms in 2004 that reorganized regional and federal level government agencies eliminated many of the agencies that addressed women's advancement. Less clear are the gender implications of other changes in electoral law initiated by President Putin, such as appointment of regional governments by the President rather than direct election and elimination of single party seats to the State Duma (ABA/CEELI 2006, 16)

There are many reasons for women's unequal representation in formal politics, but most experts point to a number of interrelated factors: women's weak integration into political institutions, lack of money, the reluctance of those who give money for electoral campaigns to invest in women candidates, party practices that put women lower on the electoral lists, public underestimation of women as politicians, women's low self-esteem that makes them reluctant to participate in politics and cultural patterns—all interact to limit women's active participation and success in politics (World Bank 2004, 117–131). As a result, what I have noted to be the pattern a decade ago remains the case in the Russian Federation today: "Women are grossly under-represented in upper echelons of state leadership. Their constitutional rights are of the declarative nature due to the underdevelopment and inefficiency of implementation measures" (Shvedova 1998, 1).

The ideological framework of the male political elite is important for understanding the climate for gender equality in contemporary Russia. In his 2006 annual address to the Federal Assembly, President Putin revealed his sense of women's social responsibility to be mothers when he stated:

> If the state is genuinely interested in increasing the birth rate, it must support women who decide to have a second child. The state should provide such women with an initial maternity capital that will raise their social status and help to resolve future problems. Mothers could make use of this capital in different ways: put it towards improving their housing situation, for example, by investing it in buying a house, making use of a mortgage loan or other loan scheme once the child is three years old, or putting it towards the children's education, or, if they wish, putting it into the individual account part of their own old-age pension. (2006)

If the views of President Putin represent the orientation of the political elite, then the key issue from the perspective of the most powerful men in the government is that Russian women are essentially mothers who should naturally assume primary responsibility for families, the well-being of children, and the burdens of social reproduction. Of course, this view was also evident during the Soviet period, but in that time the social supports for women as worker-mothers were much more extensive than they are today. According to Tatiana Lokshina, writing on behalf of the Moscow Helsinki Group, most Russian legislators view women's needs as rooted in "social protection of motherhood and reproductive rights rather than the advancement of women and provision of equal opportunities" (2005). And it is well documented that these gender stereotypes are shared widely across the spectrum of policy makers, educators, employers, and those who represent public opinion (World Bank 2004, 59).

SOCIAL AND ECONOMIC POSITION

As I have already suggested, a basic tenet of the Soviet ideology of women's emancipation was the crucial importance of their education and their contributions as laborers. And today, women's higher educational achievement rates than men and significant labor force participation are a critical inheritance of the Soviet period. Yet in spite of these important indicators of equity, an analysis of the position of Russian women within the contemporary economy tells a less equitable story and reveals that in terms of the gendered dynamics of social development, there is no direct correspondence between education and economic achievement.

Unemployment is a fact of life that Russians never faced during the Soviet period, but it has become an increasing reality. In the first years of the transition, many observers noted that unemployment had a particularly feminine face. The contemporary picture is more mixed: for example, World Bank data report that women (who make up 49% of the labor force) are slightly less vulnerable to unemployment than men. In 2004, the unemployment rate was 9.9% for males and 8.8% for females. (World Bank 2008a). However, women are more likely to register as unemployed and to experience longer spells without jobs. Of those who registered with the state as unemployed in 1996, 60% were women; in 2003, that percentage had increased to 68% (World Bank 2006, 57).[5] There are significant regional variations in the gender skewing of those who register as unemployed. Official figures in some regions in 2006 found women's unemployment rates ranging from 68% to 75% (OWL 2006b).[6] Data also reveal that women are more likely to be among the "stagnant unemployed"—that is, they have a much longer period of unemployment, averaging 8.8 months in 2001 in contrast to men's average of 7.8 months. And 40.5% of women registered as unemployed had more than a year of job searching, whereas this was the case for 33.9% of men (Roschin 2003b, 4–6). Thus, as economist Sergey Roschin notes of these unemployment data, women's longer duration of unemployment may be a product of "worse conditions for employment, lower competitive position on labour market which is the reflection among other factors of discrimination practice of Russia employers" (Roschin 2003b, 6). In a review of the literature on the gendered effects of unemployment, the World Bank concluded:

> In almost every type of unemployment—official, hidden, forced, partial or structural—women are either represented equally with men or are at a disadvantage in terms of finding a solution or assuming an employed status. . . The situation of female unemployment is especially acute among the younger population

groups, in rural areas . . . and in economically depressed regions with stagnant
industries (2004, 92)

Another feature of Russia's gendered economy is poverty, which has increased
to nearly one-third of the population. Poverty is clearly feminized, with studies
indicating that women constitute the vast majority of the poor, especially single
mothers who have insufficient family support subsidies and elderly women who
have faced a reduction in pensions (Mashkova et al. 2004). Thus, the pronatalist
rhetoric does not seem to bear itself out in terms of material supports for mothers.
Nor should we be hopeful that Russia is investing in women's development in
ways that signal future economic payoffs.

Although women have increased their share of higher education in the Russian
Federation so that now they surpass men in their educational achievement levels,
their position in the labor market has become more vulnerable. Research by Marina
Baskakova, for example, on the gendered effects of investment in higher education
suggests one of the problems in the assumption that Millennium Development
objectives can be achieved through educational equity. She points out:

> While in the 1980s, the wages of women constituted 70% of the wages of men
> on average, by the end of 1999 this figure had dropped to 52%, and in mid-2000,
> to only 50%. Obviously this process is still under way. Thus during the last ten
> years, women have become one of the socio-demographic groups most affected
> by growing wage inequality. . . . At present, an increased educational level does
> not even out the differences in the wages of men and women in Russia. This
> conclusion is especially important because it is the raising of the educational
> level of women that is usually regarded as the best way to make men and women
> equal not only in the labor and employment market, but in all spheres of life.
> (Baskakova 2002, 1)

Men, in fact, secure better returns from education than women do, even at the
lower levels—a fact that may explain the gender unevenness in higher education. As the UNDP puts it, the "labor market devalues the high level of female
education" (2005, 65). Understanding why women have not been able to move
close to parity with men requires that we think beyond formal proclamations of
equal rights and focus on the relationship between society and the economy. In
particular, it means paying attention to the underlying gender stereotypes and
latent sex discrimination that contribute to occupational segregation and low
salaries for women. The most important stereotypes are those that consign women

to a primary role in the family and a secondary role in the larger society. These have encouraged women's participation in feminized lower paid sectors of the economy and even the view that they do not need to be paid as much as men.

Government data on gender distribution across economic sectors document that occupational segregation has persisted and even gotten worse throughout the transition era and that this has had substantial consequences for gender equality. Women tend to be concentrated in service-oriented fields like education, health care, art, and culture—all of which have wage rates that are lower than the average monthly wage rate across the economy. Men are more likely to be in communications, finance, transportation, construction, and public administration and other high-wage sectors. Indeed, as the proportion of women among those employed in a particular sector increases, the average monthly wage rate declines (Roschin 2003b, 12–18). Unfortunately, during the last decade, while women have been losing voice in government, their position in the labor market has been deteriorating, and the extent of gender segregation in the labor market has increased (World Bank 2004, 147–149). Official data on the gender disparity across sectors of the economy reveal that an increasing percentage of women are employed in those sectors where wages are lower than the average wages across the entire economy. In 1998, for example, 60% of women were employed in the low-wage sectors (versus only 38% of men); in 2003, the proportion of women in the low-wage sectors had increased to 62%, and the proportion of men had declined to 32%. The reverse trend was evident in the higher-wage sectors where women lost ground, moving from 40% to 35.6% and men from 62% to 63.1% over the five-year period. Women's concentration in low-wage sectors of the economy is compounded by the fact that even within high-wage sectors such as communications, the gendered wage gap is very high (women's salaries in this sector are 40% lower than men's) (World Bank 2006, 68).[7]

Studies of gendered occupational segregation and job discrimination across the Russian Federation have documented regional differences that derive in part from the industrial structures and power of traditional gender norms in different areas. In 2001, for example, women's wages were only 52% to 57% of men's in the Republics of Komi, Astrakhanskaya, Kemerovskaya and Tyumenskaya oblasti, Yamalo-Nenetsky Autonomous Okrug, and Krasnoyarsky Krai. A study in 2003 found equivalent gender ratios (54–57%) in Belgorodskaya, Kurskaya and Tyumenskaya oblasti, and the Republic of Dagestan (World Bank 2006, 60). In two autonomous *okruygs* (Ust-Ordynsk Buryatsky and Aginsk Buryatsky), women's wages have been slightly higher than men's, a differential that has increased over time. For example, in 2001, in Ust-Ordynsk Buryatsky Autonomous Okrug, women's average wages were 104% of men's wages, and in Aginsk Buryatsky Autonomous Okrug, women's wages were 106% of men's wages. In 2003, women's wages were 113% of men's wages (World Bank 2006, 64). But these advantages appear to be the exception to the rule in Russia.

Occupational segregation is not a by-product of a gender-neutral market system. Many employers are reluctant to hire women, fearful that their enterprises will have to provide pregnancy or maternity leave or adapt to child-care needs. Although the law proscribes such discrimination, some employers demand that women signify in writing that they will not become pregnant, and such women face job loss in that eventuality. And many employers directly advertise for workers in ways that signal their gender preferences (ABA/CEELI 2006, 17–18). Women face age-based discrimination, employer preferences to lay off women rather than men in cases of economic slowdowns, and differential pay for the same work that men do. Women are often reluctant to protest these behaviors, either because they are not informed about their rights, because they fear job loss, or because they do not trust the government institutions that are supposed to enforce the law.[8] The consequence is that the horizontal gendered segregation that is well documented across occupations and economic sectors is replicated in (sometimes) more subtle ways within particular occupations, creating a vertical form of gender segregation.

It is important, however, to recognize that men suffer from some gendered disadvantages in the economy that derive from Russia's system of labor protection. The inheritance of maternalist protective labor policies has meant that men are protected less than women from a range of harmful working conditions. The irony of "protective" discrimination that excludes women from nearly 600 occupations or labor practices in the name of maternalist protection and reproductive health is that men often must work under conditions that may be equally harmful to their health (World Bank 2006, 60–61).[9] And the consequence is that "the proportion of men employed under conditions inconsistent with sanitary standards is about twice that of women" (UNDP 2005, 64).

The government's attentiveness to women as mothers and to maternal health has been shaped less by a concern for women's rights than by the demographic crisis (decline in life expectancy, a low birthrate, and decreasing population) in Russia. Reviews of Russia's compliance with CEDAW during the transition period provide evidence of improvement in maternal health care, but they also document failures on the part of the government, such as the lack of federal financial support for the system of Family Planning Centers that were developed by the government in the 1990s, the absence of effective sex education, and limited attention to many of women's health concerns (from the limited availability of effective contraceptives to the problem of increasing HIV/AIDS). The delivery of health care in rural areas is especially problematic, given the contraction in the numbers of available specialists such as gynecologists and obstetricians (ABA/CEELI 2006, 19) At the same time, an important reality is that women have a much higher life expectancy than do men in Russia. In 2005, the life expectancy for women was 72.4 years, whereas for men it was only 58.9 years (World Bank 2008b). This means that older women face a particular set of health concerns that compounds the crisis of limited pension support. At the same time, attention to gender equity would require that policy makers address the ways in which men are particularly affected by labor conditions, family policy, and the delivery of medical care.

Violence against women is another critical factor for women's health and well-being in Russia. Irina Gorshkova and Irina Shurigina surveyed more than fifty urban and rural communities across the seven regions of Russia in 2002. Their findings indicated that most women experienced psychological violence and that "half the women (50 percent) have in fact been subject to their current husbands' physical violence at least once (the husband hit or pushed, shook, caused acute pain without beating but resorting to other methods, for example, twisting her arms)" (Gorshkova and Shurigina 2003, 4). They also documented extensive tolerance of sexual violence within marriage, with 60% of men and 50% of women believing that "that rape in the state of marriage is impossible in principle" (Gorshkova and Shurigina 2003, 6). They noted that the families that did not support or show any forms of violence (psychological, economic, or sexual) were those in which resources were equally distributed and men and women shared power equally (Gorshkova and Shurigina 2003, 7). Unfortunately, the Russian government has not developed statistical measures, legal instruments, or educational efforts to address domestic violence. Nor has it done so with other forms of violence against women, such as sexual harassment. Thus, both at home and in the market, the devaluation of women may be a "normal" part of everyday life.

The chapter by Mary Buckley in this volume also addresses a significant aspect of violence against women: the problem of trafficking. Like the other forms of violence against women, she reminds us that violence is not a "private" matter but extends throughout Russian society. Yet the idea that violence is "private" or that harassment is a personal problem—not a legal issue—is shared broadly among Russians, both the public and the legal professionals (ABA/CEELI 2006, 99–104). Reports of violence against women occur in the newspaper everyday.

But these are reported as informational facts not as unacceptable social problems that should be addressed.

CIVIL SOCIETY

The emergence of an independent civil society was one of the most significant developments in the early years in Russia's transition, and women have been among the most important activists in the many NGOs. They played a crucial role in pressuring the government to address the feminization of poverty, the shrinking social benefits, discrimination in the labor market, domestic violence, and the other issues addressed in this chapter. (ABA/CEELI 2006, 20; Racioppi and See 1997; Sperling 1999) However, the government has become increasingly restive about civil society in general and advocates of democratic reform in particular. And it has been especially wary of those who collaborate with international NGOs. A law in 2006 imposed administrative restrictions on NGOs to monitor foreign funding and impose reporting requirements that may significantly limit the activities of both domestic and international NGOs and limit civic activism, suggesting another substantial challenge to gender equity as well as to democracy more broadly. Thus as noted in other chapters in this volume (Racioppi and See; Einhorn), activists cannot rely on civil society for an effective realization of gender equity. Rather, the government of the Russian Federation needs to move beyond its rhetoric and address through action the inequalities that permeate Russian government and society.

Conclusion

In this chapter, I have synthesized and built upon the findings of scholars and analysts about the state of gender politics in Russia today, with particular attention to Russia's adherence to the international norms of gender equality, which the government has endorsed in multiple international documents and in its own constitution. I have emphasized the distinctiveness of the Russian Federation, insofar as the key problems for realizing gender equality do not derive from a lack of economic development in the country or from women's lack of literacy or lesser education than men, but rather inequality is the result of women's limited political power, their lesser economic status, and the absence of political will. Women's lesser economic status is not a consequence of their being engaged in agrarian work as in many of the countries targeted by the MDGs. It is because women face structures of occupational segregation and discrimination that effectively exclude them from high-wage sectors and ensure that they are not able to get equal returns on their economic activity (UNIFEM 2005). This process means that as women age, they have lower pensions than men; and it means that they are disadvantaged by the societal wide assumption that men's work is more important than women's. Indeed, the most acute problems of gender discrimination are rooted in the traditional structure of gender roles in Russian society and the belief that a man is the main supporter of the family and that a woman is responsible for family care and household management. The widespread perception and practice that women—not men and women—are responsible for family duties spreads into the economy and into the government. It helps to reproduce occupational segregation, lower wages, and the perception that women are not suited for public office. This chapter has shown that despite the government's prohibition against sex discrimination, women face serious violations of their right to be treated equally in all spheres of society. That the media do not take these violations seriously is especially evident in the case of violence against women (from rape to sexual harassment to domestic violence), but it is also evident in the silence about the social climate that encourages stereotypes associating women with the private life of the family and men with the public life of the state. Russia needs to design policies that will ensure equal opportunities for men and women to achieve the MDG of gender equality. If improving the social and economic status of women is to be more than a formal commitment of the Russian Federation, the government has to undertake much more extensive steps and provide resources that would make this formal goal a reality through an implementation of the actions proposed by the Gender Strategy.

In relation to political participation, efforts to develop a gender equitable democracy, so that women can more fully participate, require that the government address both the limited numbers of women in government and the attitudes that foster patterns of exclusion. This would involve, for example, the development of legislative regulations that would ensure that women would be included in government and promoted in politics (such as requiring all parties to include one-third of women on their party lists and locating women candidates across the lists, rather than at the bottom; ensuring that women are represented in decision-making roles in executive authorities, in parties, and in other political institutions). These mechanisms would help to counter the prejudices against women's inclusion in formal politics and would ensure that they are given the financial resources and support to succeed in ways that are equivalent to men. But as I have pointed out, women often share such prejudices and stereotypes, and so the government needs to respond proactively with such initiatives as leadership schools for orienting women, especially young women, to politics.

This chapter has pointed out the important interaction between political equality and socioeconomic equality. But we cannot wait for women's full political inclusion to address other inequalities. Among the most important policy needs is information about the consequences of gender inequality. This requires the development of gender statistics to document and provide information about the relative status of men and women in income, access to jobs, employment, poverty, and allocation of parliamentary seats. It would also include requiring experts to assess all significant policy proposals and legislative projects for their gender impacts. Efforts should be taken to address occupational segregation, by monitoring the extent of hiring discrimination, and by harmonizing wage rates so that women are no longer disadvantaged because they are disproportionately located in particular economic sectors. It would also require increasing salary levels in state-supported areas such as health care, education, and culture so that they are equivalent to the average wage levels in the broader economy. Relatedly, economic inequality is supported by policies that make it more likely that women participate in the informal economy or in particular kinds of jobs that are more accommodating to family responsibilities. The government needs to provide greater support for child care, provide paternity as well as maternity leaves, impose greater responsibilities on fathers for child care in cases of divorce, and adopt educational policies that will counter the gender stereotypes. Similarly, preventative policies are needed to address the normalizing of the extensive violence against women. And finally, a vibrant civil society is needed to pressure the government to implement the Gender Strategy, to transform public consciousness about gender equality, and to create the sustainable development, now envisioned in international norms.

NOTES

1. The election of five women to the highest level of the executive branch has increased women's representation by more than 30%. These include Angela Merkel of Germany, Ellen Johnson Sirleaf of Liberia, Michelle Bachelet of Chile, Yulia Tymoshenko of Ukraine, and Cristina Fernandez de Kirchner of Argentina. Tarja Halonen of Finland was also reelected.

2. The presidential decrees were "On Priorities of State Policies Concerning Women" (1993) and "On Increasing Women's Role in Federal Power Bodies and Power Bodies

of RF Subjects of the RF" (1996); the government statements were "On Adopting the National Plan of Action towards Improvement of the Status of Women in the Russian Federation and Increase of their Role in Society by 2000," and "On Adoption of the National Plan of Action towards Improvement of the Status of Women in the Russian Federation and Increase of Their Role in Society by 2001–2005."

3. The roundtable was initiated by the Committee of Women, Family and Children Issues under the State Duma of the RF and the Women's Movement of Russia. Among the participants were deputies of the State Duma, members of the Council of Federation, scientists, and representatives of federal ministries, state authorities, and public organizations.

4. This document was prepared on the basis of research findings presented by the following experts: N. A. Shvedova, doctor of political sciences; O. A. Hasbulatova, doctor of history; L. V. Vasilenko, doctor of sociology; L. S. Rzhanitsuna, doctor of economic sciences; M. P. Belousova, candidate of sociology; M. I. Vronskaia, president of the NGO Goluba (Moscow); and L. B. Blokhina., chairperson of the Executive Committee of the Confederation of Business-Women of Russia.

5. Experts disagree about the methodology for measuring unemployment. According to methods employed by the International Labor Organization, unemployment rates are higher for men than for women today (World Bank 2006, 57).

6. These included Kemerovskaya, Novosibirskaya, Yaroslavskaya, Tomskaya, Habarovskaya, Kurskaya, Vologodskaya oblasti. See http://www.owl./ru/content/news/vestnik-2006/p64171.

7. In contrast to the high-wage sectors, gendered disparities are not significant in agriculture, where there are few employment opportunities for men or women.

8. See http://www.regnum.ru/news/685784html.

9. Little data have been collected on the health outcomes for men in these activities from which women are excluded. But see World Bank 2004, 89–90.

WORKS CITED

ABA/CEELI (American Bar Association and Central European and Eurasian Law Institute). 2006. *CEDAW Assessment Report for the Russian Federation.* February. Http://www.abanet.org/rol/publications/russia-cedaw-eng.pdf.

Baskakova, Marina. 2002. "Summary." In *Economic Effectiveness of Investment into Higher Education of Men and Women.* Moscow: Gelios ARV at Center for Gender Studies. Http://www.gender.ru/english/public/baskakova/2002/01.shtml.

Gorshkova, Irina, and Irina Shurigina. 2003. "Violence against Wives in Contemporary

Russian Families." Moscow, Open Women Line (OWL). Http://www.owl.ru/rights/no_violence/Bas_results.pdf.

IPU (Inter-Parliamentary Union). 2008. "Women in National Parliaments." Http://www.ipu.org/wmn-e/world.htm.

Lokshina, Tatiana. 2005. *Discrimination against Women in Contemporary Russia*. Moscow: Helsinki Group. Http://www.mhg.ru/publications/2039961.

Mashkova, Elena, Natalia Kivokurzeva, and Regina Sultanova. 2004. *Poverty in Single Mother Families*. Http://gendevelop.femin.ru/eng/002.htm.

Mayanja, Rachel. 2006. "Equal Participation of Women and Men in Decision Making Process at All Levels." *NGO CSW Interactive Roundtable Discussion*. New York. February 14. Http://www.un.org/womenwatch/daw/news/news2006/RM_NGOcswdecisionmaking14february.pdf.

Mezentseva, Elena, ed. 2002. *Gender and Economics: World Experience and Russian Practical Expertise*. Moscow: Rossiyskaya Panorama.

Ministry of Labour and Social Development. 2002. *Gender Strategy of the Russian Federation*. Moscow. Http://www.owl.ru/win/docum/rf/strategy/strategy.htm.

OWL (On-Line Women). 2006a. Http://www.owl.ru/content/news/vestnik-2006/p71744.shtml.

——. 2006b. Http://www.owl./ru/content/news/vestnik-2006/p64171.

Putin, Vladimir. 2006. *Annual Address to the Federal Assembly*. Marble Hall, the Kremlin, Moscow. May 10. Http://www.kremlin.ru/text/appears/2006/05/105647.shtml.

Racioppi, Linda, and Katherine O'Sullivan See. 1997. *Women's Activism in Contemporary Russia*. Philadelphia: Temple University Press.

Roschin, Sergey. 2002. "Supply of Labor Force in Russia: Microeconomic analysis of Economic Activity of the Population." In *Gender and Economics: World Experience and Russian Practical Expertise*, ed. Elena Mezentseva, 212–234. Moscow: Rossiyskaya Panorama.

——. 2003a. "Gender Equality and Extension of Women Rights in Russia within Millennium Development Goals." Http://www.owl.ru/rights/undp2003/eng/2.htm.

——. 2003b. "Gender Equality on the Labour Market, What Is This?" Http://www.owl.ru/rights/undp2003/eng/3.htm.

Roschin, Sergey, and Natalia Zubarevitch. 2005. *Gender Equality and Extension of Women's Rights in Russia in the Context of the UN Millennium Goals*. Office of the United Nations Resident Coordinator in the Russian Federation. Http://www.unesco.ru/files/docs/shs/publ/gender_mdg_eng.pdf.

Shvedova, Nadezda. 1998 "The Challenge of Transition—Women in Parliament in Russia." In *Women in Parliament: Beyond Numbers*. International IDEA. Stockholm. Http://archive.idea.int/women/parl/studies2a.htm.

Sperling, Valerie. 1999. *Organizing Women in Contemporary Russia: Engendering Transition.* Cambridge: Cambridge University Press.

UNDP Human Development Report. 2005. *Russia in 2015: Development Goals and Policy Priorities.*

UNIFEM (United Nations Development Fund for Women). 2005. *Gender Equality and Extension of Women Rights in Russia in the Context of the Millennium Development Goals.*

United Nations. N.d. *Convention on the Elimination of All Forms of Discrimination against Women.* Http://www.hrweb.org/legal/cdw.html.

———. 2003. Press Release. Http://www.un.org/News/Press/docs/2003/note5778.doc.htm.

United Nations, Woman Watch. 2006. .

UNPGA (United Nations, President of the General Assembly). 2005. *Revised Draft Outcome Document of the High-Level Plenary Meeting of the General Assembly.* Http://www.un.org/ga/59/hlpm_rev.2.pdf.

World Bank. 2004. *Gender in Russia: A Review of Literature (Based on Domestic Publications).* Moscow: Alex Publishers. Http://www-wds.worldbank.org/servlet/WDSContentServer/WDSP/IB/2005/09/22/000112742_20050922170036/Rendered/PDF/33605.pdf.

———. 2006. *Gender Issues in Modern Russia Based on Formal Statistics.* Moscow: Alex Publishers. Http://siteresources.worldbank.org/INTRUSSIANFEDERATION/Resources/sotr_49–52.pdf.

———. 2008a. "Gender Stats: Russian Federation." Http://devdata.worldbank.org/genderstats/genderRpt.asp?rpt=labor&cty=RUS,Russian%20Federation&hm=home2.

———. 2008b. "Data and Statistics for the Russian Federation." Http://web.worldbank.org/WBSITE/EXTERNAL/COUNTRIES/ECAEXT/RUSSIANFEDERATIONEXTN/0,contentMDK:21032960~menuPK:989684~pagePK:1497618~piPK:217854~theSitePK:305600,00.html.

6

The Past as Prologue? Challenging the Myth of the Subordinated, Docile Woman in Muslim Central Eurasia

Timur Kocaoglu

The most oppressed of the oppressed and the most enslaved of the enslaved.

—Lenin

With the demise of the Soviet Union, the newly independent Central Eurasian states, like many other post-Soviet regimes, have sought to establish new national identities;[1] they have had to reconsider many of the old guiding principles and ideologies of the Soviet era and to articulate normative bases for social and political life. Some have called for a return to tradition, to an imagined pre-Soviet national past as the basis for national identity. The Soviet mythology of the emancipation of women, discussed in other chapters in this volume, has been among these old ideologies that have been questioned. As new states have undertaken the arduous tasks of nation building, some politicians have invoked "traditional" patriarchal gender relations as a more authentic alternative to the Soviet version of women's emancipation. In Central Eurasia, such an imagined reconstruction has often been linked to Islam and its social and political role. Of course, debates about Islam and national identity and political development have a long history in the region. This chapter does not, however, focus on contemporary debates about gender politics and Islam or the gender politics of nation building, which are taken up in other chapters in this volume. Rather, it examines the transition to Soviet rule and the activism for women's equality that had developed in Muslim

Central Eurasia in the early twentieth century as part of modernizing efforts to construct national identities. In particular, the chapter examines pre-Soviet reform movements, specifically those dealing with gender issues. It demonstrates that although their numbers were small, Muslim Central Eurasian women, working with their male compatriots, were important agents of change in the pre-Soviet period, reflecting a unique development in this Muslim majority region. The chapter thus emphasizes that Soviet representations of Muslim Central Eurasian women as historically docile, subordinated subjects, rather than as active participants in public life, masked political reality and distorted the history of gender relations in this region.

Why was the significance of these reform movements unrecognized and ignored? To answer this question, it is necessary to understand the prevalent Soviet perspective. This chapter therefore begins with a brief overview of the Leninist view of Muslim Central Eurasian women and of their need for Soviet liberation. This view is then contrasted to the individual narratives of some Muslim Central Eurasian reformists, including the story of Rana, a remarkable woman I met in Turkey in the 1960s, and her husband, Raci, and Shefika Khanim (Gaspirinskaya) and her parents, Ismail and Zuhre. The experiences and activities of women like Rana and Shefika and their male reformist counterparts, however, were erased in a Soviet-era discourse that enshrined/reinforced Lenin's view of Muslim women. Thus, this chapter briefly discusses examples from both academic scholarship and fictional literature to illustrate the contours of this Soviet discourse. It then explores the development of the reform movement in Muslim Central Eurasia; it examines reformist beliefs in the power of education and the press to emancipate women, and in the necessity for women's political equality. Such attitudes could be seen not only in the actions of political activists but also in Muslim Central Eurasian literature of the pre-Soviet period. The efforts of these nineteenth- and early-twentieth-century reformists began to have an impact as autonomous and independent polities were created in the region. The chapter documents some of the constitutional and legislative actions to promote women's rights taken by these new regimes, actions that could not be fully implemented due to the advancement of Soviet power into the region and the quashing of the new governments. Arguing that the reformist movement laid the groundwork for many of the Soviet-era policies on women's behalf, the chapter concludes with a discussion of the significance of the pre-Soviet reformist movements for gender politics in Central Eurasia today.

Myth Making and Breaking: Interrogating
Soviet Constructions of Muslim Women

On April 10, 1921, the Bolshevik newspaper *Pravda* published Vladimir I. Lenin's special message to the Conference of Representatives of Women's Departments of the Peoples of Soviet Regions and Republics in the East, held in Moscow on April 5–7. Unable to attend the conference because of the pressures of other work, Lenin drew attention to the "cause of awakening the women of the East and uniting them organizationally."[2] Twelve years later, Nadezhda K. Krupskaya, Lenin's wife and close associate, explained Lenin's special interest in the women of the Soviet East:

> Lenin warmly greeted the awakening of the women of the Soviet East. Since he attached a particular importance to raising the level of the nationalities that had been oppressed by tsarism and capitalism, it is quite understandable why he so warmly greeted the conference of delegates of the Women's Department of Soviet regions and republics in the East.[3]

Lenin's phrase "the most oppressed of the oppressed and the most enslaved of the enslaved" about the Muslim women of the eastern regions of the prerevolutionary Russia became a frequently quoted slogan in Soviet, and even in some Western, discourse on gender politics in the Soviet period. In 1985, for example, the Soviet scholar Yelena Yemelyanova noted the poor status of women in the Eastern regions—that is, Muslim areas—of Russia before the October Revolution and Lenin's opinion of them: "The position of women in the outlying areas of the country with a non-Russian population was particularly difficult. Lenin said that before the Socialist Revolution the women of the East were the most oppressed of the oppressed and the most enslaved of the enslaved" (1985, 9). Thus, in the realm of fiction, we find the emancipated "positive heroines" of the Soviet period in Uzbek and other Central Asian prose fiction. One of the fictional characters most commented upon as a positive female role model is Aikiz (Ayqiz) in the Uzbek novel *The Victors* (*Ghaliblar*). Its author, Sharaf Rashidov (1917–1983), was the first secretary of the Uzbekistan Communist Party between 1959 and 1983. Rashidov introduces his heroine as follows:

> She saw the village square and the white school-house she had gone to for eight years, the statue of Lenin and the red flag on the club house; this was the club where as a long-legged first-former, she had once recited poetry, more dead than

alive with stage fright, and later had made reports and presided at meetings. . . . This could hardly be called Aikiz's permanent home for she was away most of the time, either at her job or on lengthy business trips. Never before in this sub-mountain region had a young girl, a freshly graduated agronomist, been elected chairman of the village Soviet in preference to some man of experience and prestige. (Rashidov 1958, 8)

In the next few pages, she goes on horseback near the Kizilkum desert. This desert is described as the enemy of the farmers: "Aikiz thought apprehensively of the enemy lying low there in the west, crouching before its ominous leap" (Rashidov 1958, 10). Throughout the novel, Aikiz is portrayed as always worrying about how to turn this desert land into an irrigated expanse. Very little attention is given to her personal feelings and emotions. From the way she talks to other people and the way she thinks, it is hard to tell whether the fictional heroine Aikiz is a female character or even an individual having a distinct character of her own; that is, she is a "flat" character more than a "round" one. Furthermore, the love affair between Aikiz and Alimjan is narrated very weakly (Kocaoglu 1982, 93–96). Even when Aikiz is alone with her lover, Alimjan, instead of affection toward Alimjan, her mind is busy with other things and the orders given her by the local party officials:

> Aikiz's eyes were on the tree, watching the chain of ants running up the rough bark.
> —"Aikiz"—Alimjan called tenderly.
> —"Yes, Alimjan?"
> —"When will our wedding be?"
> Aikiz touched the tree and instantly two ants climbed on to her finger; flustered and confused they hurried up her arm.
> She looked at Alimjan with a cunning twinkle in her eyes:
> —"Imagine talking about it in the middle of the street"—she said.—"Don't you know it isn't done? And then look, see all those people waiting for me at the village Soviet?" (Rashidov 1958, 34)

Throughout the novel, she talks and delivers speeches just like the party officials' speeches that were being published daily in the Soviet press. Aikiz is not concerned with feelings and emotions such as love, affection for the homeland, or the beauty of nature, but with a struggle against nature and with party discipline, it seems. The closing passage of the novel is revealing in demonstrating Aikiz's attitude toward nature. She belittles the moonbeams while praising electricity:

> Aikiz and Alimjan walked arm in arm. They came out on the highroad and turned towards the village. There was Altyn-Sai before them, flooded with electricity against which the pale beams of the moon were impotent. The lights radiated in straight, slender lines towards the centre of the village where they became intricately interwoven.
>
> —"Look at all those lights" Aikiz said. "How bright they are: It's the light of Communism shining on us from tomorrow. Oh, Alimjan-aka, all this happiness is ours." (Rashidov 1958, 201)

It is true that some Uzbek critics have found fault with the portrayal of Aikiz in the novel, calling it very artificial: "By the way, it should be noted that there are certain artificial elements in the characterization of Aikiz" (Eshimov 1968, 32). Yet Eshimov also praises Rashidov for his success in creating a positive heroine like Aikiz and advises other Uzbek writers to take Aikiz as a model for their own positive heroes and heroines (Eshimov 1968, 33, cited in Kocaoglu 1982, 95–96).

Among the Soviet scholarship dealing with Muslim women, the works of two Uzbek scholars, Rahima Aminova (1977) and Diloram Alimova (Alimova 1987, Alimova and Azimova 2000), stand out. Aminova's writing focuses on women's liberation in Uzbekistan; however, it systematically ignores the major political and social activities of Central Asian women and men to advance women's liberation in the pre-Soviet period. Aminova's work, originally published in Russian, found favor among party officials, who had it translated into English, published by the prestigious Nauka publishing house in Moscow in the series of the Central Department of Oriental Literature, and distributed worldwide. A short presentation introduces the book to the readers:

> This book deals with the radical changes in women's status in Central Asia (specifically in Uzbekistan) following the victory of the Great October Socialist Revolution of 1917. Written by an Uzbek scholar, it describes the difficult and painstaking work of the Communist Party and the Soviets in the territory of Uzbekistan aimed at securing women's equality not merely before the law, but also in actual life. (Aminova 1977, 2)

In her introduction, Aminova assigns the main reason for the inferior status of women in Central Asia to "ruthless feudal and colonial oppression," which she claims blocked any progress toward the emancipation of women. After giving credit to several Central Asian poets between the fifteenth and the nineteenth centuries for having spoken on behalf of women's rights, she skips the activities and achievements of women in pre-Soviet Central Asia between 1900 and 1920 and jumps directly to the Soviet period:

> Progressive thinkers in Uzbekistan—Navoi, Nodira, Mukimi, Furqat, and others— made attempts at upholding the rights of woman as a human being and spoke out against the brutal customs that reduced her to the status of a slave. Their efforts, however, with feudal-clerical reaction rampant, were doomed to failure. Only with the victory of the Great October Socialist Revolution in 1917 and the implementation of Lenin's programme of socialist construction under the leadership of the Communist Party it became possible to fully solve the women's question in Central Asia. (Aminova 1977, 4)

In her entire book of 238 pages, she never mentions any indigenous activity or contribution to the advancement of women's rights between 1900 and 1920. In her conclusion, she describes the pre-Soviet period as completely dark concerning women's emancipation in order to hail later Soviet achievements in this regard:

> The enormous contrast between the miserable existence of the downtrodden woman, a virtual slave in pre-revolutionary Turkistan, and the free, purposeful and manifold creative activity of the woman in Uzbekistan, who enjoys every civil right, offers the most convincing proof that the successful emancipation of women is possible in a developing country. (Aminova 1977, 220)

Thus, for Aminova and other Soviet scholars, the mention of any progressive development in the pre-Soviet period might undermine the accomplishments and glory of the Soviet period.

Dilarom Alimova's case is very interesting because of the drastic change of her position on the woman issue in pre-Soviet Central Asia between the time her book was published in the Soviet period (Alimova 1987) and her later writings of the post-Soviet period (Alimova 1998; Alimova and Azimova 2000). In the 1987 Russian-language book *Zhenskii vopros v srednei Azii: Istoriia izucheniia i sovremmennye problemy* (The woman question in Central Asia: the history of studies and contemporary problems), Alimova praises even harsh Soviet measures to emancipate women in Central Asia, but in the post-Soviet era, she begins to express critical views on her earlier work and the Leninist discourse on Central Asian women (Alimova 1998; Alimova and Azimova 2000). In the late Soviet period, she acknowledges the Soviet discourse that the Soviet campaign of the forceful unveiling of the Muslim Central Asian women in 1929–1941 was a class struggle:

> Campaign "khujum" was accompanied by the intensification of the class struggle. The growing activity of women and the dropping of *parandja* [a tradition of women and girls] met bitter resistance of conservative elements. Mullahs, top Muslim clergy [*ishans*], and rich men [*bay*] terrorized those who laughed to step over the age-long foundations of the Islamic Law [Shariat]. The tops of clergy provoked irresponsible part of the terroristic acts by the population. (Alimova 1987, 31)

According to the inside front cover note by the publisher, the History Institute of the Academy Sciences of Uzbekistan, the book was prepared for "specialists and historians as well as instructors and the university students," which explains its propagandistic tone and rhetoric. Because of Soviet press censorship, it is impossible to know what Alimova's actual thinking on topic was in 1987.

Her English-language articles published in the West after the fall of the Soviet Union, however, critically question her previous Soviet position. In an article published in the journal *Central Asian Survey,* Alimova criticizes the former Soviet doctrine that the emancipation of women was a part of class struggle in Central Asia:

> The class approach was the leading theme of all transactions and visions, handed down from the upper echelons of the party who put a label on this process: the enemies of "Khudjum" are the clergy and the rich people. However, the war over women was not a war of classes but one of mentalities. It did not depend on the social extraction of people who found it very hard to reject a conception of women's destiny which was established in the course of centuries. Confirmation of this statement may be found in the tragic events that often occurred in the families of poor people. The crude and misguided working methods of the party committees provoked this war. For instance, the agitation in favour of "Khudjum" took place at residents' meetings in mosques for prayer, special groups for taking off the *paranja* were organized by the head of the police who obtained undertakings from husbands to unveil their wives. These kinds of coercive methods exerted

a negative influence on the women's movement itself which started to decline. (Alimova 1998, 151)

In her later coauthored article in a Western study on the gender issue in Central Asia, Caucasus, and Turkey published in 2000, Alimova repeated her stand that the Soviet experiment concerning women emancipation had serious problems:

> Forcefully imposed emancipation had tragic results. Without rejecting achievements such as cultural revolution, increasing educational level and the economic participation of women, we would argue that the policy of using women as a cheap labor force and equalizing their labor with that of men in the 1930s–40s had very negative consequences. This policy continued until the 1980s. The position of the rural women is particularly noteworthy. They suffered from the negative consequences of cotton monoculture. The major emphasis was made on the full participation of women in public production and the most important indicator was quantity. (Alimova and Azimova 2000, 294)

Unlike the former Soviet official line, which ignored pre-Soviet activities concerning the promotion of gender equality in Central Asia and among the Muslims of Tsarist Russia, Alimova now gave credit to the earlier Reformist (Jadidist) movement in the late nineteenth and early twentieth centuries prior to the Soviet period:

> It would be incorrect to consider that discussions on the emancipation of women started with the October revolution. The revolution was an upheaval, a forceful penetration of the Bolshevik rule, and was supposed to have raised the question of women's emancipation in the East for the very first time. Actually, at the end of the 19th century and the beginning of the 20th century, the progressive movement of national intelligentsia, which was called "Jadidism," laid out the question of women's participation in public social and cultural life in its program of renewal and social reconstruction. (Alimova and Azimova 2000, 292)

Of course, the Soviet regime did effect a dramatic transformation of women's social position throughout the region. However, the main logic behind Lenin's message, Krupskaya's follow-up remarks, and later Soviet discursive strategy was to amplify the achievements of the Soviet period in gender issues as if they had been initiated for the first time in history. The Soviet-era attitude of ignoring any pre-Soviet-period modernization effort or reformist movement was even carried on in some Western academic writings.[4] It led a few scholars to ignore or bypass any reference to pre-Soviet-period Muslim reformist ideas and movements. For example, one contemporary British scholar of Central Asia, when commenting on the Soviet transition of Central Asia, presents modernization simply as a Soviet introduction to the area by neglecting previous developments:

> Under Soviet rule, Central Asia underwent an intensive process of modernization. In effect, the region was wrenched out of Asia and thrust into Europe. Traditional culture was either destroyed or rendered invisible, confined to the most intimate and private spheres. In the public arena, new national identities were created, underpinned by newly fashioned languages and Western-style literatures and histories. (Akiner 1997, 261)

In reality, however, Western-type modern education was first introduced by Muslim reformist educators and intellectuals in the privately run Jadid schools in the Muslim areas of Tsarist Russia, including the Crimea, the Volga-Ural region, Azerbaijan, and Central Asia, prior to the Soviet period. These schools operated from the 1880s until the early 1920s before they were closed in favor of Soviet schools. Further, the depiction of the pre-Soviet past as solely "traditional" or "Islamic" and the Soviet period as "modern" and "Western" is also a misrepresentation of Central Eurasian history, since a deep confrontation existed between the "conservative traditionalism" represented by the Islamic clergy and the "modernization" perspective initiated by reformist (Jadid) intellectuals from the mid-nineteenth century until the Soviet period. Contrary to the above scholar's claim that "Western-style literatures" were introduced only in the Soviet period, there is a very rich literature in modern genres such as plays (dramas), short stories, novels, and poetry initiated by Muslim reformist writers in the various parts of Tsarist Russia, including Central Asia, between 1850 and 1917, long before the introduction of Soviet rule.[5]

In fact, Muslim Central Eurasia, as the largest region of the Islamic world, has a relatively long history of modernization starting in the late nineteenth century. Appreciation of this history of pre-Soviet Central Eurasia not only enables a more accurate evaluation of Soviet achievements but also, as important, an assessment of the widespread mythology of the oppressed, docile Muslim Central Eurasian woman. Interrogation of this one-sided depiction of the past reveals that Central Eurasia's historical experience does not simply serve as a source of tradition but also of reform and progressivism. The gender reforms that took place during the pre-Soviet period differed from those in the Soviet era:

unlike the top-down, externally imposed Communist changes, pre-Soviet Central Eurasian reforms were carried out by a group of indigenous male and female intellectuals working at the grassroots level. Their efforts deserve attention, as they may serve as a model for Central Eurasian societies as they pass through another transition in their political, social, and gender relations.

Of course, Soviet-created myths were not only limited to the pre-Soviet past of the Muslim peoples of Central Eurasia; they also applied to pre-Soviet Russian society, where the narrative of Soviet modernization and reform was promulgated. In the Stalin period and for a while thereafter, it was claimed that the "woman question" had been "solved" in Soviet society (Edmondson 1992, 2).[6] This Soviet account did not go uncontested. There is a rich academic literature dealing with the history of the modernization drive and reforms of the pre-Soviet Russian past that challenges Soviet myths about this period and disputes Soviet claims about women's liberation under Communism (see, for example, Stites 1978; Edmondson 1984, 1992, 2001; Clements 1979; Clements et al. 1991; Ruthchild 1993; Pushkareva 1997; and McDermid and Hillyar 1998; Lapidus 1978). Specific to Central Eurasia, the modernization efforts and reform movements of the pre-Soviet period of the Muslim Central Eurasia were fairly treated in Bennigsen and Lemercier-Quelquejay (1964, 1967), Allworth (1967, 1973, 1990, 1994), Brower and Lazzerini (1997), Khalid (1998, 2007), Roy (2000), and Kocaoglu (2001). The issue of gender politics in both the pre-Soviet and Soviet periods was also treated well in Massel (1974), Hablemitoglu and Hablemitoglu (1998), Hablemitoglu (2004), Northrop (2004), Noack (2000), Heyat (2002, 2005), and most recently in Kamp (2006) and Roy (2007). Among them, the Turkish-language source (Hablemitoglu and Hablemitoglu 1998) is particularly valuable, since it includes the texts and facsimiles of both valuable publications and original handwritten documents related to the congresses and activities of the Muslim (Turkic) reformists in the tsarist period. This chapter now turns to the individual efforts of such reformist activists and their struggle for woman's rights in pre-Soviet Central Eurasia from the mid-nineteenth century until early 1920s before the tightening grip of Soviet power in the region.[7]

Challenging the Myth: Individual Reformists' Lives

When I was a youth in Istanbul, Turkey, in the 1960s, I first encountered Rana, a Central Asian woman, and her husband, Raci (pronounced as "Rahji"), a Turkish man. Their fascinating life stories captured my imagination, and Rana's experiences provided ample evidence of the reformist activism of some

Rana in 1917 in Tashkent. *Source:* Author's collection.

Central Eurasian women. Rana was born in 1900, and at the age of eighteen was appointed Russian-language teacher at the native Turan Elementary School in the Beshagach district of Tashkent, where she met her future husband, a music teacher.[8] Rana was a Muslim Uzbek, while Raci was a fugitive ex-Ottoman Turkish officer who became a prisoner of war captured by the tsarist Russian army in Ardahan city during the Turko-Russian war of 1915. After spending two years in various Russian prison camps in the Caucasus, Raci, along with other Turkish officers and soldiers, was finally sent to the Krasnoyarsk prison camp in southern Siberia. A year later, with the help of local Tatar businessmen and intellectuals, Raci and several other Turkish officers escaped the camp. After a long journey through the steppes and desserts of today's Kazakhstan, they reached the city of Tashkent. There he found several other groups of Turkish officers who had also run away from other Russian prison camps. The Turkish officers helped Raci and

Rana with a group of male teachers at the Turan secondary school in Tashkent (1919). Her husband, Raci, is standing behind her. She was never veiled. *Source:* Author's collection.

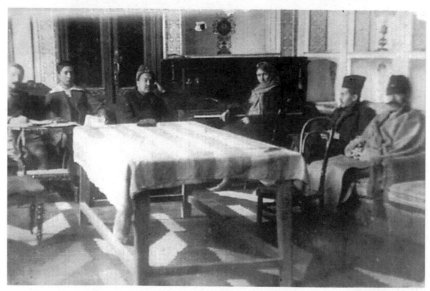

Rana in the summer palace of the former amir of Bukhara used by the new government of Bukhara (1920). The third man from the left and next to the piano is Qari Yoldash, the minister of education. *Source:* Author's collection.

his friends to get jobs in local schools, but these positions were in the modern schools in Tashkent being operated by native Central Asian intellectuals, in contrast to the Russian *tyuzemni* schools for the natives of Central Asia. After a year of friendship, Raci and Rana decided to marry. However, in 1920 it became dangerous for Raci, as an ex-Ottoman officer, to live in Tashkent; so they decided to move to the newly established independent republic of Bukhara. In Bukhara, Rana continued to work as a Russian-language teacher in various schools in the area, while Raci created and trained the military band of the Bukharan army. In 1923, conditions in Bukhara also deteriorated for the couple, as Bukhara and the rest of Central Asia were falling under the heavy grip of the Soviet Union. Rana and Raci decided to leave Bukhara and moved to Turkey. On the ship from Batum to Istanbul, Rana gave birth to their daughter (Kocaoglu 1987). In Turkey, she continued her profession as a Russian-language teacher and began to work translating into Turkish the novels, stories, and plays of various Russian writers such as Tolstoy, Dostoyevsky, Turgenyev, and Chekhov.

While detailed information about Rana's early life is limited, it is nonetheless possible to draw her portrait as representing the rare educated Muslim young woman who played an active role in the education of the native peoples during the extremely troubled years of the transition from the tsarist Russian rule to the short-lived independent republics of Bukhara and Kharazm from 1920 to 1923 and into the Soviet period. Rana definitely was one of that small number of fortunate women who lived in big cities like Tashkent, which afforded some opportunities for women like her, the daughter of lower-middle-class but educated parents. Her social status was entirely different than that of many of her contemporaries because of her education and profession. Rana was unique in that she was free to choose her husband and did not have a traditional arranged marriage. Her case clearly counterbalances the Soviet official claim that women were emancipated for the first time only under the Soviet rule in Muslim Central Eurasia. In fact, Rana was a perfect model of the "enlightened (progressive) women" that had been dreamed about since the late nineteenth century by Muslim reformist intellectuals and politicians such as Ismail Gaspirinski (1851–1914) and his daughter, Shefika Khanim (1886–1975), in Crimea; Hasan Melikov-Zardabi (1842–1907) in Azerbaijan; and Ahmad Mahzum Danish (1817–1896), Mahmud Khoja Behbudi (1875–1919), and Munavvar Qari (1878–1931) in Central Asia.[9]

Shefika Khanim, born in Bahchesaray in 1886 and died in Ankara in 1975, was one of the pioneers of the women's movement in Muslim Central Eurasia and a key participant at some of the major Muslim congresses. Her father was an educated person, but so was her mother, Zuhre Khanim, who was also an important figure among the early Muslim female reformists. The marriage of Ismail Gaspirinski and Zuhre Khanim is also very interesting from the vantage of the changes in women's status from the traditional way of life in Muslim Central Eurasia. Ismail's first marriage lasted only two years and ended in divorce, but his second was a case of secret love. His second wife, Zuhre, was the daughter of a rich Tatar family from Kazan. During young Zuhre's visit to Yalta city in Crimea with her uncle for two months in the summer of 1881, she became acquainted with Ismail at someone's house. The two fell in love. After Zuhre returned to Kazan, the lovers wrote letters to each other and even met in secret several times. Finally, they decided to marry. But when Zuhre's father, Isfandiyar Akchurin, rejected this marriage due to Ismail's poor economic conditions, Zuhre and Ismail secretly married; eventually her father accepted the relationship.

It is said that Zuhre gave her husband her expensive jewelry collection to sell and finance the private publishing house and the famous newspaper *Terjuman* (Translator) that Ismail wanted to publish. Later Zuhre helped her husband by acting as the newspaper's account manager, translator, and secretary, as well as the clerk who wrote the addresses of the subscribers on the envelopes for the post office. With the extraordinary effort by both husband and wife, between 1883 and 1918 their newspaper reached thousands of readers from the Crimea to various parts of Tsarist Russia, the Ottoman Empire, Europe, the Middle East, India, China, Japan, and even the United States.[10] When Zuhre died in 1903, her daughter, Shefika, started to help her father in the preparation and publication of the newspaper. Later, Shefika would become the editor of the first women's journal, *Alem-i Nisvan* (Women's World), which began publishing in 1906. Ismail Gaspirinski, who was very lucky to receive help from both his wife and daughter, later wrote an article entitled "One Wing Bird Can't Fly," referring to the significant role of women in helping men to enlighten society and conduct reforms in social, economic, cultural, and political fields (Hablemitoglu and Hablemitoglu 1998, 15–17).

Apart from the unusual marital team of Ismail Gaspirinski and Zuhre Khanim, another major reformist leader in Azerbaijan, Hasan Bey Melikzade Zardabi's marriage was also an odd case for the general arranged marriages of his time. When Hasan Zardabi (1842–1907) saw the name of an Azerbaijani girl in the list of high school graduates in Tbilisi in a newspaper in 1870, he immediately went to the city to find the girl named Hanife. At their first meeting, he proposed marriage to her. At first, the girl's family, relatives, and friends raised eyebrows at this strange proposal, but upon the insistence of their daughter, the family finally accepted the marriage (Hablemitoglu and Hablemitoglu 1998, 64–65).

Shefika Khanim (1886–1975), chief editor of the first woman's journal, *Alem-i Nisvan* (Woman's World) and the most prominent woman reformist in Muslim Central Eurasia. After she had to leave her homeland Crimea (late 1918) and also Azerbaijan (1921), she spent the rest of her life in Turkey. *Source:* Ismail Gaspirinski Web site: www.iccrimea. org/gaspirali/index.html.

Women's World Journal, no. 33 (1906). *Source:* Hablemitoglu and Hablemitoglu 1998: 538.

Shefika Khanim (*right*) with two other prominent women reformist leaders, Zeyneb Amirhan (*left, in white shirt*) and Ilhamiye Toktar (*center*), in the early 1900s in Crimea. *Source:* Hablemitoglu and Hablemitoglu 1998: 430.

While Hasan Zardabi published the reformist newspaper *Ekinji* (1875–1877) and contributed to the development of Azerbaijani theater, his wife, Hanife Zardabi, became the director of the private girls' school in Baku sponsored by the famous Azerbaijani oil industrialist Haji Zeynelabidin Tagiyev (1840–1924) (Heyat 2002, 49, 66–69, 74–76).

The lives of Rana, Shefika Khanim [FIG 6], and the other reformists throw into question the Leninist account of Muslim Central Eurasian women's docile subordination and the implicit reactionary conservatism of Muslim Central Eurasian men. They suggest that, even if not widespread, reformist efforts on behalf of women did occur during the pre-Soviet period and in fact formed a base for policies of women's emancipation in the Soviet era.

Challenging the Myth: Central Eurasian Reformism

The roots of reformism in tsarist-era Muslim Central Eurasia can be found in four important cultural regions: the cities of Baku and Tbilisi in Transcaucasia; the cities of Simferopol (Akmesjit) and Bahchesaray in the Crimea; the cities of Kazan and Ufa in the Volga-Ural; and the cities of Bukhara, Samarkand, and Tashkent in Central Asia (Turkistan). Among these four cultural regions,

The Ayshe Ishakova Kindergarten-Teacher's Training School in Akmesjit (Simferopol) in Crimea (1917). *Source:* Hablemitoglu and Hablemitoglu 1998: 436.

Transcaucasia was the most prosperous in terms of material wealth thanks to the advanced oil industry of Baku since the beginning of the nineteenth century. However, regardless of resources, between the 1860s and the 1910s, various groups of reformist intellectuals—among them scholars, journalists, writers, and politicians—had already started to engage in cultural, social, and political reform activities, particularly in the cities of Simferopol, Kazan, Ufa, Baku, Tashkent, Bukhara, and Samarkand.

By the early twentieth century, the situation across the empire was ripe for reformist movements. With the establishment of a constitutional monarchy following the 1905 revolution, the Russian tsar was forced to hold elections for the Duma and the State Assembly, and he promised not to interfere with legislation. In the atmosphere of freedom that began with the tsar's manifesto, many political parties, organizations, and publications came to life. This situation in Russia encouraged the Muslim Turks as well. The first political party among the Azerbaijanis was Himmet, which initially acted as a branch of the Social Democratic Party in Russia. In 1904, several new political parties appeared in Azerbaijan, such as Hurriyet (Freedom) and Ittifaq (Unity).

In addition to the political changes in Russia, political developments in the Ottoman Empire also influenced the Muslim Turks in Russia. In particular, the Young Turks (*Jeunes Turcs* in French) movement was closely followed by the

Muslims Turks of Russia. Starting as separate small secret societies, the Young Turks movement can be traced as far back as 1889. With their grand conference in 1902 in Paris, two major political divisions appeared among the members of the various Young Turks societies: one political faction supported the centralization of the Ottoman Empire (Committee of Union and Progress) while another faction had the idea of the decentralization of the Ottoman Empire (Liberal Union). The successes of the Young Turks in the Ottoman Empire in the later years inspired such secret societies among the various Muslim Turks in Russia as the "Young Tatars" in Crimea, the "Young Bukharans" in the Emirate of Bukhara, and the "Young Khivans" in the Khanate of Khiva in the 1910s. Actually, there was reciprocal influence between the intellectuals of the Muslims of Russia and the Ottoman Empire. The noted scholars on Islam in Russia, Alexandre Bennigsen and Chantal Lemercier-Quelquejay, remark that "for Russia's Muslims, the Young Turks revolution, even more than the Russian revolution of 1905, was a triumphant and clear demonstration of the fact that a democratic movement could prevail over autocracy. At the same time, while the national movement in Russia was powerfully inspired by the Turkish revolution, it exercised in its turn, particularly after 1905, an influence which was sometimes decisive on the political life of the Ottoman Empire" (1967, 34). Indeed, during the waning years of the Russian empire, when many Central Eurasian Turkic intellectuals had to escape from the tsarist empire to the Ottoman capital, Istanbul, they had a very strong impact on the Ottoman reformist intellectuals.

The Roots of Jadidism: Women, Education, and the Press

Not surprisingly, given the work of these reformists, Central Eurasia during the pre-Soviet period, like the Soviet and post-Soviet periods, saw changes in gender politics; however, there are substantial differences between the modernizations of the pre-Soviet and Soviet periods. First of all, the modernization drives in the pre-Soviet period were carried out by the initiatives of small groups of native reformist individuals in various parts of Muslim Central Eurasia, while those of the Soviet period were imposed by an alien and central power, the Soviet authority, on the native peoples, sometimes by violent force. Second, the native reformists, mostly male but a few female, strongly believed that real women's emancipation in the Muslim parts of Tsarist Russia could be achieved in three ways: through gradual reforms in the education of both men and women in modern schools of that time (the reformist Jadid schools); through dissemination of reformist ideas among the Muslim peoples via private newspapers and journals, which were increasing in number and distribution between 1883 and 1917, and finally through the establishment of democratic governments and states for Muslims both in the territories of Tsarist Russia and the protectorate states of Bukhara and Khiva.[11]

The roots of Muslim Turkic women's modern education and activism go back to the second half of the nineteenth century with the start of the reform modernization drive. At the beginning, reform movements among the peoples of Muslim Central Eurasia were based, on the one hand, on their opposition to Russian domination and, on the other hand, by their acquaintance with reform movements in the Ottoman Empire. However, reform movements first began in the Volga Ural region (Kazan, Ufa), the Crimea, and Azerbaijan and later expanded to Central Asia (the Steppe provinces and Turkistan, the Emirate of Bukhara, and the Khanate of Khiva). Reform movements developed through the press and education. In terms of press influence, the bilingual newspaper *Tercüman/ Prevodchik* (Translator) in Crimean Turkish and Russian from 1883 to 1918 played the most vital role for the development of the native press in Muslim Central Eurasia prior to the Soviet period. The reformist Ismail Gaspirinski also started the first women's journal *Alem-i Nisvan* (Women's World) in 1906 and made his daughter, Shefika Khanim, its editor.

In education, already acquainted with Russian schools, the Muslim Turks wanted to establish their own New Method (Usul-i Jadid) schools in their native tongue, but they designed them differently from their Traditional Method (Usul-i Kadim) schools. The influence of Ismail Gaspirinski was very great in the rapid spread of the New Method Jadid (Reformist) schools with modern education from Bahchesaray, Crimea, to Kazan, Baku, Tashkent, and Bukhara instead of the traditional Muslim schools under heavy religious education. Between 1898 and 1908, there were 102 New Method elementary schools and two New Method junior high schools in the Turkistan General Governorship of Tsarist Russia, six New Method elementary schools in the Emirate of Bukhara, and six New Method elementary schools in the Khanate of Khiva. In order to support the New Method schools, the Bukharan reformist intellectuals and businessmen founded a company, Shirkat-i Bukhara-i Sharif (Company of Noble Bukhara), in March 1909, which posed as a trading company but was actually a political organization (Ayni 1963, 202).[12] This company secretly provided textbooks and other supplies for the New Method Jadid schools (d'Encausse 1988, 87–88).

Secrecy was required because reformist (Jadid) educators and intellectuals were facing severe difficulties and ill-treatment in their drive to expand modern education in their New Method schools, since both tsarist colonial authorities

The Ismail Gaspirinski Teacher's College in Akmesjit (Simferopol) in Crimea (1918). This college was run by two female directors: Shefika Khanim (Ismail Gaspirinski's daughter) and Ilhamiye Toktar. *Source:* Hablemitoglu and Hablemitoglu 1998: 453.

Girls elementary school in Kostruma (Siberia, 1917). *Source:* Hablemitoglu and Hablemitoglu 1998: 434.

and regional feudal rulers, like those of the Emirate of Bukhara, joined together to prevent any reforms. Tsarist administrators and Bukharan emirs supported the conservative Muslim clergy against the reformist Muslim intellectuals (Khalid 1998, 300). Allworth gives information on the attitudes and actions of both Muslim conservative clergy and the tsarist Russian officials toward the New Method (modern) schools opened by the Muslim intellectuals in Central Asia:

> Even a small number of New Method schools frightened them [the clergy] in Bukhara and in Turkistan, just as they did most Russian officials. The establishment's anxiety became obvious when the Russian authorities in Turkistan closed more than 50 New Method schools during the 1910/11 school year. . . . The Amir of Bukhara in the 1913/14 school season closed all New Method schools known in the amirate. (Allworth 1990, 139–140)

Despite these pressures, interest in New Method education remained strong. One of the leading reformists in the Emirate of Bukhara, Osman Khodja (1878–1968), visited Bahchesaray in 1909 on his way to Istanbul and met with Ismail Gaspirinski. After studying the essential methodology of the Jadid schools with him, Osman Khodja went to Istanbul and studied the modern Ottoman school system there. Meanwhile, he and his other colleagues from Bukhara, such as Abdurrauf Fitrat (1886–1938), founded the Charity Society of Bukhara for Dissemination of Education on October 26, 1909.[13] The aim of the organization was to bring students from the Emirate of Bukhara and other parts of Turkistan (Central Asia) to continue their education in the schools of Istanbul.

After returning to Bukhara two years later, Osman Khodja immediately opened a Jadid school in his house and started to serve first the children of his relatives and later other people. When Osman Khodja and other "Young Bukharan" revolutionary group members deposed the emirate regime and established the democratic republic of Bukhara (1920–1923), Khodja first became the minister of finance in 1920 and later the president of the republic in 1921 (Kocaoglu 2001, 36–37).[14]

Not surprisingly, given Osman Khodja's role in the new government, one of the first moves taken in this short-lived non-Soviet republic was to open modern schools where both male and female students sat in classes side by side. The Bukharan government also sent three groups of high school graduates to three key cities for university education in 1921: Moscow, Berlin, and Istanbul. After the abolition of the independent republic of Bukhara by the Soviets in 1924 and later after World War II, only a few of the students who received B.A. and doctorate degrees in Berlin and Istanbul dared to return to Uzbekistan. Those who did return were later either jailed or sent to Siberia, where they served in the labor fields because the Soviet government suspected that they might have been indoctrinated while studying in Berlin and Istanbul.[15]

Muslim reformist intellectuals especially focused on the emancipation of Muslim women in their discourse and activities because they understood that without gender equality and liberation, their modernization drive could not be successful. This position was reflected in a journal article by a male reformist in 1913 in Baku, Azerbaijan: "Whoever loves his own people and wishes it a [great] future, must concern himself with the enlightenment and education of women, restore freedom and independence to them, and give wide scope to the development of their minds and capabilities" (Lazzerini 1973, 237). This writer's call is echoed more bluntly in a letter to the editor by Hariye Hanim Machabili in the newspaper *Tercüman/Prevodchik* (Translator) in Crimea in 1913: "Our rights are clearly defined in the Kor'an and in the sayings of the prophet. But, you [men], in the name of religion, are oppressing us; in the name of Shariat [Islamic law] you are destroying us. . . . Who will suffer and lose out because of this? Again it will be you [men]" (Lazzerini 1973, 237). Adeeb Khalid, in his excellent study on the politics of Muslim reformism (Jadidism) in Central Asia, summarizes the main trend in the Jadids' writings in the pre-Soviet period:

> They are marked by a great sympathy for women and a concern for bettering their position. Again, the inspiration came from Tatar and Ottoman debates. Magazines by and for women, such as *Alem-i Nisvan* (Women's World), edited by Gaspirinski's daughter Shefika Khanim in Bahchesaray, and *Suyüm Bike*, which appeared in Kazan from 1913 to 1917, had created a women's voice in the new discourses of the nation then being articulated. Veiling had disappeared among the Tatars by the turn of the century, and Tatar women in Central Asian cities were visible symbols of the change local Jadids wanted to bring about in their society; and to the extent that women had a voice in this debate, Tatar women were also agents of reform. (1998, 223)

Later, however, Khalid states that "unveiling was never explicitly raised in Central Asia before 1917, and Jadid attitudes on gender issues remained conservative" (1998, 228). It is understandable that the Central Asian reformist (Jadidist) intellectuals who were under severe attacks by the Islamic clergy and conservative circles in their societies must have realized that it was not the right time to debate the "unveiling of women" issue openly in the press.

Reformist Writers: Ideas on Education and Unveiling

The emphasis of Muslim reformists on the education of both males and females as the primary prerequisite for modernization, of course, found its way into literary works. Poems written by reformist writers in many regions of Muslim Central Eurasia between 1900 and 1920 call attention to the education of men and women. There are many stories, novels, and plays with plots that idealize educated young women in contrast to the illiterate young men who lead their communities into misery and downfall. In the novel *Unlucky Girl Jamal (Baxtsiz Jamal)*, by the reformist Kazak writer Mirjakib Duwlat-uli (1885–1938), who was killed during the Stalinist purges, the fictional female character, Jamal, commits suicide at the end because she was forced to marry someone she did not love. In contrast, in the novel *New Happiness (Yangi Saadat)*, by the reformist Uzbek writer Hamza Hakimzada Niyazi (1889–1929), the female and male characters marry in a happy ending after their parents allow their daughter to obtain an education. The Muslim reformist intellectuals (Jadids) believed that the idea of gender equality could be introduced in the Muslim communities of Russia and be gradually achieved through education of both men and women. Abdulla Avloni (1878–1934), a prominent reformist educator and poet, addresses his wife about educating their children of both sexes in one of his poems printed in 1914 three years before the Bolshevik revolution:

> Oh my wife, shouldn't we educate our son?
> Shouldn't our daughter become a teacher?
> Those uneducated will face dark days
> Youth age is like silver and gold. (1998, 14)

In reformist writer Mahmud Khoja Behbudi's (1875–1919) drama entitled *Patricide or the State of the Uneducated Child*, a modern-minded Central Asian Muslim priest (Khoja) advises a Rich Man (Bay), a conservative and narrow-minded character, on the importance of education in the following conversations between the two:

> THE RICH MAN: Oh, priest! Are you interrogating me? Son is mine, wealth is mine, and it is none of your business! Look one of the educated ones is yourself and you don't have a bread to eat. Do you give advice in your present humble condition? Hayrullah, close the guest room, I am sleepy.
> (*The servant HAYRULLA stands aside after picking up the tray and the tea cups*)

MUSLIM PRIEST: In order to be educated and become a priest one needs money. The state of our rich people is like this. Thus, God forbid, we will be disgraced in both this and the other world. Getting education was obligatory for all Muslims both male and female. What happened to this? Ah, pity to our condition! (*staring at the* RICH MAN) Sir, I told you the way of the Islamic Law (*Sheri'at*) and I did what the Islamic law required from me.[16]

At the end of the play, the Rich Man, who refuses the advice of the modern-minded priest and another reformist intellectual to educate his son, is murdered during a burglary involving his son and his uneducated friends. A reformist intellectual character, who is named as "Intellectual," reappears at the last scene of the play when the Rich Man's son and his friends are arrested and taken away in police custody:

INTELLECTUAL: Since we are uneducated and also don't educate our children, these kind of bad and unfortunate events will continue among us. There is no other way other than to be educated and to educate others. God Almighty should warn others and give you patience.

The Muslim reformists of Central Asia, who were reluctant to discuss the issue of the unveiling of women openly in the pre-Soviet press when they were under severe attack by the conservative circles of their society, were able to raise this issue in their literary works in the pre-Soviet period. One of the best testaments of this is a poem written against veiling in 1920 by the most prominent reformist Uzbek poet, Abdulhamid Sulayman Cholpan (1897–1938), who was killed during the Stalinist purges. In his poem "For an Uzbek Girl," published in 1922, the poet earnestly expresses his deep sorrows for Uzbek women behind veils:

I see: in each nation's sky
Their stars gleam brightly.
And each person drinks one's fill
Stars' sprinkled radiant on the earth!

There is no garden where there is no female rose,
There is no yard where there is no female nightingale.
There is no place where there is any female scent
There is no heart which is not captivated by a woman . . .

In each nation's garden, those roses
Are the women and girls of that people;
Each people has its own true path
That is based on their women's footsteps.

In no nation, those beautiful faces
Of women to be put behind veils.
In no nation . . . a cruel hand
Slaps a woman in rage.

Wherever I've gone, I've found
Women with their open faces;
Alas, my women are veiled in my country
Oh, Uzbek girl, I mourn in grief,
I suffocate,
I die![17]

This poem, written in August 1920, clearly rejects the Soviet notion that the ideas of both women's emancipation and the unveiling of the Muslim women were introduced first only in the Soviet period. Cholpan's poem reflects precisely the ideals of the reformist intellectuals in Muslim Central Eurasia prior to the Soviet period. The Soviet strategy of the drastic and harsh implementation of the unveiling campaign (the so-called Khujum), however, was not what the Muslim reformists had in mind.

Central Eurasian Politics: Mobilization by and for Women

Against this backdrop of nineteenth- and early-twentieth-century reformism, the first four congresses of the Muslims of Russia were held in 1905, 1906, and 1914. Unfortunately, no female delegates were in attendance. The large numbers of conservative male delegates in those initial congresses and the weakness of a female reformist movement at that time conspired to block the participation of any female delegate. However, this rejection did not stop women from mobilizing, as women reformists later began to organize as important lobbying groups. Still, when the Crimean Tatars held a meeting for the autonomy of the Crimean region on March 25, 1917, there were only two female delegates among the 2,000 participants. Nevertheless, that meeting endorsed the political rights of women

۱۹۱۷ نچی یلده ۲٤ نچی آپریـلـده قزانده‌غی مسلمه‌لر و کیللری اسییزدیڭ «روسیه مسـلمه‌لری اوچون مرکزی مؤسسه» طوغروسنده‌غی داقلاد تیکشرو و اوچون صایلانغان کامیسیه‌بو طوغریده‌غی داقلادلرنی اوقوب تو‌بنده‌گی قراریغه کیلدی.

۱) روسیه مسلمه‌لرینڭ بتون آرغانیزاتسیه‌لری برله‌شرگه تیوش بولڭ اوچون محلی کامیتیت‌لرنی رایونینی کامیتیت‌لرغه رایونینیلرنی بر سینترالنی کامیتیتکه باغلاو تیوش.
۲) مرکزی کامیتیت حاضرگه وقتلیچه‌غنه بولور.
۳) وقتلی مرکزی کامیتیت‌نڭ اورنی مه‌سکوده بولور.
٤) بو کامیتیت‌نڭ اعضالری ٥ دن کیم بولماس.
٥) کامیتیت‌نڭ مادی یاغن تأمین ایته‌رلك آقچه خلقدن تو‌بنده‌گی رهوشچه جیولور.
دوسیده‌گی مسلمه‌ار جمعیت خیریه‌لری اوچهر یوز صوم بیرورلر. ایلر جمعیت خیریه‌لر اوزلری تله‌گانچه یار ده‌م آقچه جیبارلر. هم و کیله‌لر اویلرینه قایتقاچ تورلی یوللر بلهن
٦) مرکزی کامیتیت‌نڭ مقصدینه خدمت ایتهر اوچون کامیتیت طرفندن بر ژورنال چغارلور.

One of the resolutions adopted at the First Congress of Muslim-Turkic Women in Kazan city on April 24–27, 1917. *Source:* Hablemitoglu and Hablemitoglu 1998: 468.

Another resolution adopted at the First Congress of Muslim-Turkic Women in Kazan city on April 24–27, 1917. *Source:* Hablemitoglu and Hablemitoglu 1998: 469.

مسلمه‌لر اسییزدی

خاتونلرنڭ اجتماعی وسیاسی حقوقلا حقنده تو‌بنده‌گی قرارلرنی چغاردی:

۱) قزلرنی اورتا هم عالی مکتبلرده اوقتلسون.
۲) یاشلری اوزغان خاتونار اوچون تورلی قورصلار آچلسون.
۳) خاتونلرنڭ حقوقلارن حمایه جمعیتلری آچلسون.
٤) خاتونلرنڭ طورمشن مادی ومعنوی جهتدن یاخشیرتو جمعیتلری آچلسون.
٥) هر جیرده مسلمانلو اوچون شفا خانه هم ولادت خانه‌لر آچلسون.
٦) فاحش خانه‌لر هم فحش توغروسنده زاقونلر بیتراسون.
۷) مسلمان خاتونلاری بتون سیاسی حقوقلارده ایرلر برلن بر بولسونلر.

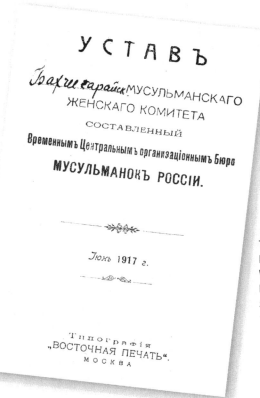

УСТАВЪ

*Бахчисарайск*МУСУЛЬМАНСКАГО
ЖЕНСКАГО КОМИТЕТА

СОСТАВЛЕННЫЙ

Временнымъ Центральнымъ организаціоннымъ Бюро

МУСУЛЬМАНОКЪ РОССІИ.

———— ✦✦✦ ————

Іюнь 1917 *г.*

———— ✦✦✦ ————

Типографія
„ВОСТОЧНАЯ ПЕЧАТЬ".
М О С К В А

The Rules and Guidelines of the Bahchesaray Committee for Muslim Women (June 1917). *Source:* Hablemitoglu and Hablemitoglu 1998: 498.

along with supporting cultural and political autonomy for the Crimean Tatars. The conservative male delegates, however, dispersed a small group of Azerbaijani women when they tried to participate at the First Congress of Caucasia on April 15–20, 1917, in Baku. Women's participation was also prevented at several other congresses in April 1917, such as the First Muslim Congress of the Ufa Region, the Turkistan Muslim Congress in Tashkent, the First Kazak Congress in Orenburg, and the First Congress of Northern Caucasia (Hablemitoglu 2004; Kocaoglu 2001).

Despite these negative developments, women continued their activities in support of gender equality. Women reformists succeeded in organizing the First Congress of Muslim-Turkic Women in Kazan city on April 24–27, 1917, at which more than 400 Muslim (largely Turkic) women from various regions of Tsarist Russia participated. This congress proved to be the most successful political step that the Muslim women in Central Eurasia had taken, because several important resolutions for woman's rights were endorsed by it. One of the first resolutions the congress adopted was related to the establishment of a Central Committee of Muslim Women of Russia as an umbrella organization to coordinate the activities of various women's groups and organizations. The resolution asserted:

1. All the organizations of the Muslim Turkic women in Russia need to be united; therefore, all local and regional committees should be united under a Central Committee;
2. The Central Committee at present will be temporary;
3. The headquarters of the Central Committee will be in Moscow;
4. The Central Committee will be composed of at least five members;
5. Financial aid for the Central Committee will come from following revenues: the charity organizations of the Muslim Women of Russia, the charity organizations of the Muslilist #2m Men of Russia; and the delegates of this congress.
6. The Central Committee will issue a journal for advocating its goals. (Hablemitoglu and Hablemitoglu 1998, 466, 468)[18]

Besides the establishment of this Central Committee, the Congress in Kazan also approved a resolution on the social and political rights of Muslim women of Russia, the key provisions of which were:

1. Girls should be educated at the middle and higher schools;
2. Special courses should be opened for the aged women;
3. An association for defending the rights of women should be founded;
4. Various societies should be established for improving the material and spiritual life of women;
5. Hospitals and maternity clinics for Muslim women should be opened everywhere;
6. New laws should be implemented for the brothel houses and prostitution;
7. Muslim women should be equal to men in all political rights. (Hablemitoglu and Hablemitoglu 1998, 466, 469)

The Muslim female delegates also endorsed a very interesting resolution, "Women's Rights in Islam," which examined the rights of women according to the Qur'an This bold initiative asserted:

1. According to the Qur'anic Law (Shariat), men and women are equal;
2. The participation of women in political and social activities is appropriate and justified by the Qur'anic Law (Shariat);
3. Covering the face of women with a "*hijab*" (veil) outside has no place in the Qur'anic Law (Shariat). (Hablemitoglu and Hablemitoglu 1998, 466–467, 470)

Following the success of the Kazan congress, the prime time arrived for the Muslim women of Central Eurasia to participate at the next major event, the Congress of the Muslims of Russia. In the First Congress of Russia's Muslims on May 1, 1917, there were 112 female delegates out of 970 total delegates (Hablemitoglu and Hablemitoglu 1998, 163). This shows that the number of the women activists between 1905 and 1917 was rapidly increasing, and their activities were becoming more effective. Another big surprise awaiting the male delegates at the congress was that they met with a new type of woman who was not shy to sit side by side with the men and not content to remain silent anymore; these women were ready to fight for their rights (Hablemitoglu and Hablemitoglu 1998, 163). Women participants succeeded in electing their female candidate, Selime Yaqubova, chairperson of the Central Office of Muslim Women, to the twelve-seat Presidency Council of the Congress. Thanks to the lobbying efforts of the women, a separate "Women's Issue" was included on the agenda, and a special "Women's Question Section" was established in order to prepare a report on this issue. One of the most heated debates between several female delegates and their conservative male counterparts at the congress was on the issue of the polygamy habits of Muslim men. The women speakers expressed strong objections against those who defended the polygamy rights of the men. According to Shefika Khanim, the following twelve-point "Women Action Plan" was endorsed with a majority vote, after long debate, which continued until midnight on May 1 (Hablemitoglu and Hablemitoglu 1998, 165–66):

1. For the sake of the nation's future, it is important that the women benefit from all political rights. Women will have rights to elect and be elected.
2. Necessary precautions should be taken in case some men will prevent their wives and daughters from going to the election polls.
3. It became a common habit to claim the right of men to have up to four wives according to the Qur'an. Since it is impossible to behave justly and equally to all four wives at the same time, acquiring more than one wife becomes void.
4. Up to the present day, women couldn't become the responsible elder of their children. Since women have been trapped like slaves between the four walls of their own homes, family life is in a state inappropriate to humanity.
5. The youngsters are being forced into marriage without their consent.
6. For the nation's survival, healthy generations are needed. Fathers need to be free from contagious diseases.

7. There are men who divorce their wives and marry another woman. These kinds of events lead to the destruction of families and make innocent women unhappy.

8. When husband and wife can't get along well, a woman can't get a divorce if the man doesn't want one. Usually children get hurt when there is no harmony in a family.

9. Since girls are being married at very young ages in Turkistan, among the Kazakhs, and in the Caucasus, young women turn into exhausted creatures by early aging and sickness.

10. When a girl is married among the Kazakhs, the bride's father receives "qalın" bride-wealth (money, property, or animal). Taking bride-wealth is nothing more than the selling of a girl.

11. Women have fallen into brothel houses for various reasons. Women should be saved from this shameful act for the sake of the nation and all humanity.

12. Women should be equal with men in all political and social rights.

When these reformist-minded Muslim intellectuals seized chances to create either independent republics in Bukhara and Kharazm or autonomous governments in Bolshevik Russia, one of their first reforms was to give equal political rights to women along with men. Turkish scholars in Turkey often are very proud of the fact that Turkish women received the right to vote and also be elected in the constitution in 1934, first among all Islamic countries and ahead of some Western European countries as well. The early constitutions of the Muslim Turkic peoples in Central Eurasia prior to the Soviet takeover, however, contest this myth. The first legislation in the entire Islamic world that granted women the right to vote and run for office was the constitution of the Crimean Tatar Autonomous Government in 1917. Article 18 of the constitution states the rights of women: "The Congress, having acknowledged the equality of humanity, approves that the women have the same equal rights with men and it orders the parliament to prepare a new law based on this equality."[19] The second legal move among the Turkic peoples in Russia was taken by the Tatars of Russia. The 1918 constitution of the All-Russian and Siberian Turk-Tatar Autonomous Government stated in Article 20: "Any male or female person 20 years old has the right to elect or be elected to the Parliament." This trend of giving women equal rights in politics was carried on in the constitutions of the independent republics of Bukhara and Kharazm in 1921. The Bukharan constitution recognized the equality of women in politics: "Article 57: Each citizen of the Bukharan

People's Counciliar Republic who is 20 years old on the election day enjoys the right of electing a parliament member or be elected as a parliament member regardless of being a male or female."

Besides granting women the right to vote and to be elected, these early pre-Soviet constitutions of the Turkic peoples of Crimea (1917), Volga-Ural region (1918), Bukhara (1921), and Kharazm (1921) also endorsed the rights of both women and men to own private property. In this respect, the constitutions of Muslim Central Eurasia between 1917 and 1921 differ from the first Soviet constitution of 1918 and subsequent versions in that the Soviet constitutions deny the right of private property and bequeathing of the land and property from parents to children.

Despite the fact that the constitutions of the autonomous governments of the Crimean Tatars in Crimea (1917), All-Russian Tatar-Muslims in Ufa (Volga-Ural region) (1918), Alash-Orda in the territory of the present-day Kazakhstan (1917), Turkistan in the city of Kokand (1917), and the independent republics Bukhara (1920) and Kharazm (1920) contained articles promoting gender equality, full implementation of these political rights for women was never achieved because the Soviet army eliminated these autonomous governments and republics one by one between 1918 and 1923. The demise of these regimes, however, does not negate the fact that some Muslim Central Eurasian men and women did struggle to promote gender equality and that their efforts bore some fruit in the short-lived republics of the early twentieth century.

Conclusion

Substantial achievements in the field of women's emancipation as well as equal political rights for women in Muslim Central Eurasia were mainly realized in the Soviet era. The struggle for gender rights by various women activists side by side with their male colleagues in the pre-Soviet-period Central Eurasia, however, should not be overlooked. Despite their small numbers and the unfavorable conditions, representatives of Muslim women bravely participated in the movement to enlighten the Muslims of Central Eurasia and acquire political and social rights for Muslim women before the firm establishment of Soviet rule in Central Eurasia. And their efforts bore some results in the constitutions and legislation of the autonomous Muslim Central Eurasian governments and republics between 1917 and 1923. However, with the onset of Soviet rule, these short-lived regimes were unable to implement gender reforms. This situation then allowed the Soviet regime to minimize the significance of the indigenous Central Eurasian efforts at gender reform and to promulgate its master narrative of Muslim Eurasian gender subordination and Soviet women's liberation.

Because the Soviet regime sought to conceal the positive and progressive ideas and accomplishments of the pre-Soviet Central Eurasia on many issues, including the gender question, new generations of Soviet Muslims could only remember and appreciate the Soviet achievements that were implemented. However, many times these were enacted through drastic and harsh measures that caused the loss of thousands of lives, such as during the mass campaigns of collectivization (1928–1933), the forced unveiling of Muslim women (1927–1930), and the Stalinist purges of politicians, intellectuals, and writers (1934–1938).[20] When the prominent Uzbek writer and poet Abdulhamid Sulayman Cholpan was pressured by the Soviet authorities to write poems in praise of these Soviet achievements, he wrote the following poem, entitled "New Me" ("Yangi Men" in Uzbek), in August 1934:

> I now have no grief,
> I'm joyous like the springs,
> To the death of the nights
> I'm the one who burst into laughter!

> I don't have the habit of longing
> Secrets from the dead souled nights,
> I don't want melancholy!
> You put your chains on the Majnun![21]

> In my new country
> There is neither Majnun nor chain!
> Here, each one who works
> His happiness comes to his arms!

> Here labor is the monarch
> It gives orders, doesn't let you to tire:
> Because the musician doesn't lose
> His affection to his own instrument.

> Here the labor creates
> Miracles with enthusiasm.

Here every day the dawn breaks
With lively songs and melodies.

As one of the millions [of people]
I sweat too each day;
Each day new excitements,
I get use to the victories!

As one of the millions [of people]
I'm also lively, I'm also joyous
To the death of the past
I'm the one who burst into laughter!

In this poem, Cholpan describes the so-called Soviet achievements by employing both dramatic irony and metaphor. All the adornments in the poem create a discrepancy between what the character in the poem believes or says and what is really happening in the Soviet Union. The main metaphor behind the depiction of the speaker of himself as a "new me" also reinforces the intensive usage of figurative speech in the poem. The speaker in the poem is a "New Me" because he is stripped of all human feelings such as longing, passion, melancholic love, grief, and exhaustion. His contentment and pleasure now simply derive from labor and work: "Here, each one who works/His happiness comes to his arms!" Joy and happiness are not something that one has to strive for; they are automatically delivered by labor, which is portrayed as the single ruler in this new realm: "Here labor is the monarch/It gives orders, doesn't let you to tire." As a result, the speaker of the poem has lost his individuality like millions of other people "in my new country" (the Soviet Union). Now he has become indifferent to his spiritual or national past: "To the death of the nights/I'm the one who burst into laughter!" Poet Cholpan's exposé of this "New Me," or actually the "New Soviet Man," only increased official criticism and pressures on him during the Stalinist purges. On July 14, 1937, he was taken to prison and executed by a rifle squad on October 4, 1938; his court verdict was issued a day later.[22]

Cholpan, of course, was just one of the numerous pre-Soviet Muslim enlighteners (Jadids) whose many progressive ideas on reforming Muslim communities were later taken over by the Soviet authorities. Although many Jadid intellectuals and politicians had to collaborate with the Soviet authorities in the execution of these reforms, they were eliminated one by one between the late 1920s and late 1930s. There is, though, a fundamental difference between the reforms that were envisaged by the pre-Soviet Muslim reformists and the way the Soviet authorities have implemented them on the Muslims by force. The pre-Soviet Muslim reformists, on the one hand, intended to introduce these reforms, especially the ones regarding gender equality and the unveiling of Muslim women, through education. They believed that they could achieve the emancipation of women only by educating the new generations of boys and girls in schools and cultivating the older generations through press and other tools of modernization. The Soviets, on the other hand, presented the emancipation of women as a class struggle on an ideological level while using it as an effective instrument to increase the labor force in the Soviet Union. In contrast, the pre-Soviet Muslim reformists treated gender equality as just another significant step in the creation of a modern society for their Muslim communities. They foresaw gender equality as one of the inseparable components of modernization, together with modern education, press freedom, private property, and freedom of consciousness—in short, many of the rights and values that were denied in the Soviet Union.

Knowledge and awareness of the reformist (Jadidist) heritage by the post-Soviet Muslims of both the Russian Federation and the republics of Azerbaijan and Central Asia are crucial for the present transition from authoritarianism to democracy. The pre-Soviet Muslim (Turkic) reformists in Central Eurasia took bold steps toward the implementation of women's emancipation and the social and political rights of women at least two decades before the Soviet period. Although influenced by political reforms and developments in Russia (1905) and the Ottoman Empire (1839, 1876, and 1908), they were not under the direction or influence of tsarist Russian administrators or the Russian elite; they acted out of their own interests and experiences. Recognition of their activism not only challenges Soviet mythology about the lack of modernization within the Muslim communities during the pre-Soviet era but also provides a more comprehensive background to the Moscow-engineered gender politics of the later years. Well-educated pre-Soviet women, although few in number, voluntarily took up key roles together with the men in the reformist movement that sought to enlighten the Muslim Turkic peoples of Tsarist Russia starting from the mid-nineteenth century until the Bolshevik revolution of 1917 and then until 1920. Their efforts demonstrate that Muslim peoples in Russia, Azerbaijan, and Central Asia today are capable of tackling the new challenges they encounter to create an equal and freer society for both genders.

NOTES

1. The terms "Central Eurasia" and "Muslim Central Eurasia" in this study refer to a larger area comprising present-day Azerbaijan and the five republics of Central Asia along with the Volga-Ural region in the Russian Federation inhabited by Muslim Turkic peoples, and Crimea in the Ukraine (all these areas were part of Tsarist Russia before 1917). Although the Xinjiang Uyghur Autonomous Region of China is also inhabited by Muslim Turkic peoples, this region is left outside the scope of this chapter since it has never been under Russian and Soviet rule. In contrast to "Central Eurasia," the term "Central Asia" includes only the former Soviet republics and the present-day independent states of Kazakhstan, Kyrgyzstan, Tajikistan, Turkmenistan, and Uzbekistan.

2. Lenin 1984, 86.

3. Nadezhda K. Krupskaya's "Preface," written on November 30, 1933, in Lenin 1984, 9. The author thanks Terri Miller, Slavic bibliographer of the Michigan State University Library, for helping to identify several sources on Lenin; also see Yelena Yemelyanova 1985 and Yedlin 1980.

4. The term "pre-Soviet period" designates the transitional period from the rule of Tsarist Russia until the establishment of Soviet power in early 1920s. For the Muslim Turkic peoples, this transitional period starts from the late nineteenth century, when several reformist leaders initiated a modernization drive in the press, new system schools, and political activities.

5. The first playwright in Azerbaijan was Mirza Fathali Akhundov (1818–1878), who wrote six comedies between 1850 and 1855 in Turki (Turkic) language. Between the 1850s and the 1910s, many plays were written and staged in Baku (Azerbaijan), Simferopol (Crimea), and Kazan (Volga-Ural region). The first Central Asian play, *Padarkush* (Patricide), was written in 1911, published in 1913, and staged in 1914. See Allworth 1964a, 1964b, esp. 214–235.

6. See also Popova 1949.

7. For other works related to this subject see Komatsu and Dudoignon 2003. For the Reformist press, see Usmanova 1996 and 1998.

8. I learned some of the details of Rana's life through interviewing her husband, Raci; see Kocaoglu 1987.

9. Shefika Gaspirinskaya ("Gaspirali" in Turkish) left Crimea for Azerbaijan with her husband, Nasip Yusufbeyli, an Azerbaijani politician, after the closing of her father's newspaper *Terjuman* on February 10, 1918, during the invasion of Crimea by the Red Army. When her husband was killed by the invading Red Army in Baku in early May 1920, Shefika also could not stay any longer in Azerbaijan, and with the help

of Turkish diplomats who provided her and her children Ottoman passports, Shefika was able to go to Istanbul and spend the rest of her life in Turkey until her death on August 31, 1975, in Ankara (Hablemitoglu and Hablemitoglu 1998, 274–290).

10. After the death of Ismail Gaspirinski in 1914, his son become the editor in chief of the paper.

11. For a list of periodicals in Muslim Central Eurasia, see Bennigsen and Lemercier-Quelquejay 1964.

12. The main source for the Jadid activities in Bukhara is the work written in Uzbek by the prominent Bukharan reformist intellectual Sadriddin Ayni (1878–1954), who later became the cultural godfather of Tajikistan during the Soviet period: "Bukhara Inqilabi Tarikhi Uchun Materiallar" ("Materials for the history of Bukharan revolution"), composed first in 1922 and later published in the first volume of multivolume works of Ayni. See Ayni 1963.

13. The original name of the organization is Bukhara Ta'mim-Ma'arif Jemiyet-i Hayriyyesi. The text and its English translation, along with the facsimile of the original source, are given in Kocaoglu 2001, 36, 469–483.

14. Osman Khodja served as the president of the Bukhara People's Conciliar Republic from September 23, 1921, to April 10, 1922, when he left Bukhara for Afghanistan. In a recent academic work, it is incorrectly stated that "Faizulla Xo'jaev . . . was the president of the Bukharan People's Republic (BPR)" (Kamp 2006, 64). The same source also states that Faizulla Xo'jaev "at age twenty-four, became president" of the republic in 1920. Actually, Faizulla Xo'jaev was the prime minister of the republic; see Kocaoglu 1973, 156.

15. The other Bukharan students who stayed on in Germany and Turkey served in universities and other institutions there, leading long and productive lives. A Uzbek scholar published a very valuable book about the lives of students who once were sent to Berlin from Tashkent and the Bukharan Republic. See Turdiyev 1991.

16. For the English translation of the play, see Allworth 1986.

17. This poem was published in Cholpan 1922, 58–60. It is also mentioned in the Allworth 1990, 186, but without giving the text, translation, or the main content of the poem.

18. For this and other resolutions, see the attached facsimile of the original documents in Arabic script.

19. The printed texts of all the constitutions in original Turkic languages and Russian are in the personal archives of the author.

20. The forceful Soviet campaigns and the death of thousands of people as a result were detailed in Massell 1974; Northrop 2004; Kamp 2006.

21. Majnun is the name of the young man who is madly in love with his darling "Layla"

(or "Leila/Leyla") in the most popular classical Middle Eastern love story (Layla and Majnun) in Arabic, Persian, and Turkish literatures. When Layla was married to another person by her father's will, Majnun loses his conscious and retreats to a desert composing songs for his love.

22. Murtaza Qarsiboev, "Cholpanning jinoiy ishi," *San'at*, no. 8 (1990): 8–11, cited in Kara 2002, 140 n.8.

WORKS CITED

Acar, Feride, and Ayse Güneş-Ayata, eds. 2000. *Gender and Identity Construction: Women of Central Asia, the Caucasus and Turkey*. Leiden: Brill.

Akiner, Shirin. 1997. "Between Tradition and Modernity: The Dilemma Facing Contemporary Central Asian Women." In *Post-Soviet Women: From the Baltic to Central Asia*, ed. Mary Buckley, 261–304. Cambridge: Cambridge University Press.

Alimova, Dilarom. 1987. *Zhenskii vopros v srednei Azii: Istoriia izucheniia i sovremmennye problemy* (The woman question in Central Asia: the history of studies and contemporary problems). Tashkent: Fan.

———. 1998. "A Historian's Vision of 'Khudjum.'" 17(1): 147–155.

Alimova, Dilarom, and Nodira Azimova. 2000. "Women's Position in Uzbekistan Before and After Independence." In *Gender and Identity Construction: Women of Central Asia, the Caucasus and Turkey*, ed. Feride Acar and Ayse Güneş-Ayata, 293–304. Leiden: Brill.

Allworth, Edward. 1964a. "The Beginnings of the Modern Turkistanian Theater." *Slavic Review* 22(4) (December): 676–687.

———. 1964b. *Uzbek Literary Politics*. New York: Columbia University Publications.

———. 1967. *Central Asia: A Century of Russian Rule*. New York: Columbia University Press.

———, ed. 1973. *The Nationality Question in Soviet Central Asia*. New York: Praeger.

———. 1986. "Murder as Metaphor in the First Central Asian Drama." *Ural-Altaische Jahrbücher/Ural-Altaic Yearbook* 58: 65–97.

———. 1990. *The Modern Uzbeks: From the Fourteenth Century to the Present. A Cultural History*. Stanford, Calif.: Hoover Institution Press.

———, ed. 1994. *Central Asia, 130 years of Russian Dominance: A Historical Overview*. Durham, N.C.: Duke University Press.

Aminova, Rakhima. 1977. *The October Revolution and Women's Liberation in Uzbekistan*. Moscow: Nauka.

Avloni, Abdulla. 1998. "Oila Munozarasi" *Tanlangan Asarlar*, 14. Tashkent: Ghafur Gulam.

Ayni, Sadriddin. 1963. "Bukhara Inqilabi Tarikhi Uchun Materiallar" (Materials for the history of Bukharan revolution). In *Asarlar*, 1: 3–260. Tashkent: OzSSR Davlat Badiiy Nashriyati.

Bennigsen, Alexandre, and Chantal Lemercier-Quelquejay. 1964. *1920*. Paris: Mouton.

———. 1967. *Islam in the Soviet Union*. New York: Praeger.

Brower, Daniel R., and Edward J. Lazzerini, eds. 1997. *Russia's Orient: Imperial Borderlands and Peoples, 1700–1917*. Bloomington: Indiana University Press.

Clements, Barbara Evans. 1979. *Bolshevik Feminist: The Life of Aleksandra Kollontai*. Bloomington: Indiana University Press.

Clements, Barbara Evans, Barbara Alpern Engel, and Christine D. Worobec. 1991. *Russia's Women: Accommodation, Resistance, Transformation*. Berkeley: University of California Press.

Cholpan. 1922. *Cholpan, Batu, Elbek, Ozbek Yash Shairlari*. Tashkent: Turkistan Davlat Nashriyati.

d'Encausse, Héléne Carrère. 1988. *Islam and the Russian Empire: Reform and Revolution in Central Asia*. Trans. Quintin Hoare. Berkeley: University of California Press (French original: *Reforme et revolution chez les Musulmans de l'empire russ*. Paris: Presses de la Foundation nationale des Sciences Politiques, 1966).

Edmondson, Linda Harriet. 1984. *Feminism in Russia, 1900–17*. Stanford, Calif.: Stanford University Press.

———. 1992. *Women and Society in Russia and the Soviet Union*. Cambridge: Cambridge University Press.

———. 2001. *Gender in Russian History and Culture*. New York: Palgrave.

Eshimov, F. 1968. "Romanda Konflict va Kharakter." *Ozbek tili va adabiyati*, no. 1: 28–34.

Hablemitoglu, Necip. 2004 *Çarlık Rusyasında Türk Kongreleri*. Istanbul: Toplumsal Dönüşüm Yayınları.

Hablemitoglu, Necip, and Şengül Hablemitoglu. 1998. *Şefika Gaspıralı ve Rusyada Türk Kadın Hareketi (1893–1920)*. Ankara: n.p.

Heyat, Farideh. 2002. *Azeri Women in Transition*. London: Routledge Curzon.

———. 2005. *Azeri Women in Transition*. Baku: Chasioghlu.

Kamp, Marianne. 2006. *The New Woman in Uzbekistan: Islam, Modernity, and Unveiling under Communism*. Seattle: University of Washington Press.

Kara, Halim. 2002. "Reclaiming National Literary Heritage: The Rehabilitation of Abdurauf Fitrat and Abdulhamid Sulaymon Cholpan in Uzbekistan." *Europe-Asia Studies* 54(1) (January): 123–142.

Khalid, Adeeb. 1998. *The Politics of Muslim Cultural Reform: Jadidism in Central Asia*. Berkeley: University of California Press.

———. 2007. *Islam after Communism: Religion and Politics in Central Asia*. Berkeley: University of California Press.

Kocaoglu, Timur. 1973. "The Existence of a Bukharan Nationality in the Recent Past." In
    The Nationality Question in Soviet Central Asia, ed. Edward Allworth, 151–158. New
    York: Praeger.

————. 1982. "Nationality Identity in Soviet Central Asian Literature: Kazakh and Uzbek
    Prose Fiction of the Post-Stalin Period." Ph.D. diss., Columbia University.

————. 1987. "Türkistan'da Türk Subayları." *Türk Dünyası Tarih Dergisi* [Istanbul] 1–11
    (various pages in each issue).

————. 2001. *Reform Movements and Revolutions in Turkistan.* Haarlem, Netherlands:
    SOTA.

Komatsu, Hisao, and Stéphane A. Dudoignon. 2003. Central Eurasian Studies (18th–20th
    Centuries): A Selective and Critical Bibliography of Works Published between 1985
    and 2000. Tokyo: Toyo Bunko.

Lapidus, Gail Warshofsky. 1978. *Women in Soviet Society: Equality, Development, and Social
    Change.* Berkeley: University of California Press.

Lazzerini, Edward. 1973. "Ismail Bey Gaspirinskii and Muslim Modernism in Russia,
    1878–1914." Ph.D. diss., University of Washington.

Lenin, V. I. 1974. *On the Emancipation of Women.* Moscow: Progress Publishers.

————. 1984. *The Emancipation of Women: From the Writings of V. I. Lenin.* New York:
    International Publishers.

Massel, Gregory. 1974. *The Surrogate Proletariat: Moslem Women and Revolutionary Strategies
    in Soviet Central Asia, 1917–1929.* Princeton, N.J.: Princeton University Press.

McDermid, Jane, and Anne Hillyar. 1998. *Women and Work in Russia, 1880–1930: A Study
    in Continuity through Change.* New York: Longman.

Noack, Christian. 2000. *Muslimischer Nationalismus im Russischen Reich. Nationsbildung
    und Nationalbewegung bei Tataren und Baschkiren, 1861–1917.* Stuttgart: Franz Steiner
    Verlag.

Northrop, Douglas. 2004. *Veiled Empire: Gender and Power in Stalinist Central Asia.* Ithaca,
    N.Y.: Cornell University Press.

Popova, Nina. 1949. *Women in the Land of Socialism.* Moscow: Foreign Languages Publishing
    House.

Pushkareva, Natalia. 1997. *Women in Russian History: From the Tenth to the Twentieth Century.*
    Armonk, N.Y.: M. E. Sharpe.

Rashidov, Sharaf. 1958. *The Victors.* Moscow: Foreign Languages Publishing House.

Roy, Olivier. 2000. *The New Central Asia: The Creation of Nations.* New York: New York
    University Press.

————. 2007. *The New Central Asia: Geopolitics and the Birth of Nations.* New York: New York
    University Press.

Ruthchild, Rochelle Goldberg. 1993. *Women in Russia and the Soviet Union: An Annotated*

Bibliography. New York: G. K. Hall.

Stites, Richard. 1978. *Women's Liberation Movement in Russia: Feminism, Nihilism, and Bolshevism, 1860–1930.* Princeton, N.J.: Princeton University Press.

Turdiev, Sherali 1991. *Ular Germaniyada Oqighan Edilar.* Tashkent: Ozbekistan Respublikasi Fanlar Akademiyasi Fan Nashriyati.

Usmanova, Dilara M. 1996. "Die tatarische Presse 1905–1918: Quellen, Entwicklungsetappen und quantitative Analyse" (The tatar press, 1905–1918: sources, development stages and quantitative analysis). In *Muslim Culture in Russia and Central Asia from the 18th to the Early 20th Centuries,* ed. Michael Kemper, Anke von Kügelgen, and Dmitriy Yermakov, 239–278. Berlin: Klaus Schwarz Verlag.

———. 1998. "The Activity of the Muslim Faction of the State Duma and Its Significance in the Formation of a Political Culture among the Muslim Peoples of Russia (1906–1917)." In *Muslim Culture in Russia and Central Asia from the 18th to the Early 20th Centuries,* ed. Anke von Kügelgen, Michael Kemper, and Allen J. Frank, 417–456. Berlin: Klaus Scwarz Verlag.

———. 1999. *Musul'manskaia fraktsiia i problemy "svobody soveti" v Gosudarstvennoi Dume Rossii (1906–1917)* (The Muslim fraction and the problem of the "free Soviets" in the Russian State Duma (1906–1917). Kazan: Izdatel'stvo "Master Layn."

Yedlin, Tova 1980. *Women in Eastern Europe and the Soviet Union.* New York: Praeger.

Yemelyanova, Galina M. 2002. *Russia and Islam: An Historical Survey.* New York: Palgrave.

Yemelyanova, Yelena. 1985. *Revolution in Women's Life.* Moscow: Novosti Press Agency Publishing House (English translation of *Revolutsiia, partiia, zhenshchina*).

7

Gender Politics in Transitional Societies: A Comparative Perspective on Azerbaijan, Kazakhstan, Kyrgyzstan, and Uzbekistan

Ayşe Güneş-Ayata and Ayça Ergun

For over a decade, the successor states of the Soviet Union have been experiencing an ongoing social, economic, and political transformation. The transition to democracy, building new states and almost new nations, and the shift to a market economy have resulted in radical changes in every aspect of social life. Moreover, the fact that the previous regimes continue to have considerable impacts on the definition of state-society relations constitutes yet another burden for post-Soviet states, since the Soviet heritage is competing with new policies of liberalization and democratization. For example, one can observe authoritarian and semiauthoritarian tendencies in the current governing elite, persistence of nomenclatura-type administrative structures, and shortcomings in the process of democratization. Both state-building and nation-building processes remain incomplete, and there are other problems associated with the shift to a market economy and privatization. Poverty, unemployment, and the loss of reliable foundations for a social security system have been the main challenges for societal development. However, the collapse of the Soviet Union has had different impacts on each of the states concerned, leading to differing outcomes in the various regions and countries.

In the context of these challenges, the gender dimension of the post-Soviet transformation has been mostly neglected and often undertheorized by students of transition and democratization. However, the simultaneous changes taking place at the social, political, and economic levels have paved the way for the emergence of new gender problems, including the redefinition of male and female roles in both the public and private spheres, the exclusion of women from economic and political life, and a search for alternative life strategies for women.

Along with other authors in this volume, we argue that gender as a unit of analysis should be integrated into the study of post-Soviet transition in order to establish a better understanding of the process of democratization. De jure gender equalities were part of the Soviet system since its foundation. This should be considered as a very important advantage for establishing gender equity in the newly independent states. However, as with many of the other "equalities" of the old regime, gender relations had two problems. First, the legal framework was not fully implemented, so there were deficiencies in achieving gender equality, leading to some major de facto inequalities between men and women. Second, Soviet notions of equality failed to correspond to emerging international norms of the late twentieth century. There have been concerted efforts to address these two problems in all transition countries in the last two decades. These efforts have included attempts to integrate gender into policy decisions in the light of emerging norms.

Therefore, gender appears to be a new issue for the post-Soviet transition agenda. Despite the fact that the gender dimension has increasingly become an integral part of the democratization agenda and has been addressed both by state officials and civil societal actors, old cultural and social traits neglecting and/or undermining gender equality are still widespread in these countries. This shows that Soviet policies initiated and implemented to solve the "women problem" did not prove to be fully successful (Werner 2004, 65; Kamp 2005, 405). The assumption that gender equality was achieved under Soviet rule seems invalid, as inclusion of women in the economic and political sectors did not necessarily result in women's empowerment and emancipation. More important, it did not result in the elimination of a gender-biased understanding of women's roles and identities in any of theses states.

A new framework for gender equality has been introduced by the international community to the countries in transition. As a result of guidance, advice, and training provided by international governmental and nongovernmental organizations (NGOs), gender as a theme, as a priority issue, and as an integral part of democracy building has already partly been incorporated into new institution building, policy making, and activities of civil society organizations in Central Asia and the Southern Caucasus. Numerous projects have been initiated by international organizations and implemented by both states and local NGOs. Significant amounts of funding have been allocated in order to increase gender awareness and create sensitivity to women's problems.

In this chapter, we discuss the social, political, and economic aspects of gender problems in four republics of the former Soviet Union, namely Azerbaijan, Uzbekistan, Kyrgyzstan, and Kazakhstan. All of these have significant Muslim majorities and a Turkic population, and all have experienced significant problems of national identity formation and state building in the last fifteen years.

A comparative analysis of the status of women in these cases shows that patriarchy is still dominant in Central Asia and Azerbaijan, and perceptions about male and female roles are still gender biased and informed by cultural patterns. Women are seen to predominantly belong to private spheres, their roles as mothers and wives are often prioritized, and they often face discrimination in social, political, and economic spheres. Moreover, traditional gender roles seem to be highly internalized and reproduced by both men and women.

In this chapter, we argue that despite the similarities of post-Soviet countries' experiences after independence and also due to a shared past, which includes the period before the Soviet Union, there are still significant differences. We conclude that these differences can be traced back not only to their history but also to their economic and social development. In this comparison, we argue the countries of this region can be divided into two groups: first, Azerbaijan and Uzbekistan, where women and gender issues constitute a core identity problem reflecting the desire to move away from both the West and their Soviet past; and second, Kazakhstan and Kyrgyzstan, where gender identity is a secondary issue, more important as an ethnic concern as opposed to a national identity, and one that is certainly not anti-Soviet and anti-West.

In the first part of the chapter, we briefly discuss the status of women in the Soviet period in order to explore the extent of continuity and change in the status of women in the post-Soviet period. We also examine changes in the perceptions about male and female roles and the significance of cultural patterns in defining gender relations. In the second part, we analyze the post-Soviet nation-building process and show how new perceptions of national identity pave the way for the preservation of gender-biased approaches to the status of women. In the final part of the chapter, we focus on the representation of gender at both the state and civil society levels; the outcome of institutional arrangements, such as state policies to achieve gender equality; and the local NGOs' initiatives to address gender issues. The role of the international community will also be addressed both in introducing and "teaching" gender to state and civil societal actors and in shaping the state's policies and local NGOs' activities in gender equality promotion.

This chapter is based upon research undertaken during frequent visits to the region starting in 1993, backed up by statistics and secondary literature.

Numerous interviews were conducted during these visits, discussing gender issues with gender experts, representatives of NGOs, members of the national machinery, members of international organizations, politicians, and representatives of the media.

Women Under Soviet Rule

The Soviet Union was certainly a country of de jure equality between men and women. How much this was reflected in the actual lives of women and men varied from state to state, as well as between social groups. Although there were formal equality policies to ensure women's participation in public life, some authors are rather skeptical about the extent to which Soviet policies actually achieved women's integration. Marianne Kamp argues that the socialist system was not able to "eradicate women's double burden" (both working in the labor force and doing housework) and was unsuccessful in ensuring women's political representation in administrative positions (2005, 405). Cynthia Werner similarly points out the double burden of Soviet women, arguing that Soviet policies had little impact in transforming gender relations (2004, 65). Recent surveys conducted by international organizations similarly show that gender relations, role models, and perceptions about masculinity and femininity are still partly informed by the cultural patterns that were highly preserved under Soviet rule (Paci 2002; see also Asian Development Bank 2005a, 2005b, 2005c, 2006a). Despite the fact that most people in Central Asia were accustomed to women's participation in economic and political life during the Soviet period, women's work today is approved of only if it is necessary. The man is considered to be the main breadwinner in the family, and politics is seen as a male domain by the majority of both men and women.[1] However, one cannot deny the social and economic benefits the Soviet system provided to women, such as education, participation in the labor force, and political representation through a quota system that increased women's participation in public life. In politics, there was an imposed 30% quota for women. Even though in many positions women's presence was symbolic, if not tokenistic, there was significant encouragement for women to participate in the public sphere and take up positions of authority.

Educational attainment is a key factor in ensuring women's empowerment in public life. The Soviet Union successfully ensured the right to education for all. More important, this right was cemented through equal access to education for both boys and girls even in the remotest parts of the Soviet Union. Education was considered the main tool to create "true Soviet citizens," since it facilitated the legitimization of the political regime and served as a tool of propaganda. Uniformity in the curriculum, along with Russian-language classes (also education in the Russian language), created homogeneity at all levels of education throughout the Soviet Union. Almost everywhere illiteracy was minimal. Not only was education universally available and free, it was obligatory. This meant that girls did not and would not face significant discrimination.

Everybody had, in principle, the right to work, and there were state provisions for employment and full social security, including health care. In fact, even though there were variations between the republics of the Soviet Union, in general there was a high level of participation in the labor force by women. Free preschool day care and monthly subsidies for children facilitated keeping women in the workforce. However, the Soviet system did very little to lift the double burden of women. While encouraging (and in some cases pressuring) women to participate in the labor force, the system did not necessarily contribute to reducing women's domestic burdens. Being less of a consumer society than the West, there was little potential to own time-saving domestic devices; men were not specifically encouraged to take over some of the household responsibilities; and domestic help was available to only a few members of the Politburo. As there was little attention paid to the domestic division of labor, intrafamily inequalities survived despite a strong emphasis on the equalities in the public sphere by the state. In fact, this enduring family tradition in the Muslim states of the Soviet Union facilitated the revival of traditional gender roles in the transition period.

The Soviet system, especially in republics with Muslim populations, controlled some of the activities of its citizens and communities in both the workplace and at home. Political opposition and Islamic rituals, for example, were suppressed. Similarly, excessive oppression of women by the community was strongly overseen. In our visits to the region, many feminists told us that they remember the Soviet era as a time when the Communist Party kept an eye on the "fair" treatment of women in the home. Some NGO activists of the post-Soviet period recall Soviet times and argue that men could not dare to commit domestic violence since they were afraid of "being punished" by the local party branch.[2] Frequently they would say domestic violence would have been condemned, not sending girls to school would have been impossible, and divorces would have been settled to the benefit of women, imposing obligatory financial duties on men for the care of their children. In many ways, this was an imposed modernization, where the Soviet ideology was considered as progressive, rational, and modern. In the same period, the Soviets conducted a very successful battle toward eradicating polygamy, bride price, underage marriage, and girls dropping out of school (Werner 2004, 65).

At different points in time, the Soviets had pronatalist policies encouraging childbirth by giving significant child benefits (Kamp 2004, 37). However, such policies did not necessarily reduce women's burdens in the home. Men, especially in Muslim communities, saw this encouragement of women's participation in the labor force as a threat to their patriarchal community structure and values. The ideology of Soviet gender equality led to "life choices" for both women and men. Therefore, this system can be also perceived as overburdening women's self-actualization so that it would be possible only through public achievement. In this respect, the fall of the Soviet Union changed some of the basic features of this de jure equality of women in the public sphere.

Gender and Nation-State Building in the Post-Soviet Period

Post-Soviet states are still "nations in the making" and "nationalizing states" as well as states in the making (Brubaker 1996, 9). Some authors argue that the Soviet policy toward the titular nationalities defined the current boundaries of identity formation (Brubaker 1996; Suny 1990; Saroyan 1989; Lapidus et al. 1992). Instead of eliminating national affiliations, Soviet nationality policy unconsciously created and consolidated ethnicity and fostered a "growing cohesion among the major nationalities" (Suny 1990, 6). That policy provided the "reconstruction of [an] ethnic identity that embraces the nation as a whole" (Saroyan 1989, 150). In the post-Soviet period, the emergent nation-states made specific efforts to distinguish themselves from one another and to distance themselves from the Soviet past in three areas: the introduction of a market economy, pressures for the democratization of society, and cultural specificity.

The challenge of building a nation-state varied across the region. Those countries with no clear sense of national identity had to generate new ideas about the meanings of the nation-state and citizenship, while others had an easier path toward self-identification. The main task of all of these countries was the construction of a national identity that was an alternative to that produced by the policies of Sovietization and Russification.[3] The Soviet myth of the "creation of the Soviet man" regardless of ethnicity and religion has been replaced by the construction of a national identity that is respectful of both. In this respect, what is referred to as nation building is a process in which the boundaries of the "national" have been redrawn, and the content of "being national" has been rediscovered and redefined and in some sense reformulated in accordance with new ideas of independence and sovereignty. The process of new nation building was informed by overcoming the Soviet heritage; the emergence of nationalizing elites, particularly in cases where there were nationalist independence movements; and the "rediscovery" of cultural, social, political, and national origins. It is a process that has involved the "re-examination of the past; invention of tradition, [the] validation of present national territorial claims and [the] re-installment of 'traditional' social, cultural and ethnic values as the basis of new state ideologies" (Akiner 1997, 363). As can be deduced from the above discussion, the presence or absence of different ethnic groups within one country made significant differences. The attitude of the new regime toward Soviet and/or Russian policies was influenced by the way the regime was perceived in each country by the majority and by minorities that composed a significant proportion of the population. Because the Slavic/Russian and Christian minorities were a significant proportion of the population, accommodation of these minorities into the regime was important in distancing the regime from its Soviet past.

All these processes have significant impacts on gender. Nira Yuval-Davis (1997) has argued that in the process of redefining nationhood and national identity, women were conceived as the main agents of transmitting national values, as "mothers" of the new "nations-in-making." Reconsolidation of traditional gender roles became a part of the new national identity and was incorporated into the national mentality, particularly in Azerbaijan and Uzbekistan. A strong emphasis on customs and traditions, which define women's roles and identities in the private rather than the public sphere, has replaced de jure equality between men and women achieved under Soviet rule. Problems associated with the transition period—namely the high level of unemployment, the demolition of social security and support systems for working women, and the migration of mainly male members of families—also facilitated the reaffirmation of women's roles as mothers and wives. Thus, in the post-Soviet nation-building process, women found themselves in a disadvantaged position both in private and public life.

Gender and Ethnic Composition

In the post-Soviet period, one of the important factors that contributed to the consolidation of national identity of the majority population (that is, Muslim and Turkic) and the emphasis on cultural specificity is the extent of migration of Christian/Slavic minorities in each of the four republics. According to the final census of the Soviet Union (1989), Russians and Armenians constituted around 12% of the Azerbaijani population.[4] As of 2004, these groups only constituted 3.3% of the entire population due to the emigration of Russians and the Karabagh conflict between Armenia and Azerbaijan (*Statistical Yearbook of Azerbaijan* 2004). The remaining Christian population now mostly consists of intermarried people and the elderly. In the case of Uzbekistan, there were only 8% Russians before independence, and this decreased to 5.5% after the disintegration of the Soviet Union.

Among the ex-Soviet republics, Kazakhstan represents a distinct case in terms of the demographic composition of its ethnic groups. According to the 1989 census, ethnic Kazakhs constituted approximately 40% of the population, Russians constituted 37.8%, and Ukrainians constituted 5.4%. After the collapse of the Soviet Union, ethnic Kazakhs remained the dominant majority, constituting 53.4% of the population, whereas the total percentage of the Slavic population (Russians and Ukrainians) decreased to 33.7% (Alekseenko 2001). Before the collapse, Russians and Ukrainians constituted almost 25% of Kyrgyzstan's population, whereas the ethnic Kyrgyz population was around 52%. The total percentage of Russians and Ukrainians decreased to 13.5%, whereas the ethnic Kyrgyzs became the dominant majority in the republics, with 64.9%.[5] So after the disintegration we see that two of the countries (Azerbaijan and Uzbekistan) became significantly homogeneous in terms of religion and ethnicity, with the percentage of the Russian population at less than 5%. However, the two others had higher Russian/Slavic populations, and so the Kyrgyzs and Kazakhs could not overwhelmingly dominate the country without significant contributions from the other ethnic groups. As the population figures indicate, this was a more serious problem in Kazakhstan in comparison to the other countries. As it will be argued here, the ethnic composition of these countries had a direct impact not only on their nation-building processes but also on their gender policies.

Problems of Transition and Their Impact on Gender

Economic changes during the transition have received substantial attention in the literature. The introduction of the market economy had enormous impacts on daily lives, including on employment structure and living standards. These changes have had different impacts on rural and urban areas and on different communities and gender groups.

Women in the rural areas have not benefited equally from the shift to private farms. In countries like Uzbekistan, where the rural population is larger, the impact of privatization on women was more visible. Under the Soviet regime, there was a tradition of unpaid family labor of women; for example, in 1980 "only 46.3% of women were employed compared to the national average of 84.9% in the Soviet Union" (Marnie and Micklewright 1992),[6] and women were not given their share of jobs through the process of transition. Similar experiences are cited in Azerbaijan and other states of Central Asia with similar consequences. In all these countries, wage gaps between earnings of men and women are significant. The gap is 22.3% in Azerbaijan, 38.3% in Kazakhstan, and 35.1% in Kyrgyzstan (see Asian Development Bank 2006a, 9).

The post-Soviet transformation led to massive unemployment. This was a new experience for the whole region. Women suffered more than men. This is most striking in Azerbaijan, where the female unemployment rate is 40.5% in comparison to 16.4% for males. The respective figures for Kazakhstan are 10.8% and 8.8%, and they are 14.3% and 11.2% in Kyrgyzstan (see Asian Development Bank 2006a, 9). The social security systems were demolished, and support systems for working women suffered. For example, day-care centers were closed or became unaffordable. Monthly subsidies for children were no longer sufficient (Kamp 2004, 38–39). The breakup of the social security system also led to a triple burden on women, who then had to substitute for the state security system as caretakers for the elderly and children as well as functioning as crisis managers.

Women as well as men were de-skilled in the transition. This led to job losses or underemployment as people were forced to take jobs that paid less and that had much lower status. As a result, both women and men found themselves in poverty. There were not many new employment opportunities for women, and only a limited few could find work in middle-class positions, such as private businesses, international companies, and NGOs. The majority became petty traders and day laborers. Those who were in the minority and found good jobs, particularly young women, were often said to have those positions due to their physical beauty and Western outlooks as well as their knowledge of English (see Azerbaijan Human Development Report 2007). For other young women in the labor market, temporary work was the only option. This made them vulnerable to all kinds of abuse, including trafficking. Migration is also a new phenomenon in the region. Even though most of the migrants are men, there are also female migrants. In either case, this leaves families separated and leads to all kinds of social problems.

Despite the problems stated above, a significant number of women are employed in some sectors of the economy. Even though the number of men employed in administrative positions is increasing, the remnants of the Soviet structure still continue in other occupations. Women are dominant among teachers and doctors, as these occupations are seen as part-time and compatible with family life. For instance, in Kazakhstan, 74.2% of education sector employees and 80% of health sector workers are women, whereas men tend to occupy secure, high-prestige jobs in government or to engage in business (Asian Development Bank 2006b). Similar figures can be found for all four countries.

Economic burdens experienced in the post-Soviet period resulted in the reconsolidation of the traditional gender roles. Women who used to have job security in the Soviet period have faced the problem of unemployment and/or low level of income. They not only have to generate income but also have to fulfill their household chores. Moreover, male unemployment challenges the men's role as "breadwinner" as well as their status as "head of the household," which in turn threatens traditional authority patterns within the family (see Azerbaijan Human Development Report 2007). This may result in increasing problems within the family, including domestic violence, divorce, and migration. Thus, the post-Soviet economic transition and the shift to a market economy triggered women's problems and increased gender inequalities.

Another very important impact of the transition has been on demographic structure. The four countries had different experiences in terms of their population structures. From the beginning, the percentage of people living in rural areas was higher in Uzbekistan (64%) and in Kyrgyzstan (62%) than in Azerbaijan (45%) and Kazakhstan (44%). So it is not surprising that in Uzbekistan and Kyrgyzstan, community control and pressure on the individual to adhere to the traditional roles will be stronger because of the prominence of closed rural communities.

The transition also led to changes in life expectancy at birth. Whereas changes of life expectancy in Kyrgyzstan and Kazakhstan were very significant (an increase of about four years), there was a much smaller increase (on average, one year) in Azerbaijan and Uzbekistan between 1989 and 1999. Currently, in Kazakhstan and Kyrgyzstan, the difference between the male and female life expectancies is ten and nine years, respectively, whereas in Azerbaijan it was seven years as of 1999 and in Uzbekistan four years as of 1990.[7]

In the transition period, the fertility rate in all these countries is also falling. However, the divorce rate, the number of children born out of wedlock, and the abortion rate differ considerably. In Kazakhstan, 27% of marriages ended in divorce in 1989. In 1999, it was 29.8%. In Kyrgyzstan, the figures were 19.7 %

and 24.2%, respectively. In contrast, there has been a drop in the divorce rate in Azerbaijan (15.9% to 13.4%) and a much sharper drop in Uzbekistan (14.9% to 5.9%) in the same period. Parallel with these figures, we see that in Kyrgyzstan, the percentage of children born out of wedlock increased from 12.7% in 1989 to 27.4% in 1999 and to 32.7% in 2002. There has been a similar increase in Kazakhstan, whereas the increase has been comparatively marginal in Uzbekistan and Azerbaijan. Abortion had been used as a means of birth control in the Soviet Union, and so the rates of abortion are high in these countries in general, but in Uzbekistan we have seen significant drops in pregnancies ending with abortion during the transition.

Education, as we suggested earlier, is a very important indicator of the emerging gender problems in Central Asia and Azerbaijan. Education, previously free, has become costly in the transition period, especially given the fact that private education became the preferred option, and school expenses had to be covered by the families. This pushed some poor families into situations where they had to choose which children to educate, sometimes leading to female students dropping out.

In almost none of the countries is there a gender discrepancy in enrollment at the level of basic education. However, in secondary and tertiary education, we see that there are emerging gendered trends. In Azerbaijan, Kyrgyzstan, and Kazakhstan, there is a slight tendency for girls to be attending schools at higher rates than boys. However, in Uzbekistan, there has been a dramatic increase in the rate of dropouts in the education system as a whole, and by secondary school, there is already an increase in the number of girls dropping out. This trend continues in higher education. In 2003, according to the State Statistical Committee of Uzbekistan, the share of female students in tertiary education was 38.8%. In Kazakhstan, there has been a tendency toward another extreme. Boys have higher dropout rates in secondary education (usually because they have to help their families as labor or income providers). At the tertiary level, the ratio of boys to girls has been 1:1.30 since 1995 (Paci 2002). This raises significant questions about the value of education and the commitment of boys to the education system.

In all of these countries, there have been dramatic political changes during the transition. After gender quotas were abolished, there were dramatic drops in female political representation. None of these states have deep-rooted democratic traditions; all have lived under the authoritarian rule of the former Soviet *nomenklatura*. The new ruling elites see little problem in women dropping out of public life. On the contrary, most see this as an opportunity to satisfy their new male supporters. Although women's roles in politics have decreased, as will be discussed in the coming section, women have been active through civil society and have received significant support from the international community.

In short, despite many similarities in the impacts of transition in the afore-mentioned countries, there are some divergences. The divergences are in the dimensions of society that are related to family, patriarchy, gender stereotypes, and the characteristics that may lead to the strengthening of gender roles. For example, declining divorce rates, increasing numbers of school dropouts, the concentration of women in stereotypically female jobs, the reinstatement of patriarchy in agriculture, rising female unemployment, and low female labor force participation are more serious problems in Azerbaijan and Uzbekistan. In Kazakhstan and Kyrgyzstan, these trends are either less significant or more localized in particular ethnic groups.

Globalization and International Influences on Gender Equality

The process of new state building in Eurasia required institution building and policy making for liberalization and democratization. Moreover, the post-Soviet states had to find a space for themselves in the international community. Their will to be integrated into the Western world necessitated becoming members of international and regional organizations, as well as the ratification of international treaties. These countries were required to act in accordance with international norms and comply with internationally recognized values, such as democratization, respect for human rights, and gender equality. By the 1990s, women's rights were incorporated deeply in human rights norms, thereby becoming a yardstick for a country's prestige in the international community. To provide a thorough analysis of gender politics in post-Soviet countries, recent trends of globalization must to be taken into account. Attitudes of states on the issue of gender equality have not been uniform, even though all of them readily accepted these norms on two grounds. First, they were accustomed to de jure equality in the Soviet period, and they realized this was one of the essentials for international recognition; second, such acceptance was a symbol of their readiness to become an integral part of the West.

As an important step toward integration into the international community, the Convention on the Elimination of All Forms of Discrimination against Women (CEDAW) and its optional protocol were ratified by all the Central Asian and Caucasian states. The importance of CEDAW is multifold. First, it urges states to have a state policy on gender. Second, it monitors the development of gender equality at a national level. Third, it forces governments to have a national machinery on gender. Fourth, it encourages and expects the machinery to be in dialogue with the civil society and to empower the civil society and women's movements. Finally, it is a channel for international funding, particularly from United Nations (UN) bodies but also from other donors. Thus, CEDAW ratification may lead to significant capacity building in the post-Soviet states as well as the establishment of the international norms. Through this process, gender courses have been developed, feminist NGOs established, gender sensitivity introduced to some segments of government and society, and expertise on gender equality enhanced.

Through the process of CEDAW ratification, all Commonwealth of Independent States (CIS) countries established national machineries for gender equality. These are usually political offices under the president or attached to one of the ministries. The national machinery in each state in the region is, in general, constituted of a senior person, a chairwoman, a committee, and a few staff with clout but little political power. There may also be a committee whose members are of similar backgrounds as the chair. The position of chairwoman is seen as highly respectable. Women with significant achievements in their professional life (not necessarily as a gender specialist) and close to the government are appointed. However, the committee has only symbolic power, if any. The staff of the national machinery in all four countries is limited to very few people, including the support staff, some of whom can be gender experts employed on specific projects. In general, the national machineries are understaffed and, except for the salaries paid, have a meager disposable budget, if any at all. This makes them totally dependent on international funding.

The national machinery has no field offices in any of the four countries. Even though the staff realize the problems of women on the periphery, the structure of the machinery and the state bureaucracy limit their activity to the center and policy level only. One very important activity that is carried out by the national machinery in all the countries is to show a presence on important days such as the Eighth of March–International Women's Day and its ceremonies. This ensures high-level visibility and reaffirms the state's commitment to gender equality. For a long time, the national machineries in all these countries were technically supported by United Nations Development Program (UNDP) projects. The UNDP gave funding toward the establishment of the machinery. In most cases, this included office equipment (from computers to desks) and usually a supplementary salary/stipend paid to the chair or to a project leader designated by the chair (usually a woman with a profession that may have a gender connotation such as doctor, teacher, and so forth).

Within the national machinery, the UNDP has held numerous training sessions on gender awareness and international gender norms. Even learning what gender means and distinguishing it from sex have been major achievements. In none of the official languages of the four countries is there a word that can be translated as "gender." Gender experts therefore use the English word, further alienating the concept from ordinary people. The UNDP has also helped to write periodic CEDAW reports, and it has fostered collaboration between the state and NGOs to organize study visits abroad to observe best practices. It has even helped local people to write project proposals for funding. Thus, the UNDP has been the most important catalyst for the advancement of gender equality norms in these four countries. In some countries, this international support continues, whereas in others it is fading away. Kazakhstan and Kyrgyzstan still keep this technical support system, and gender in development units exist in these countries under a variety of names. The main activities of such bureaus have concentrated on specific areas such as enhancing women's participation in public life, particularly in politics, and combating domestic violence. In both of these countries, there have been attempts to pass laws to fight against domestic violence.

In 2006, the Azerbaijani and Uzbek UNDP gender offices were closed down. In both countries, gender issues have been structured under the auspices of the government and related state institutions. Projects by international donors, including the United Nations Development Fund for Women (UNIFEM) and the United Nations Population Fund (UNFPA), are implemented through their project offices and/or through support of NGOs. There may also be cases of support for the national machinery and its projects but not always in the form of new offices that have been established on a permanent basis. In both countries, national machineries have been under political pressure. In Uzbekistan, they have been subject to frequent purges. In 2006, new cadres replaced almost all of the members of the national machinery. In Azerbaijan, such political pressures are also exercised, but these are usually limited to warnings to the committee and to the chair. The national machineries are often only mouthpieces of the state ideology. They have little power and space for initiative in policy making. Interviews conducted with their chairs provide evidence that their influence on policy formulation is limited and that they function only as executors and advocacy agents. They try to make up for their weakness by using the leverage of international norms. In a sense, they become the mediator among state apparatuses, international expectations, and civil society. Moreover, the shortage of funding for such offices and their staff (limited to salaries and travel grants) hinders their capacity for policy implementation. Their relations with the feminist movement, gender experts, and local NGOs are usually conjectural and are guided by the international politics of the country rather than their own choice.

In Central Asia, the Soros Foundation has been very supportive of gender experts. In many countries, it has built the capacity of gender NGOs, trained them in gender studies, organized international conferences, and helped build networks. In some countries, such as Kazakhstan, the foundation gave seed money to establish refuges and hotlines for women facing domestic violence. However, the governments of Kazakhstan and Uzbekistan considered the Soros Foundation to be a threat. As a result, not only was the Soros Foundation's Open Society Institute expelled from these countries, but the NGOs that the institute supported and funded immediately lost their favored status. The situations in Kyrgyzstan and Azerbaijan were different. The chair of the Kyrgyz national machinery was a longtime cabinet minister, and because Kyrgyzstan sought international recognition, there was more stable support for the committee and gender NGOs. The attitude of the Azerbaijani government toward the activities of international NGOs is quite positive. NGOs are not subject to open critique by the existing government since gender-related issues are not considered as "threatening the stability" of the country.

These four countries have seen some improvements in gender equality since independence. Azerbaijan has passed a gender equality law, whereas Uzbekistan implements a gender quota in politics. Kyrgyzstan has a Presidential Decree on the Improvement of Gender Policy and a special representative of the president on gender development in the parliament. Kazakhstan has adopted a Gender Action Plan. In all these countries, in comparison to the 1980s, there is, by far, greater gender awareness; the number of gender experts has increased; and studies on gender equality are more common. Through international projects, a significant number of academics, media professionals, and politicians, as well as members of NGOs, have been trained about gender equality. In this respect, the international community contributed significantly to the creation of gender awareness in the post-Soviet countries.

Civil Society and Gender Equality

In terms of civil society development in Eurasia, starting in the mid-1990s one can witness a growing number of NGOs throughout the region, headed by a professionalized NGO elite who had acquired the necessary skills to engage in civil societal activity. However, Western-style civil society organizations are rarely found in the region not only because there is the lack of a heritage of inclusion of societal forces in the political transformation and democratization processes but also because local organizations did not have the necessary experience prior to the collapse of the Soviet Union (Ergun 2005a, 105). Numerous international organizations are engaged in supporting local NGO development in the post-Soviet countries through funding, guidance, and training for the realization and implementation of projects. The UN and its related programs—such as the UNDP, UNIFEM, United Nations Children Fund (UNICEF), and UNFPA, as well as the Organization for Security and Co-operation in Europe (OSCE) and the Office for Democratic Institutions and Human Rights (ODIHR), were particularly prominent in the early years of the independence period, when international NGOs were scarcely operating in the region. In this respect, the UN was the first organization to provide guidance and assistance to both state and civil society actors when dealing with the problems of regime change.[8]

Although there were women's organizations in the Soviet period, their activities mainly concentrated on charity rather than the elimination of gender inequality or dealing with women's problems in social, political, and economic spheres. Therefore, the international recognition of gender equality and women's problems has become a concern of local actors and has been "nationalized" only in the postindependence period. Moreover, the recognition of women's problems, combating all forms of discrimination against women, and the necessity for gender sensitivity and awareness have been learned by national civil society activists and incorporated into their agendas.

The increase in the number of local NGOs is a result of the introduction of a civil society dimension as an integral and essential aspect of democratic transformation. It is well known that the numbers do not fully reflect the content and the effectiveness of NGO activities. Most of them are reregistered NGOs formerly affiliated with the Communist Party. Accurate data on the number of NGOs in each country is hard to discover, as the information is either incomplete or outdated. However, estimated numbers can give an idea of the percentage of NGOs engaged in gender- and women-related issues. In Kazakhstan, about 150 out of 4,500 NGOs are involved in feminist activity, "protecting the rights and legal interests of women."[9] Kyrgyzstan has almost the same number as Kazakhstan: 150 out of 3,019 NGOs are women's NGOs.[10] In Azerbaijan, there are 123 women's NGOs out of approximately 3,200 and 68 NGOs "implementing gender-related projects."[11] According to the UNDP *National Human Development Report* (2003), women's NGOs constitute 3.5% of the all NGOs operating in the country. In Uzbekistan, 412 out of 2,300 NGOs deal with women's organizations, and 40 of these were established by women (see Asian Development Bank 2005c). It should also be noted that gender-related activities are quite fashionable among NGOs, and this implies that local NGOs that do not specialize in the protection of women's rights and/or the improvement of the status of women also conduct gender-oriented projects and activities.

Gender and women's organizations in the four countries are engaged in a wide range of activities. A review of the goals declared by the local women's organizations reveals that they aim to improve the social status of women, promote gender equality, protect women's rights, empower women in the public and private spheres, eliminate all kinds of discrimination against women, increase women's participation and representation in politics, raise consciousness and create awareness among women, prevent domestic violence, and provide psychological and medical assistance for victims of domestic violence. In each country, women's organizations have also been established to promote women's participation in economic life, support female entrepreneurs, and foster income-generating activities. A significant number of NGOs are also working with single mothers and mothers with many children. There are projects to protect orphans, to raise awareness of reproductive health, and to provide child care for working mothers. In Kazakhstan and Kyrgyzstan, women's organizations have established umbrella groups to strengthen solidarity and cooperation.[12] Although there is no formal union among Azerbaijani women's organizations, they are in close cooperation.

Women's organizations, like other NGOs in the region, work on a project-by-project basis. The outcome of these projects is usually in the form of reports, publications (including educational and training materials, books, and leaflets), training sessions, monitoring, and the organization of seminars, conferences, roundtables, and workshops. Local NGOs are considered to be important agents for democratic consolidation and gender equality promotion by the international community. International governmental organizations and NGOs not only are the main financial providers for the NGOs in the region but also provide guidance, training, and assistance in the process of learning how to become an NGO and what the relevant themes are in civil societal activity (Ergun 2005b, 324). Funding provided by international organizations has supported efforts to situate gender and women's problems at the center of local civil societies' agendas. As mentioned earlier, international actors have greatly promoted the raising of gender sensitivity and consciousness at both the state and society levels. They have mainly taught local actors what gender is, how gender equality can be promoted, and what tools are available for the elimination of gender inequality. In this respect, it can be argued that local NGOs have first incorporated a "gender dimension" to their activities, then learned its content through international guidance and training.

The chairs of NGOs in the region, particularly women, have been invited to international conferences and seminars and gender sensitivity trainings. These are learning processes for those engaged in civil society activity; they not only train people but also become centers for trainers. Therefore, international input to create gender awareness and gender equality in the region and to solve women's problems resulted in the formation of a group of NGO activists who are experts on gender and women's issues. The shortage of competence, knowledge, and skills common immediately after independence has been replaced by the emergence of professionals familiar with the international vocabulary of women's rights, who channel their activities toward women's empowerment and the creation of gender awareness.

Dealing with issues related to gender inequality and women's problems is becoming quite fashionable among local NGOs in these countries. One should also note that the funding priorities provide a motive for engaging in the work on women's problems on the part of the civil societal actors. Significant amounts of funding provided by international donor organizations are attractive for all local organizations and eventually result in encouraging local NGOs to work on gender-related issues. Even organizations that are not women's organizations started to work on gender-related issues because they were seen as worthy of funding. Grants are mainly allocated to projects on domestic violence, women's participation in politics, trafficking of women and children, and reproductive health. International funding usually constitutes seed money for local NGOs. This requirement limits the activities to the duration of the project, and these activities are unlikely to be sustainable since local NGOs lack the necessary funding to follow up on projects and are not engaged in income-generating activities, and local donors are not available. The scope of projects is limited to very specific target groups, and the population reached by these projects is generally urban since most activities are conducted in capital cities.

In Eurasia, women's participation in civil society activity is quite high (Tohidi 2004; Handrahan 2001, 73). There are a number of reasons for this. First, women's active participation in politics is low. After the elimination of the quota system of the Soviet period, a smaller number of women have participated in the parliaments and held administrative positions, as well as taken part in political parties. Politics as a male-dominated sphere is hard to penetrate for most women, whose roles are primarily defined in the private sphere. Moreover, men often consider women's engagement in civil societal activity as "legitimate" and "acceptable" since they attribute a less important role to civil society, whereas politics is viewed as "men's work" (Handrahan 2001, 75). Second, NGO activity is often defined as "light" business leaving time for women to fulfill their roles as mothers and wives. Third, as a result of economic transformation, most women either became unemployed or received low salaries. Civil societal activity is an income-generating activity in the region, creating job opportunities in particular for unemployed professionals (Herzig 1999, 38).

In post-Soviet democratization, the interrelationship between the state and civil society has two contradictory features: "encouragement and antagonism" (Ergun 2005a, 113). At the level of state discourse, presidents as well as state officials are very keen on the development of civil society in their respective countries, often making supportive declarations and statements concerning the need in civil society for democratization. As a result of both the growing number of local NGOs and their impact and the advice and guidance of international actors, the state-building project was restructured to include "civil society" or the "citizens' community" in political transformation. This resulted in the establishment of new units and departments within the presidential apparatus and within parliament (Ergun 2005a, 113). In terms of regimes' attitudes toward NGOs, however, these organizations are supported and encouraged only if they are considered as loyal to the regime or at least do not directly challenge the regime's policies. Those who are labeled as "opposition," however, have to face arbitrary practices, oppression, and delays in or rejection of their registration (Ergun 2005a, 115).

Women's NGOs are not seen to challenge fundamental regime policies and so enjoy a relatively greater freedom in civil society. In many cases, there appears to be a less hostile attitude toward women's organizations from governments. In part this is because women's organizations are not considered as dealing with "political issues" like NGOs working on human rights, democratic reforms, and the rule of law. Therefore, they are not seen as a challenge to state authority. Moreover, gender in general and women's problems in particular are seen as "soft" themes and are not associated with "threatening stability" in the country. These perceptions by current governments about women's organizations, along with the consideration of "civil society as a female domain" of social and political transformation, facilitate women's activism and empowerment in public life. Women not only acquire the necessary skills compatible with international norms and standards to represent their interests and further democratize society, they also actively take part in the redefinition of gender relations in the post-Soviet era. As Tohidi (2004) points out, women's social activism is gradually gaining gender consciousness.

Thus, the weak but emerging civil society in Central Asia is getting more gender sensitive. Even those organizations that do not particularly deal with women's problems are keen on addressing gender-sensitive issues or at least "working" on gender. The fact that gender is integrated into the NGOs' work is promising for the creation of gender awareness at the societal level. Although the national machineries work with local NGOs on gender-related issues, the mechanisms for further collaboration between state and civil societal actors are still to be found. Further collaboration between state and civil society actors will contribute to a more gender-sensitive democratization at both the political and social levels.

Similarities and Differences in Gender Roles

So far, we have argued that there are significant similarities and differences between the four above-mentioned Muslim states of the former Soviet Union. As a result of the Soviet legacy of de jure equality, they share many similar experiences. Their commitment to adopting international norms on gender is one dimension of their similarities. However, despite this commitment, all have very weak state-level implementation of these norms. Thus, we argue that they all have low capacity and expertise to ensure gender equality. Although there are these similarities, we maintain that there are very crucial differences in their attitudes toward gender and how gender is located in their national identity. As earlier, we divide the ex-Soviet Muslim states into two groups for comparative purposes: on the one hand, there are Azerbaijan and Uzbekistan; on the other, Kyrgyzstan and Kazakhstan.

Azerbaijan and Uzbekistan appear to be close to what Kandiyoti calls the "classic patriarchy," referring to a sharp gender division of labor, at least at the attitudinal level (2002). Men are breadwinners; women are mothers and homemakers. There is the expectation that men should have control over the women in their families. There are patriarchy and, in some cases, extended patrilineal families. In both countries, the family is very important for solidarity and is the main milieu of transmission of values and norms. It is the tool for the preservation of cultural values. This is the sphere into which Soviet rule, its ideology and policies, could not penetrate and/or challenge pre-Soviet cultural patterns. As has been cited previously, in the Soviet period in both of these countries, especially in Uzbekistan, female labor force participation was relatively low compared to the other Soviet successor states. As of 2006, high unemployment in both countries means there is little chance of women being employed. This leads to a heightened ideologization of housewives. In both countries, opinion polls indicate that people hold strong images of women as homemakers. This attitude is shared by men and women, including educated professional women who stated that the money earned and brought home by a husband is "sweeter" than their income. This widespread belief in men as breadwinners leads to diminishing pressures on employment as the female labor force is driven out of or exits the labor market. It also leads to strengthened patriarchal solidarity within the family. Decreasing divorce rates in these two countries reflect such a patriarchal domination, as do the number of girls who drop out of school and the number of early marriages. But such an ideology does not necessarily reflect real life. Women may become petty traders in response to unemployment, or work in the *mardikor* (daily labor market), or even be trafficked as cheap labor or sex laborers to the West. Still, the perception is that women and unmarried girls should not live away from home, they should not engage in physical work, and they should not work in jobs that do not fall into the stereotypical professions compatible with duties at home.

We argue that this perception reflects what we call a national mentality—that is, a way of life that distinguishes the Uzbek and/or Azerbaijani from the rest of the world. This national mentality is based on the control of women. It is often used to legitimize women's exclusion from the public sphere (political and economic), to emphasize men's role as the head of the family and main breadwinner, and to relegitimize the unequal division of labor within the family, defining male and female roles as well as male and female jobs. In both countries, the discussion of family and gender (and usually these two words are used together in these countries) is very often referred to as national mentality. The national mentality, as many informants in our interviews describe, usually extends beyond gender, but is centered on gender. For example, they may be hesitant in approving the migration of men (and women) to foreign countries. They argue that this leads to dissolution of the family, men having illicit relations, and women (wives) left behind "on the loose" without male authority. They would very often compare this with attitudes on migration of minorities, such as Russians, and argue that female migration is acceptable for the "others."

This national mentality distances itself from the Soviet past, which forced women to take part in public life, especially in the labor force. It also distinguishes itself from Western society because it is based on family solidarity, a key to national identity. The national mentality requires children to be raised at home, tries to limit divorces, expects solidarity within the extended family, and cares for the elderly. This ideology also tries to resist the impact of globalization and consumerism. It tries to replace consumerism with family values and a national identity. Pressures to conform to this identity are being sustained through traditional culture and in some cases also by Islam.

In the case of Uzbekistan, there is also the control within the *mahalle* (neighborhood) community. This local unit even maintains official powers of control (Kamp 2004, 39). Islamic and traditional discourse says women must be good mothers, kind and righteous, pious and compliant to the husband. Increasingly, family is central to societal life. The value of sons is becoming so high that in Azerbaijan, there is a growing number of selective abortions. Men are considered as the guardians of moral values and customs, safeguarding their lifestyles.

This national mentality is a very important tool for the state. It draws the boundaries of the past and present as well as the boundaries between different pathways of development. Neither Azerbaijan nor Uzbekistan is against a formally egalitarian public order. On the contrary, since 2006, they have been quite progressive on these grounds. For example, Azerbaijan has adopted a gender equality law, and Uzbekistan has a gender quota in politics. However, they do not want to interfere in the private life of their citizens, as they see this as an important asset in their political and economic development. In both of these countries, the Russian/Slavic/Christian minorities have a very limited role. So this "national mentality" policy is also safely being used to increase distance from the Soviet past and to build homogeneous national communities where patriarchy and hierarchy between genders still dominate. Traditional male roles in Azerbaijan are also fostered due the country's defeat in the Karabagh war; the notion of the "guardians and protectors" of the nation is attributed to men, with an emphasis on their being brave and strong.

We have not come across evidence of the notion of a "national mentality" in either Kazakhstan or Kyrgyzstan. Rather, they represent different cases, where gender is a still a central issue but cannot be seen as part of the core national identity. In both countries, there is a considerable number of national minorities, each with different gender perceptions. Achieving distance from the Soviet past is tricky for the Kazakhs because this may lead to the alienation of the Russian/ Slavic minority. In fact, Kazakh gender identity exists, but it is very much an ethnic identity among ethnic Kazakhs and Kyrgyzs. There is a tendency to differentiate from the Russians, as a form of national culture. However, it is less of a complete ideology in comparison to that of the Uzbek and Azerbaijani cases, where there is a stronger patriarchal culture. Both Kazakhstan and Kyrgyzstan have majority urban populations, which has made Soviet-style modernization easier. Nevertheless, in both of these countries the transition economy has led to major social problems. This has been reflected in the dissolution of the family. Divorce and abortion rates are both very high and increasing. There is a very high percentage of births out of wedlock, especially in young age cohorts. Gender-based violence is very common. The family crisis is so significant in Kazakhstan that the government has defined single-parent families as one of its social security targets.

In a way, this process is the opposite of the one in Azerbaijan and Uzbekistan. The transition economy in both countries has led to significant levels of unemployment. Men have faced major problems, including alcoholism and health problems associated with the lack of work. As a result, male life expectancy has fallen. In both countries, the gap between life expectancy at birth for men and women has grown to over ten years. In such situations, women have managed to find survival strategies. For some, the remedy was in petty trade; for others, it was in illicit sex. The moral and ethical breakdown affected both men and women, finding themselves in despair. In this situation, rural and urban differences as well as generational discrepancies are quite important. The rural population and older generations found themselves pushed toward traditional values, including Islam, whereas urban populations and the young were inclined toward consumerism and global linkages.

More ethnically heterogeneous communities found it more difficult to define the "old," the authentic, and the traditional. Women define their national culture through items of food and dress; men define it through masculinity, such as bride kidnapping, violence, and sheep polo (Handrahan 2004). This definition is significantly different from the Uzbek and Azerbaijani "mentalities."

In fact, the transition in Uzbekistan and Azerbaijan has strengthened the patriarchy, leading to reinforced solidarity, community control, and reiterated gender roles. In Kazakhstan and Kyrgyzstan, it has led to a crisis of patriarchy, especially at the community level as men lost their position within the family as the main breadwinner. Moreover, patriarchy cannot be embraced as a state ideology because of the ethnic tensions it may involve. Nira Yuval-Davis discusses how women participate in ethnic and national state processes (1997). A mirror image of the same theoretical point is to analyze state-building processes through the gender lens. The transition societies suggest that nation-state-building processes may be impacted by gender relations as well as determine them.

Conclusion

This chapter has reviewed the status of women in four Central Asian countries while they were part of the Soviet Union and as they went through the transition to independent nations. While all of these nations shared a common past as Soviet republics, they differed in their ethnic composition and in the traditions that they carried through the Soviet period. From the data collected through interviews in each country, it is possible to divide the four countries into two groups based on ethnic composition. Both Azerbaijan and Uzbekistan are quite homogeneous, and the majority population is Muslim; Kazakhstan and Kyrgyzstan are more diverse, with significant numbers of Russians in the population.

While the gender roles in each of these countries have been shaped by similar forces, including the transition to the market economy and privatization and the influences of an international community with clear gender equality norms, the result has been different in the two groups of countries. In the largely Muslim and majority rural countries, a traditional patriarchal system has been reinscribed and become part of the national identity. In contrast, in Kazakhstan and Kyrgyzstan, which are more urban and more ethnically heterogeneous, women's roles are not so clearly delineated and may vary depending on the ethnic group and the environment—urban or rural—in which the women live.

De jure gender equality promoted and implemented in the Soviet period proved not to be very successful in the post-Soviet period. Traditional gender roles, which are largely determined by local sociocultural patterns, are still persistent in the successor states. In this respect, Soviet policies were not fully internalized at the national level, both in the public and private spheres. Moreover, stereotypes associated with womanhood and manhood have been reconsolidated after the achievement of independence. On the one hand, the problems of the transition period, such as a high level of unemployment and poverty, decreasing standards of living, and the demolishing of social security and support systems, have resulted in fostering gender inequalities. On the other hand, the transition period has also necessitated the establishment of new democratic nation-states with new national law making and institution building. Through the advice and guidance provided by the international community, gender equality as a theme for democratization has been introduced into the discourses of both state and civil societal actors. As a result, governments ratified international treaties to promote gender equality and included a gender dimension in the new institutionalization, and NGOs are engaged in the creation of gender sensitivity and in consciousness-raising and have become active advocates of women's rights. Yet new arrangements at the state level, advocacy at the civil society level, and the impact of the international community to create gender awareness are not fully successful due to the predominance of the national mentality at the local level.

Comparing four countries in post-Soviet Eurasia in terms of gender politics, we have come to conclude that modes of transition are reflected in the shaping of gender roles, and this is based on two different models. In Azerbaijan and Uzbekistan, reshaping of national identity is predominantly based on recon-solidation of traditional gender roles. In this respect, national mentality and emphasis on customs and traditions have paved the way for the preservation of inequalities between men and women, attributing a private rather than a public role to women. However, in Kazakhstan and Kyrgyzstan, where the non-Muslim Slavic minority remains significant, there is a less strong patriarchal culture, and perceptions about gender roles are not based on national mentality. Roles attributed to men and women are not defined with reference to national identity. Rather, perceptions about gender roles are seen as differentiating factors in terms of national cultures of the Muslim-Turkic majority and non-Muslim Slavic minorities. Thus, how the transition process is experienced and to what extent it is affected by previous social and cultural patterns determine redefinition as well as reconsolidation of gender roles in these four post-Soviet countries. Such comparative analysis is crucial to understanding the factors that shape women's engagement in post-Soviet transition and gender empowerment as well as those that support patriarchal practices in this region.

NOTES

1. Authors' interviews in Kazakhstan, Kyrgyzstan, and Uzbekistan (April–November 2006). See also the UNDP Gender Attitudes Survey in Azerbaijan Human Development Report 2007.
2. Authors' interviews in Azerbaijan (April–May 2006) and in Uzbekistan (September 2006).
3. What we refer to as Sovietization is the aim of creating the "Soviet man" regardless of national and religious identities. What we refer to as Russification is the widespread use of the Russian language, both in education and daily life.
4. The data related to the final census of the Soviet Union (1989) can be found at *Demoscope Weekly*, an Internet version of *Naseleniye i Obschestvo* (Population and Society), available at http://demoscope.ru/weekly/ssp/sng_nac_89.
5. See National State Statistical Committee, *Main Results of the First National Population*

Census in the Kyrgyz Republic of 1999 (Republic of Kyrgyzstan, 2000).

6. Cited in Asian Development Bank (2005c) *Country Gender Assessment Report*, 6.

7. See TransMONEE 2006 Database, www.unicef-irc.org/databases/transmonee, UNICEF IRC, Florence.

8. The entrance of international NGOs multiplied not only the funding and resources allocated to the development of civil society and democracy assistance but also introduced the new vocabulary to the transition period and created local partners for the realization of projects. The Open Society Institute (OSI) and the U.S. Agency for International Development (USAID) are still the main donors for civil society actors who are competing to get grants from these organizations. The ISAR, NDI, NED, NRI, Eurasia Foundation, Westminster Foundation of Democracy, and Counterpart Consortium (particularly in Central Asia) have also contributed to the formation of the large network of affiliated local NGOs in each of the respective countries. Foreign embassies such as the U.S. embassy, the British embassy, the Norwegian embassy, and the Dutch embassy occasionally provide funding for the projects of the local NGOs.

9. See Report on Implementation of the Convention on the Elimination of All Forms of Discrimination against Women, Kazakhstan, Second Periodic Report of States Parties, 2005, 8, accessed December 15, 2006.

10. See Report on the Implementation of the Convention on the Elimination of All Forms of Discrimination against Women, Kyrgyzstan, 2005, 7, accessed December 15, 2006.

11. See www.gender-az.org, accessed on December 25, 2006.

12. For example, there is the Women's NGO Forum in Kyrgyzstan and the Political Alliance of Women's Organizations of Kazakhstan, later renamed as the Democratic Party of Women of Kazakhstan.

WORKS CITED

Akiner, Shirin. 1997. "Melting Pot, Salad Bowl-Cauldron? Manipulation and Mobilisation of Ethnic and Religious Identities in Central Asia." *Ethnic and Racial Studies* 20(2): 362–398.

Alekseenko, Alexandr. 2001. "About Some Results of Population Census in Kazakhstan/Migration in CIS and the Baltic: Through Differences to Common Information Space." Http://www.demoscope.ru/weekly/2002/057/analit04.php.

Asian Development Bank. 2005a. *Country Gender Assessment Azerbaijan.* Http://www.adb.org/Documents/Reports/Country-Gender-Assessments/cga-aze.pdf.

————. 2005b. *Country Gender Assessment Kyrgyz Republic.* Http://www.adb.org/Documents/Reports/Country-Gender-Assessments/cga-kgz.pdf.

————. 2005c. *Country Gender Assessment Uzbekistan.* Http://www.unece.org/stats/gender/publications/Uzbekistan/UzbekistanGenderAssesment.pdf.

————. 2006a. *Central Asian Republics: Gender Assessment Synthesis Report: Azerbaijan, Republic of Kazakhstan, Kyrgyz Republic, Tajikistan.* Http://www.adb.org/Documents/Reports/Country-Gender-Assessments/cga-synthesis.pdf.

————. 2006b. *Country Gender Assessment Republic of Kazakhstan.* Http://www.adb.org/Documents/Reports/Country-Gender-Assessments/cga-kaz.pdf.

Azerbaijan Human Development Report. 2007. *Gender Attitudes in Azerbaijan: Trends and Challenges.* Baku: UNDP Azerbaijan.

Brubaker, Rogers. 1996. *Nationalism Reframed.* Cambridge: Cambridge University Press.

Ergun, Ayça. 2005a. "Democratization from Below: The Role of Civil Society in Azerbaijan." In *Black Sea Politics Political Culture and Civil Society in an Unstable Region,* ed. Ayşe Ayata, Ayça Ergun, and Işıl Çelimli, 103–115. London: IB Tauris.

————. 2005b. "International Challenges and Domestic Preferences in the Post-Soviet Political Transition of Azerbaijan." In *Central Asia in Global Politics,* ed. Mehdi Parvizi Amineh and Henk Houweling, 321–364. Leiden: Brill.

Handrahan, Lori. 2001. "Gendering Ethnicity in Kyrgyztan: Forgotten Elements in Promoting Peace and Democracy." *Gender and Development* 9(3): 70–78.

————. 2004. "Hunting for Women Bride-Kidnapping in Kyrgyztan." *International Feminist Journal of Politics* 6(2): 207–233.

Herzig, Edmund. 1999. *The New Caucasus: Armenia, Azerbaijan and Georgia.* London: RIIA.

Kamp, Marianne. 2004. "Between Women and the State: Mahalla Committees and Social Welfare in Uzbekistan." In *The Transformation of Central Asia States and Societies from Soviet Rule to Independence,* ed. Pauline Jones Luong, 29–58. Ithaca, N.Y.: Cornell University Press.

————. 2005. "Gender Ideals and Income Realities: Discourses about Labor and Gender in Uzbekistan." *Nationalities Papers* 33(3) (September): 403–422.

Kandiyoti, Deniz. 2002. "Post-Colonialism Compared: Potentials and Limitations in the Middle East and Central Asia." *International Journal of Middle East Studies* 34:279–297.

Lapidus, Gail, Victor Zaslavsky, and Philip Goldman, eds. 1992. *From Union to Commonwealth.* Cambridge: Cambridge University Press.

National Human Development Report of Azerbaijan. 2003. UNDP. Http://www.un-az.org/UNDP/nhdr2003/45.html, accessed December 15, 2006.

Paci, Pierella. 2002. *Gender in Transition.* Washington, D.C.: World Bank.

Saroyan, Mark. 1989. "Beyond the Nation-State: Culture and Ethnic Politics in Soviet Transcaucasia." *Soviet Union, Union Sovietique* 15(2–3): 219–244.

Statistical Yearbook of Azerbaijan. 2004. Http://www.azstat.org/publications/yearbooks/ SYA2004/pdf/02en.pdf.

Suny, Ronald Grigor. 1990. "The Revenge of the Past: Socialism and Ethnic Conflict in Transcaucasia." *New Left Review* 184:5–37.

Tohidi, Nayereh. 2004. "Women, Civil Society and NGOs in Post-Soviet Azerbaijan." *International Journal of Not-for-Profit Law* 7(1): 36–41.

Werner, Cynthia. 2004. "Women, Marriage, and the Nation-State: The Rise of Nonconsensual Bride Kidnapping in Post-Soviet Kazakhstan." In *The Transformation of Central Asia States and Societies from Soviet Rule to Independence,* ed. Pauline Jones Luong, 59–92. Ithaca, N.Y.: Cornell University Press.

Yuval-Davis, Nira. 1997. *Gender and Nation.* Thousand Oaks, Calif.: Sage.

8

Labor Migration in Central Asia: Gender Challenges

Eleonora Fayzullaeva

This chapter addresses one of the most crucial public issues in post-Communist Central Asia: the impact of labor migration on the Newly Independent States (NIS) and particularly its effects on gender order. The key questions I aim to address are: What are the causes, extent, and consequences of labor migration in the four NIS Central Asian states: Kazakhstan, Tajikistan, Kyrgyzstan, and Uzbekistan? And how do the different patterns of migration affect the gender order in these states? This chapter examines the difficulties researchers face in answering these questions and discusses what current findings reveal about migration within and emigration from the NIS of Central Asia. It also emphasizes the differences within the region, differences that are crucial to understanding the region and the individual cases, as well as to developing an appreciation of the gendered dimensions of migration in the post-Communist world. It is clear that much work remains to be done to provide an adequate understanding of the role that gender plays in shaping the migration process.[1] As my Kazakhstani colleague Eugenia Kozireva, the president of the Feminist League of Kazakhstan, said, "There is practically an absolute vacuum when it concerns gender challenges of labor migration."

The first section of this chapter examines the usefulness of extant theoretical frameworks for understanding migration in this region. This is followed by a brief exploration of the extent, forms, and gendered dimensions of labor migration in the NIS of Central Asia. A discussion of policies and patterns of labor migration across the region during the Soviet era then provides a historical framework for understanding current trends. The chapter next turns to the patterns and problems of migration in four NIS states of Central Asia (Kyrgyzstan, Tajikistan, Kazakhstan, and Uzbekistan), with particular attention to the gendered dimensions of migration in each of these countries. The gendered complexity of migration will be underscored to emphasize the reductionism in explanations that view women either as simply victimized or empowered by migration. The chapter concludes with a brief review and analysis of state policies toward labor migration.

Causes and Major Types of Labor Migration

Labor migration is defined as "territorial dislocations of population based on the motivation of changing their employment through moving to another location and concluding new labor agreements" (Melikyan 1994, 267). Scholars delineate major types of labor migration in a variety of ways—for example, internal (movements within the boundaries of a country) or external (emigration and immigration across state boundaries). Migration can also be classified as legal or illegal as defined by national and international legislation or interstate agreements. Some researchers distinguish permanent migration from a temporary or seasonal pendulum, differentiating seasonal economic migrations that occur when an additional labor force is needed in a particular sector of the economy (for example, harvest seasons in agriculture) or those that occur for sociocultural reasons (for example, travels for education, medical treatment, tourism) from more permanent migrations (Ribakovskiy 1995). Researchers also identify two opposite patterns of how labor migrants behave in situations where the stay in the receiving country is long term. In general, migration researchers argue that as migrants accumulate time in receiving societies, they begin to put down social and economic roots. The difficulties inherent in maintaining relations over long distances lead to an attenuation of migrants' ties to their homeland. But if there is a pattern among some migrants of viewing themselves as permanent settlers, there is also evidence that many sustain connections to their countries of origin, particularly given frequent experiences of intolerance and threats of deportation in the host countries (Wellman and Wortley 1989).

Whether migration processes occur on the local, national, or international scale and whether the migrations are temporary or more permanent, they are usually stimulated by a combination of push and pull factors. Push factors are more often associated with forced migrations and are characterized by such things as societal conflicts, natural disasters, or a dramatically deteriorating economic situation. Pull factors, on the other hand, tend to be associated with voluntary migration, as potential migrants perceive more attractive economic or social opportunities elsewhere. Thus, labor migration may be caused by a range of factors from the parameters of the actual workplace to the perception of more desirable social, economic, or environmental conditions. However, while all analysts of migration conceptualize the phenomenon as a combination of such push and pull dynamics, scholars have adopted different theoretical approaches to explain these dynamics.

Modernization theorists conceptualize massive migration as an inevitable by-product of industrialization, urbanization, and concomitant social, demographic, and economic changes in both sending and receiving societies. Thus, for example, high degrees of unemployment will push a populace to immigrate to a site of high labor demand. In contrast to modernization theory's emphasis on impersonal market processes and demographic changes, the more critical world systems theory roots migration in the dynamics of capitalism. This approach contends that structural factors in the capitalist world economy have historically shaped and continue to generate and direct international labor migration (Jonas and Thomas 1998, 70; Portres and Walter 1981; Sassen-Koob 1984). In this chapter, I build from the historical structural perspective of world systems approaches; however, I also argue that sustained attention must be paid to the political context within which these global processes occur, a context that is particularly important for understanding migration in the NIS.

The mass exodus of labor migrants from some of the NIS states has been to a large extent a consequence of the policy orientation of ruling powers in these states. There are three reasons for this. First, migration has helped to address problems in the economies of the individual states. When citizens emigrate to work abroad, the majority send money back to their families and relatives, thus simultaneously solving two problems: decreasing the number of mouths who need to be fed in the country and increasing the flow of currency into the country through the remittances. Second, emigration has had political benefits to the ruling elites. While labor migrants living abroad remain the citizens of their native country, their physical absence has left a convenient loophole for manipulating their votes to support the policies of the elite in various referenda and elections. Third, the major migrant streams have been from among the proletariat and the intelligentsia, the two most active components of any potentially oppositional electorate. Their exodus from a country can diminish social discontent among the population, while simultaneously increasing the capital flow into the country. Thus, migration may meet multiple political and economic interests of the political elite.

The Scale of Labor Migration in Central Asia

How significant is migration in post-Communist Central Asia? Even a brief glimpse at the scale of labor migration in the NIS should make the reader aware of its dramatic social impact. But we must first recognize that there are no absolutely reliable methods of defining exact numbers of labor migrants in a country. Methodologically, ascertaining the number of migrants is difficult because the data are collected by a great number of groups but have not been organized into a coherent database. Certain groups and/or categories are registered by different state bodies, ranging from the Ministry of Labor and/or Social Maintenance, to the Department of Migration under the state Department of Statistics. In addition, law enforcement bodies provide data through registrations of criminal activity associated with migration, and national banks through the systems of registering remittances. Other data are collected by private labor agencies, tourist companies, border posts at the frontiers, and so forth. Ideally, the data collected in such organizations should create the basis for summary, analysis, and generalization so that we might define basic types and numbers of labor migrants, amounts of income, and the impacts of migration on economic and social life. But in reality the data available from different sources are rarely combined to depict the entire picture. Also, official data on registered unemployment rates need to be considered with caution, as they do not provide a complete picture of real trends and their impacts on men and women.

In addition to the problem of incomplete and erratic data collection are the many problems that researchers face in getting access to data. In some countries of Central Asia, it is extremely difficult to obtain even official statistics and even more so to undertake research and collect data related to labor migration. For example, in many cases a researcher must obtain an official permit from local authorities, who are usually reluctant to give it. In other cases, in particular under authoritarian regimes, people have become extremely cautious and refrain from giving any interviews or information, especially to foreigners; thus, the topic of labor migration has become a kind of taboo and not discussed in public. As a result of such problems, migration data cannot be seen as absolutely reliable; nonetheless, as the following discussion suggests, the available information indicates that the scale of migration in Central Asia is extensive and that it varies across the region. To get a sense of that scale and variance, I provide a brief look across the region at migration patterns in Kyrgyzstan, Tajikistan, Kazakhstan, and Uzbekistan.

KYRGYZSTAN

Studies of labor migration trends in Kyrgyzstan document substantial internal migration from rural areas to Bishkek and other large towns and high rates of external migration, especially to Russia and Kazakhstan. According to information from the Department of Migration under the Ministry of Foreign Affairs in Kyrgyzstan, the level of illegal labor migration to Russia has been around 300,000 to 600,000 people annually (Department of Migration 2005). And each year about 70,000 to 100,000 citizens of Kyrgyzstan from the Osh and Jalalabad regions migrate to work in the tobacco fields in Kazakhstan. According to estimates from the International Organization for Migration (IOM), from 1990 to 2002 nearly half a million people—approximately 10% of the total population—emigrated. Although both men and women have responded to increasing unemployment and to the erosion of the social welfare system in Kyrgyzstan by leaving the republic, the National Statistics Committee has documented a higher number of women than men emigrating each year between 1996 and 2003 (Glodenyte 2003). The emigration of the educated has been especially substantial. During the period 1990 to 2001, about 70,000 specialists who had completed higher education, many women among them, left the country. That figure represents about one-third of the total specialists in the country (Glodenyte 2003). At the same time that Kyrgyzstan has faced emigration of its educated populace, it has also been a locus of recruitment of poor women for commercial sexual activity (ADB 2006b).

TAJIKISTAN

The official state statistics on employment and migration from Tajikistan differ considerably from those presented by international sources. The government claims the official level of unemployment to be 16.8% and also stresses that one-third of the population may be potential migrants. In contrast, statistics provided by independent sociological agencies and nongovernmental organizations (NGOs) indicate that a total of one-third of the population, over 1.5 million people, are unemployed, suggesting a huge pool of potential migrants.

According to data obtained in a national poll conducted in August 2003 by the Ministry of Labor and Social Maintenance, from 1999 through 2003, 347,556 Tajik citizens left the country in search of employment opportunities. Of these emigrants, 94% are men, and only 6% are women. The major streams of labor force migration have been to Russia (336,754, or 96.9%), Kyrgyzstan (4,870, or 1.4%), Kazakhstan (2,382, or 0.71%), and other NIS countries (0.9%). According to IOM data, 84% of labor migrants from Tajikistan are in Russia, with many fewer in Central Asia countries: Uzbekistan—5%, Kyrgyzstan—3% and Kazakhstan—1% (IOM 2003).

KAZAKHSTAN

The patterns of migration in Kazakhstan underscore the importance of understanding each particular case in post-Communist Central Asia. Since gaining independence from the Soviet Union in 1991, more than 2 million people have emigrated from Kazakhstan. According to the official data, in the period 1989 to 2000, over 3.5 million people, mostly of Slavic or German origin, emigrated from the country; even with substantial immigration, the loss in population was over 2.1 million (Statistical Agency of the Republic of Kazakhstan, 2000). Only in 2004 did Kazakhstan experience a positive migration balance that allowed it to reverse the overall population decline. In part, the reversal can be attributed to implementation of a policy of repatriation of ethnic Kazakhs (*oralmans*). In the period from 1991 to 2000, over 183,000 ethnic Kazakhs from NIS and the "Far Abroad" returned to their homeland; the major stream (over 65,000) came from Mongolia. But in addition, the rapidly developing economy and needs for labor have made Kazakhstan attractive for migrants from neighboring Central Asia (Kurtov 2006). Moreover, given its geographic position and developed communication and transport systems, Kazakhstan has become a transit zone for illegal migration flows to Western countries, flows that are often accompanied by the smuggling of drugs and arms as well as people.

According to the Ministry of the Interior, in 2002 alone, 730,000 migrants from NIS countries arrived in Kazakhstan, 33% of them to the city of Almaty. This constitutes practically one-fourth of the official population of Almaty. Of this migrant stream, 71,000 are citizens of the Russian Federation, 53,000 are from Kyrgyzstan, 35,000 are from Uzbekistan, and 15,000 are from Tajikistan (Sadovskaya 2001).

UZBEKISTAN

Decreasing employment opportunities, constrained trading possibilities, and a poor social support system, which deteriorated after the fall of the Soviet Union, forced many people in Uzbekistan to seek income sources abroad so as to support their families. The proportion of Uzbekistan's population seeking employment opportunities abroad increased in the 1990s and particularly intensified after 1999 (IOM 2005). Migration has been especially prevalent among the populace in rural areas. Clampdowns on trading activity in 2004 further reduced the capabilities of entrepreneurs to engage in importing/exporting and in the sale of goods in Uzbekistan. Increasingly restrictive economic policies, unreasonably high taxes, and stalled banking reform facilitated the expansion of an underground or shadow economy. The only official statistical information was found in research conducted under the supervision of the President's Office. But government findings that indicate a total of 281,200 migrants from Uzbekistan in the period 1997 through 2001 do not fully depict the picture in the country. Estimates of labor migration from Uzbekistan to Southern Kazakhstan alone range from 200,000 by state officials to 1,000,000 by NGOs. So it is difficult to get an accurate picture of the extent of migration. Most of the migrants are unskilled or semiskilled, and many are commercial migrants. Their destinations vary: about 60% travel to Russia, 26% choose Kazakhstan, and for about 14%, South Korea is the final destination (IOM 2005).

Shipping and reselling agricultural goods and fuel lubricant materials are the major kinds of "shuttle" businesses not only to Southern Kazakhstan but to Almaty and its suburbs. Enterprising citizens from the neighboring country open bakeries for national Uzbek bread (Uzb "non") and restaurants and cafés with Uzbek cuisine, and they trade in local wholesale and retail markets. Labor migration significantly alleviates the problem of unemployment in Uzbekistan, with the highest migration from *viloyats* (regions) that have the greatest strains in their local labor markets—the Samarkand, Jizzak, Ferghana, and Syrdarya *viloyats*. Even though official unemployment levels in these regions range from 0.2% to 0.4% of the economically active population, only about 52% of the working-age population in Uzbekistan are registered to be employed. Thus, one can make logical assumptions on the real scale of labor migration even with the exclusion of those employed in informal sectors of economy.

A considerable number of illegal migrants (males in the majority) migrate to Russia, where demographic trends and the needs of a growing economy have produced a demand for migrant labor. According to the experts' estimates, at least 800,000 external workers are needed annually. Recently, the Russian State Duma considerably softened restrictions on migrant labor and approved the extension of Soviet passports through 2007 to serve as the basis for obtaining Russian Federation citizenship. Turkey has also become a relatively new migrant destination, largely for female labor. In the old part of the city of Tashkent, the women in *mahallas* (local communities) are hired by intermediaries who have created networks with partners in Turkey. In the destination country, the women are met by a hiring company representative and sent to be employed mostly as housemaids, nannies, and cooks; but family medical doctors and nurses are also in special demand.

It should be clear from this brief summary that international migration has become an integral part of the world economy today. Transference of people across state frontiers in the NIS is no longer the destiny of a limited social group. The processes of regional integration, the growing amalgamation of the international labor market, and the world economy have made migration an important facet of globalization, one having both positive and negative aspects (Kurtov 2006). According to International Labor Organization (ILO) statistics, global labor migration in the beginning of the twenty-first century constituted 128 million people, that is, 2.3% of the world population (Tyuryukanova and Malysheva 2001). However, labor migration is a comparatively new and unfamiliar phenomenon for the NIS subregion.[2]

Migration Patterns during the Soviet Era

During the Soviet era, the patterns of population mobility differed radically from the current ones. The outside borders were blocked with the "iron curtain," and one needed to pass through a number of special procedures, including a KGB investigation and *sobesedovaniye* (instructions procedure), to go abroad. The permission and visa for all citizens of the Soviet Union were issued centrally in Moscow, and the entire permit process could take months. Special cases when technical engineering personnel were contracted out to the "friendly" countries of the socialist camp or to support construction of some big projects like the Aswan hydro-power station in Egypt were exceptions rather than the rule at that time. In accordance with centralized social-economic priorities, experts from certain sectors of the national economy were sent to the Soviet national republics to work as well as to train local specialists.

Thus, processes of labor migration in the Soviet Union were controlled within the centralized model, limited by the general policies of economic development in the various regions and by particular Soviet policies. Some ethnicities, for example, were forcibly deported from their native lands for political reasons, such as Crimea Tartars, Meskhetin Turks, or Koreans during the Second World War. And for individuals, the requirement of the *propiska* (residence permit) radically limited their mobility within Soviet space. The state provided permits for seasonal migrations, such as the compulsory work of students and employees in agriculture during the sowing or harvest periods. In addition, the Soviet Union often adopted very limited seasonal permits for a portion of citizens to travel to central regions of the Russian Federation, such as youth going for education in Russia and other Soviet republics. There were also popular campaigns to send students to Siberia and the Far East to contribute to oil and gas mining, and to participate in nationwide projects like the Virgin Land or Baykal Amur Mainline (BAM) construction or to assist in places where there had been a natural disaster, such as the reconstruction brigades that were sent to Tashkent after the earthquake of 1966 to assist in restoring the ruined city (Olivnova et al. 2006). A considerable proportion of youth from rural areas went to the cities to study in higher educational institutions or vocational colleges. But the mechanism of *raspredeliniye* (distribution) obliged the graduates to return to their native regions and pay back the free education by three years of compulsory work in their professional field. Only then were they granted diplomas. In short, the patterns of migration during the Soviet era were a consequence of policies adopted by the centralized state for political purposes and for socioeconomic development.

Post-Soviet Labor Migration

After the fall of the Soviet Union, as we have already seen, migration became a strong feature of life in all the NIS of Central Asia. However, in contrast to what occurred during the Soviet period, the recent processes of labor migration have been a spontaneous response by the population to the changing political and economic environment. Today, labor migration has become a part of everyday life in the NIS. Extensive economic changes, including dramatic and radical impoverishment, especially in Central Asia, have led to daily migration of hundreds of people (many of them males) to other NIS countries in search of more favorable economic and social climates. Indeed, there has been a sharp shift from the psychology of settlement, which characterized the populace during the Soviet period, to a more nomadic sensibility today. The loss of confidence in a secure, planned, and state-guaranteed "tomorrow," which had been fostered by the economic and social safety net of the Soviet era, has been coupled with the reality of harsh choices, as people across post-Communist Central Asia face the need to leave their families and migrate outside their native place to earn a living. Combined with the common language, background, and mentality, the comparatively easy visa regimes have made labor migration within the NIS borders much more popular and widespread.

Although all of the NIS countries have experienced a dramatic shift from the state-controlled population policies and economic safety nets of the Soviet period to more open visa regimes and migration, they still differ considerably in terms of the contemporary experience of labor migration. Some—Azerbaijan, Armenia, Kyrgyzstan, Moldova, Tajikistan, and Uzbekistan—have become donor countries. Others—Kazakhstan and Russia—have turned into destination and sometimes transit countries. And a third group—Georgia and Ukraine—are both donor and transit countries for illegal migration. Moreover, migration tendencies have changed dramatically recently, as may be illustrated with a few simple examples. In comparison with 2000 data, the number of emigrants from Kyrgyzstan in 2005 increased by 450% (IOM 2005). Another example is the dramatic increase in the number of airline flights from Tashkent, Uzbekistan, to Moscow. In 2006, only three flights a week were provided between these cities by the National Airways Company. More recently, Uzbek Airways offered two flights daily in both directions. These flights are usually overbooked, and an observer can see that the majority of the passengers are labor migrants (mainly males). The labor migrants are easily recognized by their hardworking hands, by their clothes, and by their diffident, homesick eyes. When returning to Tashkent from Moscow, the migrants can often be seen transporting a large box with a television set for their homes.

As mentioned earlier, labor migration on the global level has both positive and negative impacts. The major world monetary institutions usually focus on its positive effects, emphasizing its economic contributions to both sending and receiving countries. They stress that labor migration increases the income and welfare of migrants' households; that migrants' remittances reduce the proportion of people living in poverty; that migrants' incomes facilitate the formation of a new middle class; that migration attenuates popular discontent and social conflict by providing a partial solution to the problems of unemployment; and that migration may also contribute to women's empowerment. Migration, it is also argued, provides specific benefits to the NIS region. For example, many commercial migrants and foreign employees state that they discovered the world, became mobile, learned foreign languages, and gained rich vocational and life experiences. The most successful migrants are currently forming a "new" middle class, characterized by a capability of independent thinking and decision making. It is well known that during the Soviet era, the prevailing characteristic features of an individual were an incapacity for independent decision making and a lack of initiative. The representatives of this new class are overcoming the paternalistic ideology of being dependent on the social policies and benefits of the state. They assume the burden of risks and responsibilities for themselves, their families, and their businesses. To some minor but growing positive trends one can add the success stories of the new middle class coming from labor migrants who have positively affected the household welfare levels. Labor migration has begun to influence career choices made by youth, as significant increases in enrollment in construction colleges and cooking courses. But it is also important to recognize the mixed impact of migration on this region.

The impacts of globalization and consumerism on the emerging NIS new middle class have, some argue, fostered a "money talks" culture in which humane values and "high morality" have eroded. Migration in the NIS of Central Asia has also resulted in a wide-scale process by which hundreds of thousands of highly qualified professionals and experts have lost their professional qualifications, as they discontinue their vocational careers. Members of this class are usually employed in the receiving society as part of the general labor force. Thus, the "old" middle class is being wiped out by migration, losing its social and economic status. At the same time, enrollment in medical, teacher, and mechanics colleges is decreasing. The class effects must be added to the negative impacts of global migration that are most frequently stressed: increasing poverty, trafficking in human beings, HIV/AIDS pandemic, expansion of tuberculosis and other contagious diseases, a growth in criminal activities and drug smuggling, and an increase in xenophobia and ethnic conflicts, based in part on the perception that migrant communities form the basis for subversive activities of extremist organizations. There is no clear calculus for weighing the costs and benefits of migration across NIS Central Asia, but a comprehensive analysis requires consideration of these myriad effects.

Gender Challenges of Migration in Post-Communist Central Asia

At the heart of a full analysis of labor migration is a recognition of its gendered nature and implications—a subject that is receiving some attention from international agencies like the ILO, the IOM, and the Joint United Nations Program on HIV/AIDS (UNAIDS). Trafficking and exploitation; physical, sexual, and verbal abuse; double discrimination (as women and foreigners) in the labor market; xenophobia; and marginalization of women, who constitute about 46% of all international migrants, have been the focus of studies of the above international agencies.[3]

However, most of these agencies concentrate their activities on female migrants in the destination countries. Few have attended to the gendered impact of migration on the donor countries. This section of the chapter looks particularly at the gendered impact of migration within and emigration from the NIS Central Asian countries.

More than seventy years' experience of the Soviet economic and social system, ideology, mentality, and language have produced common gendered experiences in the post-Communist era. The abolition of the well-established system of state-provided child care that characterized the Soviet period led to the closure of almost two-thirds of the nurseries and kindergartens in these countries. The widely exercised practice of "prolonged day groups" in primary and secondary schools vanished all together during the transition period. Many of the additional social support services provided by the former Soviet Union, such as nursing, health care, and pensioner care, have also disappeared, placing increasing pressure on women to fill these roles. In rural areas today, child care is almost nonexistent. Although a very limited number of kindergartens operate in urban areas, most are well beyond the financial reach of the average family in the countries of Central Asia. Women still predominantly carry out the responsibilities for the household and for the care and socialization of children. Because it is generally necessary for women to work outside the home and because so many women migrate to support their families, the absence of state-subsidized child care has imposed double and triple burdens on women's shoulders.

Migration has presented additional dramatic challenges to the structure and dynamics of families in the former Soviet republics of Central Asia. In the Soviet Union, the state seemed to guard the integrity of the family, which was viewed as a primary source for the reproduction of labor. A well-developed system of sanctions and institutions—including the Communist Party, trade unions, and public opinion—functioned to keep families intact. Under the conditions of the transition period, however, national and cultural traditions have remained the only resource for preserving family integrity. Still, these traditions have become generally insufficient to provide for the strategies that might allow traditional families to survive. In many cases, when they are far from their families and outside their own homeland, NIS migrants develop a sense of "freedom" from the inclusivity of family ties. Migrant workers (mainly males) can lose ties with their families at home and, without divorcing their spouses at home, start new relations and develop informal families abroad through the so-called civil marriages. In many cases of civil marriages, the male migrants minimize or cease providing financial aid to the home family. For example, the data on labor immigrants in Kazakhstan show that only 22% of migrants provide regular economic aid to their families; 9% provide incidental financial aid to their relatives and dependents (Sadovskaya 2000). The wives of such male migrants stay at home as "grass widows." They cannot remarry, as they are not officially divorced, and they cannot make claims for state allowances for children as single mothers. Such patterns are broadly shared across the post-Communist region of Central Asia. But there are also important gendered dimensions of migration specific to each country, and I turn to these now.

KYRGYZSTAN

The gendered impact of the transition from Communist rule has been stark in Kyrgyzstan, where women have been especially affected by higher rates of unemployment, by the erosion in social services, and by the development of an informal labor market. The gendered effects of the structural changes in the economy are particularly evident in wage labor. World Bank data indicate that 83% of women in the Kyrgyz Republic were in the official labor force in the years before Soviet rule ended. After independence, however, the adoption of programs for economic restructuring and the contraction and privatization of social services led to a precipitous decline in women's employment. Indeed, the employment rate for women plummeted following the dissolution of the Soviet Union, so that by 2002, only 47.4% of women in the labor market had jobs (Government of the Kyrgyz Republic 2001, 15). Simultaneous with these gendered changes in employment, child care costs rapidly escalated, so that women have been less able to combine childrearing and wage labor. According to the World Bank data, the 2001 per capita gross domestic product (GDP) fell to about $300, at the same time that public kindergartens were charging monthly rates of 500 soms (US$12). The private rates of 2,500 to 5,000 soms (US$60–$120) per month have been beyond the resources of most Kyrgyz families (World Bank 2003, iii). The impact has been especially dramatic in rural areas where child-care facilities are very rare. And similar effects have been felt in other areas where the Soviet state provided a safety net: support for the aged and nursing care for invalids. Not surprisingly, these changes have had a disproportionate impact on women, who have been more likely than men to lose their jobs and to experience persistent unemployment. And, according to research by the Women's Support Centre (WSC), more than half (56%) of the women who did report themselves as employed said that they were employed "without a contract," suggesting the extent of their vulnerability to the vagaries in the labor market (WSC 2003). Although slightly more women (20.6%) than men (15.6%) who had registered as unemployed indicated that they had been laid off, official unemployment rates are not a good measure of joblessness (WSC 2003, 69). Stringent requirements have inhibited application for the increasingly meager unemployment benefits.

One of the consequences of the high rates of joblessness and the limited social supports has been the emergence of an informal labor market, ranging from unpaid family businesses to urban food markets and small trades, to home produce and domestic work. As noted earlier in this chapter, some urban areas in Kyrgyzstan have become a destination for sexual trafficking. A research report to the Convention on the Elimination of Discrimination against Women (CEDAW) indicates that in Bishkek, women have dominated not only the informal economy in markets but also the "shuttle trades," where products made outside the formal economy are shuttled illegally to markets in Kazakhstan, Uzbekistan, and Russia (CEDAW 2002, 42). According to an assessment of gender relations in Kyrgyzstan by the Asian Development Bank (ADB):

> a significant (although as yet unquantified) number of women engage in "shuttle tours" and the "suitcase" trade (or the *chelnochny* business) by selling goods brought in from neighboring countries. It is also predominantly women who are traveling to other countries in the regions to sell cheaper Kyrgyz-made goods. Many of these women are married with children and leave husbands and other family members to care for children in their absence. (ADB 2005b, 30)

Seasonal migrations from Kyrgyzstan to the southern regions of Kazakhstan, where whole families travel to work in the tobacco fields, also have had a substantial social impact. Tobacco processing is demanding work that poses significant health problems for the migrants. In most cases, children work with their families in fields and cannot attend schools during the season of migratory work. For example, in the Nookat region of Kyrgyzstan in September 2005, about 30% of children were absent from schools due to these reasons. In addition to raising concerns about the exploitation of children, NGOs from the Nookat region have also stated that many women in seasonal labor in the tobacco fields are sexually abused by their masters/farmers and feel so stigmatized by the experience that they cannot return to their communities. Although field research on women in the tobacco fields is limited, overall it is clear that as in more permanent migrations, sojourning has substantial gender impacts (ADB 2005b, 62).

TAJIKISTAN

Among the most important aspects of the transition from Soviet rule was the civil war during the early years of the transition (1992–1997), which produced social and economic deterioration in Tajikistan. In the subsequent years of economic turmoil, reliance on Russia as a source of employment has become a structural feature of the Tajik economy. Since demand for labor from construction and the oil and gas sectors in Russia is heavily biased in favor of physical work, young men have a comparative employment advantage over women. A survey conducted in Khatlon oblast revealed that about 18% of the total economically active population in Tajikistan (28 out of every 100 economically active Tajik men) worked abroad in 2005; only 8% of all migrants were women (Mughal 2006).

Some specific aspects of the Tajik society shape the experience of migration. In the rural areas of Tajikistan, the *avlod* (also known as *qaymi* or *toyfa*) plays a significant role in community life. The *avlod* is a kinship group, patriarchal in structure, where members share property and productive means, and even coordinate household budgets. Still quite strong in rural areas, the *avlod* can play a very important role for migrants, determining who should migrate and then functioning as the basic institution for those who have emigrated. Findings by the ILO indicated that "in the countries where the members of the *avlod* work, migrants tend to establish insular groups exclusively made up of relatives and fellow villagers. It is standard practice for construction brigades and *artels* (associations) of agricultural workers to live under the laws of the *avlod.* The foreman plays the role of the head of the *avlod*. He exercises undisputed authority over the brigade" (Olimova and Bosc 2003). These findings suggest that migration has reinforced traditional patriarchy in Tajikistan. However, among migrants in urban areas of Russia, the *avlod* is countered by factors that can weaken family ties. As migrants enter urban workplaces, they experience new freedoms and personal independence that can undermine traditional kinship obligations. Many male migrants marry Russian women, a practice that simultaneously weakens the traditional family structures and provides the migrants with a bridge between the *avlod* and the host society.

Male migration from Tajikistan has also resulted in gendered changes in family and society in the home country: women who remain in Tajikistan often start to carry out functions of the "head of household" in their families. These women fall into one of three categories: women who head their households during the migrant husband's absence; women who have been abandoned by their migrant husbands; and women whose migrant husbands return to see the family once every few years. In all three cases, the households are usually poorer than those headed by men. During a father's absence, most households comprised of several migrant families do remain under male authority, be it the head of the *avlod*, a grandfather, or a brother; these patriarchal households tend to be financially better off than migrant households consisting only of women and children. Although contributing to the family budget can strengthen a woman's hand when it comes to household decision making, women also encounter male resistance to their growing independence both within households and in neighborhoods and communities. Therefore, if there is no male in a household, it is much more complicated to solve serious social problems.

Moreover, women who are left heading households face discrimination outside the family. Among the most devastating inequalities that women suffer are related to land acquisition and farming. Women are at a severe disadvantage when it comes to obtaining plots of land from privatized corporate farms, and it is especially difficult to get a land plot for families without a male family member acting as the household head (IOM 2003, 113–114). In short, it appears that Tajik society is not ready to accept women in positions of authority, even as migration patterns impose greater responsibilities on women.

KAZAKHSTAN

As in the rest of Central Asia, many people in Kazakhstan are moving from rural to urban areas in search of employment, and here, too, there is a substantial gendered impact. Jobs or alternative income-generating opportunities are extremely limited in isolated rural areas, and young people do not see a future for themselves in these communities. At the same time, good jobs for inexperienced and unskilled workers are not easy to come by in urban centers like Almaty or Astana, and many young workers are consigned to casual day labor or become vulnerable to human traffickers (ADB 2006a, 57). Trafficking appears to be a particular concern for the daughters in poor rural families, as recruiters solicit these young women for domestic service positions. Families receive some modest remuneration—for example, about 100,000–200,000 soms (about US$100–200)—and the young women may be able to send remittances back to their siblings; but the trafficked women are vulnerable to exploitation—both sexual and otherwise. The Asian Development Bank estimates that there were about 50,000 commercial sexual workers in Kazakhstan in 2006 (ADB 2006a, 57). In the course of gathering the information, the Center for Public Opinion survey participants presented numerous cases when parents (most often mothers) sent their minor daughters to engage in prostitution on the streets. During interviews, the respondents also shared cases of rural village parents who have sent their sons to work as farm laborers. However the researchers were unable to find out whether the boys were also victims of sexual exploitation (Center for Public Opinion 2006).

The population migrating within Kazakhstan is clearly vulnerable to a broad range of labor exploitation, but so are migrants to Kazakhstan, especially those who have arrived illegally or who have overstayed their visas. As indicated earlier in this chapter, the republic has been identified as both a source and transit country and a destination for trafficking. Documentation of human trafficking is very difficult. In 2003–2004, the IOM, for example, indicated that only 139 cases of trafficking in Kazakhstan had been reported to it. Eighty-five of these were trafficked out from the country (seventy-one women and fourteen men); fourteen were trafficked within the country; and the remainder were trafficked to Kazakhstan from other Central Asian republics, primarily Uzbekistan. Women constitute the vast majority of trafficking victims who have been assisted by the IOM. Emigration for purposes of commercial sexual activity is particularly problematic. Such prostitution is most widespread in the regions neighboring Kyrgyzstan and Kazakhstan, where attitudes toward commercial sexual activity seem to be more tolerant (Bureau on Democracy 2005).

UZBEKISTAN

The Soviet Union fundamentally changed the image and role of Uzbek women. As part of its ideology of modernization, all Uzbek women were unveiled in a compulsory manner. And as in the other Central Asian republics, the Soviet ideology of gender equality made access to education, health care, and employment equal for men and women. Still, the Soviet-style egalitarian system laid a double burden upon women: labor outside the home was mandatory at the same time as they continued to carry major responsibilities for the household and the children.

Since independence, there has been a reaction against Soviet ideas of sexual equality, and one can observe in Uzbekistan a growing conservatism toward women's roles and an embrace of traditional values, including the traditional patriarchal order. This growing conservatism and traditionalism have been enhanced by the officially proclaimed policy of reviving national identity and values. There is strong support in both urban and rural areas for a return to traditions, which include gender disparity and the disempowerment of women. The influence of clergy in the formation of public opinion and livelihood strategies within the *mahalla* reinforces this. Ordinary citizens live according to community-established norms and regulations rather than official laws. Within the local community, the major criterion of social behavior is "what will people say if . . ." Thus, archaization and enhancement of patriarchy have been taking place simultaneously with the process of democratic reforms.

Along with the support across the country for a return to traditional patriarchy has been an increase in social stratification, producing radical economic disparities between the largely poor rural areas and economically developing urban areas. The rural population constitutes 67% of Uzbekistan, according to recent World Bank data. The official poverty rate is 27%, but 70% of the rural population exists in poverty (ADB 2005a). Employment and income-generation problems are becoming more acute, and one of the outcomes has been an increase in informal and formal migration.

As in the other NIS, the substantial internal migration within Uzbekistan has been gendered, especially after the intensification of the passport regime following the 1999 terrorist acts in Tashkent, which made it much more difficult for men to come from rural areas to cities, while less so for women. Thus, in recent years internal labor migration has become a predominantly female activity. The phenomenon of *mardikor* bazaars (day labor markets) is not new in Uzbekistan. But these unofficial day labor markets, where unemployed persons come to "sell their hands," have expanded significantly as rural work has declined. What is entirely new for that phenomenon is that the *mardikor* bazaars are becoming more and more feminized, as women are willing to do *any* kind of work alongside males: work in the construction sites, in agricultural fields, and so forth (International Crisis Group 2005, 25–26). Traditionally, day labor markets used to be a male preserve, as it was considered a family shame for a woman to sell her labor in such an unprotected place. Women working in such markets are much more vulnerable than men because they face a constant risk of sexual discrimination and exploitation. Greater access to *mardikor* bazaars has also produced greater recruitment of Uzbek women to labor abroad because a significant proportion of recruitment for external labor migration takes place at these bazaars. And as in the other NIS, the *mardikor* bazaars have also become a trap for victims of human trafficking.

Women's emigration patterns from Uzbekistan have also shifted. In 2002, 14.1% of emigrants from Uzbekistan were female. This proportion increased to 23.7% in 2004. Higher numbers of women participating in emigration can be explained by three interrelated factors: obviously, the physical proximity makes nearby Kazakhstan an easy destination for migrants. Second, the cultural similarities between the two regions make migrating to Kazakhstan less intimidating for Uzbek women than migrating to Russia. Third, there has been a growing demand for labor in traditionally female occupations in the spheres of agriculture and services in Kazakhstan.

Despite the embrace of traditional values, the changing gender balance among labor migrants has had some effect on women's position and roles in Uzbek society, particularly in the rural areas. Whereas in 1999 less than 2% of women labor migrants considered themselves heads of households, currently 57.6% of female respondents indicated that they are the breadwinners of the family and thus view themselves as heads of household. In fact, in Tashkent, Djizak, Syrdarya, and Ferghana *viloyats,* one can identify entire villages where almost all of the women migrate to Kazakhstan for work, leaving their unemployed husbands for up to three to four months during the agricultural season to take care of the children and the elderly.

Another gendered impact specific to Uzbekistan and Kyrgyzstan has been the growth of polygamy in the home country that has resulted from male emigration. According to the numerous surveys conducted by NGOs, many Uzbek and Kyrgyz women agree to become second wives in the face of their economic vulnerability, their impoverishment, and the revival of traditional stereotypes. This implies that the status of a married woman is much more preferable and respected than a single life. If a woman is divorced or widowed and she has grown-up children, especially daughters, it will be difficult to get her daughter married to a respected family unless the mother has the status of being a wife.

Like women in other Central Asian countries, such as Tajikistan, women in Uzbekistan face substantial challenges when their migrant husbands start new families in the destination countries. But in comparison to Tajik migrants, the traditional kinship relations among the Uzbeks have weakened. The Uzbek communities abroad do not preserve the strong structure of *avlod,* where kin relations have both vertical and horizontal structure. As described earlier in this chapter, alongside their implicit obedience to the head of the *avlod,* members of the Tajik *avlod* preserve strong horizontal relations with one another. In contrast, members of Uzbek families tend to have vertical connections with the head/patriarch of the family, while the horizontal connections inside the family become weaker with each successive generation. Thus, the third generation of Uzbek migrants do not tend to maintain strong and regular connections within the extended family, especially after the elder members pass away. This trend has numerous impacts on migrants' families. The patriarch of the family (mainly the eldest male) usually does not migrate due to his mature age. Simultaneously, the younger male family members who have migrated do not have authority among the other relatives and/or compatriots who might come from the same family and/or village; hence male migrants from Uzbekistan are not able to create sustainable and strong units within the migrant community that could serve as a bridge for preserving strong relations with the family back home (Azimova, Fayzullaeva, Yakupov, 2008).

Another factor contributing to weaker ties between migrants and their families in Uzbekistan has been the burden of traditional norms that prescribe that men be economically capable of sustaining the family. Such traditional views of manhood are especially strong in Muslim societies (Shahrani 2006, 26). If the man fails to fulfill the breadwinning function, there are strong implications of shame for this man. The dramatic drop of job opportunities in the home country and large-scale unemployment make it much much harder to be a "real" man. At the same time, the majority of the population is either unaware of or has not embraced ideas and values of gender equality. As a result, the traditional masculine identities in Uzbekistan conflict with the reality that more and more women are becoming breadwinners and managers in the family. Indeed, from the NGOs data as well as my observations, in cases of female out-migration, the males who stay home and care for children and households hardly ever openly speak about this situation with their friends or relatives; instead, they try by all means to preserve the formal signs of masculinity in public. Such an environment has produced what is often perceived as a "crisis of masculinity," which some argue is manifest in the dramatic increase in the number of suicides and nervous breakdowns among men (Rasuly-Paleczek 2006).

The revival of a gender-biased traditional identity is in clear conflict with those factors that are supporting women's empowerment and that are eroding the traditional family. These conflictual processes in their turn result in growing domestic violence, and women often use migration as an avenue of escape from unhappy marital relationships and domestic violence. In many cases, one of the reasons for conflicts in the families of labor migrants is the way in which money earned in the hardships of migration is spent—in particular, for celebrating ceremonies and rituals. For many, significant portions of their earnings go to conduct magnificent celebrations of wedding parties, *sunnat tuy* (a circumcision party), *beshik tuy* (a party celebrating a newly born child), or other traditional rites. Substantial funds are also expended on the renovation and construction of houses. Although these expenditures may reflect traditional gendered values, they cannot preserve the gender order that has been undermined by migration.

Public Policy and Migration in Central Asia

The foregoing sections of this chapter underscore the dramatic and multiple impacts of migration on the NIS. In this section, I discuss briefly the problem of public policy in the sphere of migration. Goals such as the creation of the common labor market in NIS countries, development of economic collaboration, and strengthening of national security are impossible without the formation of effective migration policies. And these policies require legislation, institutional development in the sphere of migration processes management, and bilateral and multilateral agreements. Regulating labor migration is a quite complicated issue, inseparably connected to social, economic, and historical contexts.

The relative inexperience and often the reluctance of the NIS governments to manage and legalize labor migration, as well as the gaps in existing legislation that are often exploited by corrupt officials and criminal structures, frequently result in severe violations of migrants' rights. The issue is sometimes compounded by popular perceptions of fluid borders and poor awareness among individual migrants and their employers about foreign labor legalization procedures. Unregulated or poorly organized labor migration results in flows of illegal labor migrants who are highly vulnerable to human rights abuses, including exploitation and human trafficking.

Currently throughout post–Communist Central Asia, there is a tendency toward "shadowization" in all public life—that is, the development of unofficial economic and social structures paralleling the official ones. A legal infrastructure for social and economic reforms is needed for sustainable development and in response to the deep and systemic changes in social relations and institutions. Unfortunately, policies to regulate ongoing and expanding labor migration processes in Central Asia are far from ideal, and the major streams of migrants are illegal and constitute the shadow sector of the economy in these states. Moreover, the avoidance of taxes is perceived in the public mentality not as a violation of law but as a response to the large-scale robbery by the state of its citizens (Barsukova 2000). After millions of people have lost their savings in the wake of inflation and state-sanctioned mass financial machination schemes, it has become normative for people to conceal their incomes from the state. "Hypertrophied honesty out of any social economic context is the destiny of moral stoics who may deserve respect but their honesty cannot be accepted as a norm" (Barsukova 2000, 63). In this context, this last section addresses the policies of three of the four Central Asian governments in relation to labor migration.

KAZAKHSTAN

Given the dramatically growing scale of migration in the transition period, the need for legislative regulations of labor and migration processes is urgent. But creation of a solid basis for such regulation remains one of the many unresolved issues in the Kazakhstan legislature. The issues lie in a problematic legislature. Compared with Russia, for example, which recently introduced a strict migration regime, Kazakhstan is moving in the opposite direction. The job authorization issuing system has been beyond the control of law enforcement bodies. This function is located within Departments of Labor under local *akimats* (mayors' offices). An employer must apply to the *akimat* and present grounds why she or he needs a foreign employee. Then, a commission in the *akimat* considers such applications and makes decisions. Each city and region has a definite quota for a foreign workforce. For example, the quota for Almaty in 2003 was 5,000 people. But that scheme is very easy to manipulate and avoid. Employers can easily choose not to apply to the *akimat* and not to declare that they hire foreign workers, since there is little risk in unofficially hiring labor for the so-called black cash, which does not require any permit and registration. According to Kazakh legislation, the penalty for employing such illegal labor includes an administrative fine of twenty-five minimal salaries (17,000 tenge) and deportation of the worker when the illegal character of employment is proved. But only a single clause in legislation refers to this kind of crime (Kozyreva 2005, 3–4).

TAJIKISTAN

In Tajikistan, there is a sufficient legislative basis for regulating labor migration. Two major laws and a number of state programs, strategies, and concepts reflect a coherent state policy in the sphere of labor migration. The law on migration was adopted in 1999 and amended on May 10, 2002. The government's External Labor Migration Program for 2003–2005 was authorized by the parliament in 2002. Under Article 8 of this law, the government can render assistance to the organized external migration of workers with their consent and only to countries where their rights are protected. Tajik citizens who plan to take a job abroad need to have a signed contract, an international passport, and an entry visa, if required. A state strategy on the labor market is also reflected in a Poverty Reduction Strategy Document initiated by the government and a number of international financial institutions. Stressing the link between unemployment and migration, the government acknowledges the importance of coordinating antipoverty and migration policies.

UZBEKISTAN

In Uzbekistan, in contrast, state policy does not cover labor migration. A single state agency under the Ministry of Labor deals with labor migration issues, and the volume of its operations covers a very small portion of the issues related to labor migration. It supervises only the labor force exchange with South Korea. The single official research conducted under the President's Office states that labor migration is a positive process for Uzbekistan, as labor migrants migrate mainly to Russia to find temporary jobs to feed their families and start small businesses. The research does not analyze the other aspects of migration, providing no information on its causes and consequences, human trafficking, or the gendered aspects of migration.

Conclusion

Labor migration has been one of the most powerful social and economic consequences of political transition and market liberalization in Central Asia. As this chapter has shown, the centralized Soviet system strictly controlled population mobility across the areas under its control in Central Asia, regulating migration in light of state policies of economic and social development. This system also promoted women's participation in the labor market through extensive child-care systems and other social supports. During the early years of the transition, restrictions on migration were significantly liberalized; at the same time, the social support for women began to be dismantled. There is no singular pattern to the substantial emigration and sojourning across the region that resulted from the dramatic economic and political changes. In all cases, we can document a significant rural-to-urban migration within the countries. But the extent of emigration has depended on the economic and social contexts. In economies like Uzbekistan, Kyrgyzstan, and Tajikistan, emigration has been significant, whereas Kazakhstan and other rapidly developing or resource-rich states have become destination countries, attracting substantial migrant labor, as well as becoming source countries, contributing labor elsewhere.

There has also been great variability in the gendered composition of the migration streams. In Tajikistan, most of the emigrants have been men, whereas in Kyrgyzstan, more women than men have migrated. The consequences of migration do differ for men and women. Women who migrate or are trafficked are especially vulnerable to sexual exploitation, as occurs among women working as sojourners in the Kazakh tobacco fields and among poor girls who migrate to serve as domestic workers and workers in the day markets of Uzbekistan. The consequences of gender imbalances in the home regions and countries as a result of migration are also very powerful. Many men form new families in the host societies, attenuating their ties to the families at home and support for traditional gender orders. But, as is evident in the differences between Tajik and Uzbek emigrants, the social structure and networks within the emigrant communities seem to affect the stability of the patriarchal order at home. Efforts to reinscribe patriarchy and return to traditional norms and values have also been affected by the gendered patterns of migration. In Uzbekistan, where the call to return to tradition has been particularly strong, massive male emigration has placed women in charge of households and created a crisis for those men left behind who cannot achieve normative masculinity. At the same time, women who are increasingly independent feel the stigma of those norms that associate respectability with marriage and therefore are ready to enter into polygamy as a route to gender respectability.

The labor migration that has become one of the most central impacts of globalization on Central Asia has had dramatic and complex gendered implications. The largest international financial agencies have emphasized the positive gender impacts of global labor migration processes, stating that global migration adds to the welfare of states, families, and individuals. But they barely focus on the adverse sides of labor migration. As I have suggested in this chapter, the situation of labor out-migration *can* contribute to women's empowerment through allowing greater economic independence, leadership, and autonomy; increasing the share of women in paid employment situations; and providing opportunities to weaken patriarchal controls and promote gender equality. But such empowerment seems far from the reality across post-Communist Central Asia. Much more attention has to be paid to the often devastating effects of the extensive migration on the destinies of women in Central Asia. Unless states adopt policies that view women as partners in social reconstruction and agents of development, the vision of migration as a source of empowerment seems an illusory dream.

NOTES

1. Perhaps not surprisingly, most studies that have begun to examine migration as a gendered process are done by female scholars (e.g., Brettell 1996; Davis and Heyl

1986; Fernandez-Kelly and Nash 1986; Grasmuck and Pessar 1991; Pedraza 1991, Maksakova 2005; Morokvasic 1983; Sadovskaya 1999, 2000 and 2001; Zayonchkovskaya 1999; Ward 1993; Sassen-Koob 1984, 1988; Wolf 1992; Tyuryukanova 2004a, 2004b; Tyuryukanova and Malisheva 2001; Rakhmanova 2005.

2. For example, any description of this phenomenon was missing in the encyclopedic dictionary *People and Population* published in Moscow in 1994.

3. The following websites are useful for background and current data on migration in post-communist Central Asia:

   - Asian Development Bank (ADB): http://www.adb.org
   - Central Bank of Russia: http://www.centralbank.ru
   - Eldis: http://www.eldis.org/
   - International Labour Organization (ILO): http://www.ilo.org
   - International Organization for Human Rights: http://www.ihf-hr.org
   - International Organization for Migration (IOM): http://www.iom.int
   - United Nations Development Fund for Women (UNIFEM): http://www.unifem.org.

WORKS CITED

ADB (Asian Development Bank). 2001. *Women in the Republic of Uzbekistan.* Country Briefing Paper. February. Http://www.adb.org/Documents/Books/Country_Briefing_Papers/ Women_in_Uzbekistan/women_in_uzbekistan.pdf.

———. 2005a. *Uzbekistan: Country Gender Assessment.* (December) Http://www.adb.org/ Documents/Reports/Country-Gender-Assessments/cga-uzbekistan.pdf.

———. 2005b. "The Kyrgyz Republic: A Gendered Transition Soviet Legacies and New Risks." *Country Gender Assessments—Kyrgyz Republic.* December. Http://www.adb.org/ Documents/Reports/Country-Gender-Assessments/cga-kgz.pdf.

———. 2006a. *Kazakhstan: Country Gender Assessment.* May. Http://www.adb.org/Documents/ Reports/Country-Gender-Assessments/cga-kaz.pdf.

———. 2006b. *Kyrgyzstan: Country Gender Assessment.* December. Http://www.adb.org/ Documents/Reports/Country-Gender-assessments/cga-kgz.pdf.

Azimova, Nodira, Eleonora Fayzullaeva, and Saurjan Yakupov. 2008. "Voices of Labor Migrants." In *Labor Migration in the Republic of Uzbekistan: Social, legal and Gender Aspects.* Tashkent: UNDP and Gender Program of the Embassy of Switzerland in Uzbekistan.

Barsukova, Svetlana. 2000. "Shadow and Ficticious Labor Markets in Contemporary Russia." *Pro et Contra.* Moscow: Carnegie Center, 5(1). Http://www.carnegie.ru/en/pubs/ procontra/55575.htm.

Brettell, Caroline B. 1996. "Women Are Migrants Too: A Portuguese Perspective." In *Urban Life: Readings in Urban Anthropology,* ed. George Gmelch and Walter P. Zenner, 245–258. Prospect Heights, Ill.: Waveland Press.

Bureau on Democracy, Human Rights and Labor. 2005. *Annual Report on Human Rights.* Almaty: Bureau on Democracy, Human Rights and Labor.

CEDAW (Convention on the Elimination of Discrimination against Women). 2002. *Second Periodic Report of State Parties. Kyrgyz Republic.* CEDAW/C/KGZ/2. Submission Under Article 18 of CEDAW. New York: United Nations.

Center for Public Opinion/El Pikar. 2006. "Situational Analysis of Commercial Sexual Exploitation of Children in Uzbekistan." Bishkek: Center for Public Opinion/El Pikar.

Davis, James F., and Barbara Sherman Heyl. 1986. "Turkish Women and Guest worker Migration to West Germany." In *International Migration: The Female Experience,* ed. Rita J. Simon and Caroline Bretrell. Totowa, N.J.: Bowman and Allanheld.

Department of Migration under the Ministry of Foreign Affairs in Kyrgyzstan. 2005. Unpublished migration data.

Fernandez-Kelly, Maria Patricia, and June Nash, eds. 1984. *Women, Men, and the New International Division of Labor.* Albany: State University of New York Press.

Glodenyte, A. 2003. *Overview of the Labor Migration Trends and Management Initiatives in Selected CIS and Neighboring Countries.* Vienna: International Organization for Migration.

Government of the Kyrgyz Republic. 2001. *The Kyrgyz Republic: New Development Prospects. Comprehensive Development Framework of the Kyrgyz Republic to 2010.* Bishkek: Government of Kyrgyz Republic.

Government of Uzbekistan. 1995. "Health Examination Survey." Www.measuredhs.com.

———. 2005. "The Millennium Development Goals." Draft National Report. Tashkent: United Nations Office in Uzbekistan. 2005.org/upload/Uzbekistan/Uzbekistan%20MDG%20April%202006.pdf.

———. 2006. *The Millennium Development Goals Report.* Http://planipolis.iiep.unesco.org/upload/Uzbekistan/Uzbekistan%20MDG%20April%202006.pdf.

Grasmuck, Sherri, and Patricia Pessar. 1991. *Between Two Islands: Dominican International Migration.* Berkeley: University of California Press.

International Crisis Group. 2005. "The Curse of Cotton: Central Asia's Destructive Monoculture." *Asia Report,* no. 93 (February): 1–56. Http://www.crisisgroup.org/library/documents/asia/central_asia/093_curse_of_cotton_central_asia_destructive_monoculture.pdf.

International Organization for Migration. 2003. *Labor Migration from Tajikistan.* Http://www.iom.int/jahia/webdav/site/myjahiasite/shared/shared/mainsite/published_docs/studies_and_reports/.

————. 2005. *Labor Migration from Uzbekistan in the Southern Regions of Kazakhstan*. IOM Assessment Report.

Jonas, Susanne, and Suzanne Dod Thomas. 1998. *Immigration: A Civil Rights Issue for the Americas*. Wilmington, Del.: Scholarly Resources Books.

Kozyreva, Yvgenia. 2005. "Illegal Migration in Kazakhstan." Feminist League of Kazakhstan. Unpublished materials.

Kurtov, Ajdar . 2006. *Chinese Migration in Kazakhstan: Is the Future of This Phenomenon Defined?* Almaty. Http://www.apn.kz/index.php?chapter_name=advert&data_id=420&do=view_single; Http://www.stat.kz/stat/index.aspx?p=migr.

Maksakova, Lyudmila. 2005. *Trudovaya migratziya nasyeleniya Uzbekistana: Tendentzii i regionalniye osobyenosti*. Tashkent: Centre for Effective Economic Policy, Ministry of Economics in the Republic of Uzbekistan.

Maksakova, Lyudmila, and Valentina Chupik. 2003. *Migration Tendencies in Uzbekistan*. Materials for the conference "Trafficking in Human Beings," OSIAF, OSCE Center in Tashkent.

Meladze, G. G., B. N. Kutelia. 2003. "External Migration in Georgia in 1996–2001." *Sociological Journal* 1.

Melikyan, G. G, ed. 1994. *People and Nations*. Moscow: Big Russian Encyclopedia.

Morokvasic, Mirjana. 1983. "Women in Migration: Beyond the Reductionist Outlook." In *One Way Ticket: Migration and Female Labor*, ed. Annie Phizacklea, 13–31. London: Routledge and Kegan Paul.

Mughal, Abdul-Ghaffar. 2006. "Leveraging International Migration for Empowering Women in Tajikistan." Panel paper. CESS Conference, University of Michigan.

Olimova, Saodat, and Igor Bosk. Саодат Олимова, Игорь Боск. 2003. *Трудовая миграция из Таджикистана* (Labor migration from Tajikistan). Moscow: International Organization on Migration in collaboration with "Shark" scientific-research center.

Olimova, Saodat, Sobir Kurbonov, Grigory Petrov, and Zebo Kahhorova. 2006. "Regional Cooperation in Central Asia: A View from Tajikistan." *Problems of Economic Transition* 48(9) (January): 6–86.

Pedraza, Silvia. 1991. "Women and Migration: The Social Consequences of Gender." *Annual Review of Sociology* 17: 303–325.

Rakhmanova, Nilufar. 2005. "Access of Health Services for Women of Reproductive Age with Anemia in Uzbekistan." CESS Conference, Poverty Reduction Strategy Paper, released by the government of Tajikistan.

Rasuly-Paleczek, Gabrielle. 2006. "Dislocating Gender, Family and Kinship: The Uzbeks of Afghanistan and Beyond." Paper presented at panel on State, Family and the Crisis of Masculinity/Femininity in Muslim Central and Southwestern Asia, CESS Conference (September 28-October 1), University of Michigan.

Ribakovskiy, L. L. 1995. *Migration Exchange of Population between Central Asia and Russia.* Moscow Social Survey 9.

Sadovskaya, Elena U. 1999. *Migration Processes and Migration Policy in Kazakhstan.* Moscow: Center for Forced Migration Study in CIS and Independent Council on Migration of CIS and the Baltics. Russian Academy of Science. Collection of papers, editor-in-chief J. Zayonchkovskaya.

———. 2000. *Migration in Kazakhstan on the Boundary of the 21st Century: Major Trends and Prospects.* Materials for the seminar "Migration in Kazakhstan–Present and Future," Astana, January 26–27.

———. 2001. *Labor Migration as Means of Adaptation to Economic Crisis in Kazakhstan.* Alma-taa.

Sassen-Koob, Saskia. 1984. "Notes on the Incorporation of Third World Women into Wage-Labor through Immigration and Off-Shore Production." *International Migration Review* 18(2): 1144–1167.

Schiller, Click, Nina Linda Basch, and Christina Szanton Blanc. 1992. *Towards a Transnational Perspective on Migration.* New York: Academy of Sciences.

Shahrani, Nazif. 2006. "Causes and Conditions of Crisis of Masculinity/Femininity in Muslim Central and Southwestern Asia." Paper presented at panel on "State, Family and the Crisis of Masculinity/Femininity in Muslim Central and Southwestern Asia," CESS Conference (September 28–October 1). University of Michigan.

Statistical Agency of the Republic of Kazakhstan. 2000. "About the Migration of the Population of the Republic of Kazakhstan." Almaty: Statistical Agency. 1/3/2000. Http://www.stat.kz/stat/index.aspx?p=migr.

Tyuryukanova, Elena. 2004a. Трудовая миграция из стран СНг и новые практики эксплуатации труда (Labor migration from NIS: New forms of labor exploitation). Paper presented at conference International Migration, Cairo.

———. 2004b. Исследование для МОМ о миграции в Московской, Ставропольской и Омской областях Российской федерации (A survey on migrants in Moscow, Stavropol and Omsk regions of Russia Federation, in the Pro et Contra journal of Carnegie Center, Moscow Russian Federation). Http://www.carnegie.ru/en/pubs/procontra/.

Tyuryukanova, Elena. Malysheva. 2001. Женщина, миграция, государство (Women, migration, state). Moscow.

Tzovinar, Nazarova. 2004. "What It Means to be a Russian Repatriate in Israel" Interview with Zvika Shetnfeld, professor at Tel-Aviv University.

Uzbekistan State Statistical Committee. 2004. *Women and Men of Uzbekistan.* Tashkent, Uzbekistan: State Statistical Committee.

Ward, Kathryn. 1993. "Reconceptualizing World System Theory to Include Women." In

Theory on Gender/Feminism on Theory, ed. Paula England, 43–68. New York: Aldine de Gruyter.

Wellman, Barry, and Scott Wortley. 1989. "Different Strokes from Different Folks: Which Type of Ties Provide What Kind of Social Support?" *Research Paper No. 174*. Centre for Urban and Community Studies, University of Toronto.

Wolf, Diane Lauren. 1992. *Factory Daughters: Gender, Household Dynamics, and Rural Industrialization in Java*. Berkeley: University of California Press.

World Bank. 2003. *Uzbekistan Living Standards Assessment Report No. 25923*. Human Development Sector Unit, Europe and Central Asia. Washington, D.C.: World Bank.

———. 2004. *The Kyrgyz Republic. Recent Economic Developments: January–December*. Washington, D.C.: World Bank.

WSC (Women's Support Center). 2003. *Gender Dimensions of HIV/AIDS in the Kyrgyz Republic*. Bishkek: United Nations Development Fund for Women.

Zayonchkovskaya, J. A. 1999. *Migration Situation in CIS*. Moscow: Center for Forced Migration in CIS and Independent Research Center on Migration in CIS and the Baltics, Russian Academy of Science.

9

The Complexity and Multiplicity of Gender Identities in Central Asia: The Case of Tajikistan

Zulaikho Usmanova

This chapter takes up the issue of gender roles and identities in Tajikistan, the multiplicity of which can be seen at different levels of social life, including family and community relationships. It examines these roles and identities through a case study of Khujand, the regional center of the Sughd region of Tajikistan, including some rural areas around the city of Khujand. While Khujand is an inalienable part of Tajikistan, the social practices in this region manifest differences that are reflected in a particular Khujand culture and identity. Not surprisingly then, gender roles and identities are at once both illustrative of greater Tajikistan and unique to Khujand. A considerable body of scholarship suggests that Central Asian women have been, historically and currently, suppressed, badly treated, and discriminated against. This observation is partly true, but if one wants to understand gender relations and the situation of women in Central Asia, an analysis that takes women's agency into account is required (Harris 2004). While the gender situation across Tajikistan is on the whole similar, there are some geographic areas, predominantly urban ones, and some fields of life where women make their voices and their presence known in society. This chapter highlights the activity of selected women in Tajikistan, particularly in Khujand, who have special status and authority not only among women but in society more broadly.

Between February and July 2005, I was a part of a group research project exploring individuals' expressions of social and ethical values in the daily life of small communities (*mahallas*) in Khujand.[1] Beyond the city, I visited two villages adjacent to Khujand, Konibodom City (70 km from Khujand), and several villages in the Mastchoh region to explore the perceptions that both urban and rural inhabitants in these areas have about Khujand and Khujandi people, their values, and their social behavior. During this research, I observed public and life-cycle events: weddings, funerals, birthday parties, official meetings and student conferences at Khujand State University, Bozihoi Milli (the National Children's Games, including traditional games), the girls' sports competition held on March 8, International Women's Day, and other events. To explore issues of Islam and gender, I visited several mosques in Khujand, where I had conversations and taped interviews with mullahs and other mosque workers. I also attended various religious events with female cultural-religious leaders, *otunbuchas* and *folbins*. Research methods included observation; open-ended, taped interviews; conversations that were not taped; participant observation; and archive work at Toshhuja Asiri regional library.

This study thus takes up an area of Tajikistan that has received little attention in women's studies. Western scholarship on gender relations in Tajikistan has focused mostly on the southern part of the country, giving less attention to the oldest cities like Khujand, which have their own traditions and strong identity and where women have been playing significant roles in both the public and private sectors for decades. This chapter complements and extends that scholarship by situating its analysis of gender politics in Khujand in a broader discussion of the historical and contemporary context in Tajikistan.

Women's lives in Tajikistan during the transition from Soviet rule to the present have been affected by legal, political, economic, and social circumstances at the local level as well as at the national level. These circumstances have, in turn, been affected by at least three factors: the previous Soviet regime, the recent civil war (1992–1997), and the whole system of traditional gender roles and expectations, including local customs and religious influences (Harris 2004, 20).

Safarova et al. (2007) point out that Soviet-era gender relations in Tajikistan, as well as in other Soviet Central Asian republics, were shaped by official directives that sought to encourage women's emancipation, particularly through participation in economic production and political affairs. These policies, especially those that advanced women's education and social services, did effect a certain degree of liberation as they fostered more active participation of women in public life (Safarova et al. 2007, 5). But despite socialism's achievements in improving women's situation, there was no true gender equality in Soviet Tajikistan. The public sector was characterized by a quite high proportion of women at lower levels of government and only isolated examples of female managers at the highest levels. And even at high-level administrative posts, women were confined to addressing social issues, generally related to the family. Most young women and girls worked in the cotton fields, without the benefit of elementary norms of labor protection and personal hygiene. Payments to and privileges for mothers with many children encouraged closely spaced births, which had an effect on both women's health and well-being. Thus, the Soviet state policy of "liberating women of the East" had many positive aspects, but history shows it is impossible to emancipate one gender without emancipating the entire population from total control and state intervention. Moreover, despite tremendous changes in the public involvement of Tajik women during the Soviet era, their position in the private sphere remained almost the same. Although formal equality was provided by the constitution, there were no effective mechanisms for emancipating women.

The civil war of 1992–1997 dragged many Tajiks into violence, poverty, and suffering. With more than 50,000 people dead, the war inevitably disrupted family structures, "leaving many young women to look after their children without a male breadwinner" (Falkingham 2000, 14). The civil war and its negative impacts contributed to the way that the gender policies were developed in the mid-1990s to early 2000s and were subsequently implemented. Since the demise of the Communist system and the civil war in Tajikistan, women's roles have been changing rapidly in both the public and domestic/private spheres. Jane Falkingham argues that "one of the biggest transformations in gender roles in Tajikistan has been the withdrawal of women from public life" (2000, 25). Another has been the revival of traditionalism. It is insufficient, however, to view the gender transformations in Tajikistan as a trajectory of return to traditional gender roles and relations. Social changes over the last few years, shaped in part by globalization, suggest an increase of women's involvement in the public and social life of the country, mainly in urban areas. An analysis of the political, economic, and social spheres reveals not only the persistence of traditional gender inequalities but also the emergence of new problems for Tajik women. In this next section of the chapter, I turn to the participation of women in political and economic life.

Gender Policy and Women in Political and Economic Life

POLITICS AND LAW

From the mid-1990s forward, legislation in Tajikistan has specified an official policy of nondiscrimination against women. The state has ratified a number of international conventions and agreements on human rights and is a participant of the Convention on the Elimination of All Forms of Discrimination against Women (CEDAW). As Safarova et al. (2007) document, post-Communist Tajikistan has adopted legislation and policies that promote women's equality and protect their rights within the family and in the labor market. These include the National Action Plan on Increasing the Female Status and Role (1998–2005) and subsequently a set of directives embodied in a state policy, Providing Equal Rights and Opportunities for Women and Men (2001–2010). The state has also adopted regulations meant to support women's welfare through programs related to reproductive, maternal, and children's health. However, formal policies are no guarantee of gender equality (Safarova et al. 2007, 5–6).

The main inequality in politics lies in the fact that the policies of state institutions do not always consider the interests of women. Gender stereotypes persist, making consideration of women's interests secondary to socioeconomic concerns. Almost all laws lack consideration of a gender-based approach. Clear identification of what constitutes sex discrimination is missing in legislative acts, and there are no mechanisms to specify and punish those responsible for discrimination against women.

In terms of formal political representation, the current Tajik government inherited a Soviet system of quotas according to which a certain percentage of women should be visible at different levels of political power. Indeed, the representation of women in the lower house of the Tajik Parliament remains comparatively high (18%) (Safarova et al. 2007, 6). But still there is insufficient women's representation in power structures at all levels. By 2003, there were no women ministry chairpersons, and women made up a little less than 9% of department chairs (Safarova et al. 2007, 7). At the same time, however, the last decade has witnessed an increased role for women in local power structures. In the *mahallas,* some women have become Heads, and women make up 23% of Jamoat Heads and 43% of Deputy Jamoat Heads in Tajikistan (Safarova et al. 2007, 8).[2]

ECONOMICS

The most significant gender problems and inequality can be seen in the economic sector. In general, hard economic conditions have deeply affected traditional gender identities, because many men cannot effectively execute the role of breadwinner anymore, and women are often forced to assume this role in the family. For many men, the most visible economic loss has been losing the job that had given them a stable income. However, women cannot easily take on the mantle of breadwinner and retain the family's economic status. For women, economic losses have been aggravated by the disappearance of the social supports that the Soviet system provided for the family and for protection during maternity and childhood. The loss of these benefits has been exacerbated by the increase in unemployment, the rise in poverty, and the continuing problem of occupational segregation.[3]

The world of female labor continues to differ from the world of male labor by the types of work, payment, position, and character of hiring and dismissing. In some professions, women are prevalent (as a rule, low-paid ones). Women predominate in the social sphere and agriculture, where salary rates are four to eight times lower than those in industry and construction, and twenty times lower than in the banking system and business.[4] In other spheres, men are prevalent; they generally become the owners of privatized businesses, where women are hired labor. Thus, at present, women play an increasingly important role in the survival of their families, and they need jobs; but they have to compete with men in an unfavorable labor market.[5] At the same time, the post-Soviet situation has seen a rise in poverty due to unemployment and underemployment. Combined with high birth rates and diminished state supports to families, circumstances have become untenable for many Tajiks. The situation is especially difficult in those families where a woman is the only breadwinner and she alone is responsible for rearing and educating her children. Such stresses, along with other consequences of economic reforms, such as poverty, have had an impact on people's health and well-being as evidenced by reduced life expectancy, increased mother and infant mortality, increased numbers of homeless children and children in orphanages, the growing number of cases of teenage pregnancies, drug trafficking, the reappearance of traditions of early marriage and polygamy, growth in crime and prostitution, and trafficking in women and children.

Finally, the increasing economic instability and poverty have prompted many Tajiks to migrate for work. Both genders suffer from migration. But the migration itself is different from that of five to six years ago, when migration was largely by males moving to Russia and other countries to make money. Now a new trend can be seen, especially in urban areas of the country. For example, in Khujand it has become more usual for spouses to go to Russia together, leaving children with grandparents temporarily. This migration trend seems positive because at least the family survives together, and joint labor migration does not necessarily lead to divorce, as was often the case when a man migrated by himself. However, it is unclear how women's socioeconomic status will shift as a result of migration trends.

The Social Context for Gender Equality

Like other institutions of Tajik society, family relations in Tajikistan have been affected by the transformations of recent years. Two trends can be seen in the structure of the family. On the one hand, there is an increase of patriarchal models because under difficult economic conditions and meager state support, one can count only on one's family. As a consequence of the increased role of families in shaping gender roles, there is evidence of some regression in comparison with the emancipation of women under Soviet rule. Education, for example, is increasingly not seen as positive for females, especially for girls in rural areas. A girl in a family with many children might marry earlier because her family is too poor to educate her and even to feed her.

On the other hand, certain antipatriarchal trends connected with modernization processes can also be observed. In education, for example, a state-imposed quota system encourages young rural women to be educated in institutions of higher education. Women continue to have high levels of education and continue to work in the public sphere, and there are new opportunities for women who may occupy positions in business, nongovernmental organizations (NGOs), and international organizations in Tajikistan. Although the economic situation has deteriorated, thus far basic indicators of education for women have not declined. There are no differences in the literacy rates for men and women nine to forty-nine years old, and there is equality in the general literacy level among men and women. In elementary schools, there is almost no difference between the numbers of boys and girls. Indeed, seven out of ten families interviewed indicated that parents would encourage their daughters to continue education and to get a profession: "Because it is no guarantee that her husband will be making money enough for the family, her being a professional will help," says a fifty-three-year-old head of a family in Khujand (author's field notes). However, there are reasons for future concern. In the high schools of Tajikistan, the difference between the numbers of boys and girls is already 24–25%, and in institutions of higher education, the percentage of girls is down to 24.3% overall (Gender and Development 2003).

Society's return to certain patriarchal values has strengthened the inequality between men and women and complicated their relationships. The traditional models of relationships between men and women have been strengthened among the population.

More and more young men and women obtain education abroad, and this promotes acceptance of new values and practices. Furthermore, globalization also has had a significant impact on decreasing patriarchal models. More and more young people use the Internet and read and watch mass media, through which they can become familiar with new ideologies and images of femininity and masculinity. One upshot of these changes is attitudinal, as suggested by my interviews. My urban female informants mentioned a certain progress in family relations. They reported that men in general have become more tolerant and more open and supportive. Also telling, in the interviews, most of my informants, even more senior ones, would discuss issues of sex and sexuality.

Relations between husbands and wives in urban areas are also not as strict and male dominated as has been accepted as a general view. Again, the economic sphere provides an interesting lesson. Women are more flexible in the job-seeking process and more goal oriented. A woman may be more willing to move slowly toward upper positions; she can wait and manage with not as high a salary. But men seem to be not as flexible and patient as women are and, as a result, may stay without a job for months and even years. In such cases, women's and men's positions in the family may be far more equal than generally expected.

FAMILIAL RELATIONS IN TAJIKISTAN

Other traditional familial relations remain powerful despite the changes prompted by the transition from Communism. In Tajik society, there is a religiously supported ethical ideal of the child who respects his or her parents intensely. In the Qur'an we read: "Your God decided that you should not worship anyone but Him, and loyalty [is due to] parents. If either of them or both reach old age, do not spit on them! Do not shout at them, but say a [good] word to them. And do bow in your humility to both of them and say: 'God forgive them, for they raised me from a baby'" (17:24–25). Traditional ethical rules prescribe that children obey parents, listen to their advice and preaching, and never act so that parents feel bad in respect to the people around them, because the shadow of the children's bad acts falls on the parents. A popular saying attributed to the classical Persian poet Sa'adi, famous for his ethical and social observations, goes, "Whoever does not respect his parents, will never be beloved or happy."

Children are considered to be a "result" of their parents, as is acknowledged in formal, celebratory speeches at personal life-cycle events. A forty-seven-year-old man gave a toast in Russian at his friend's birthday party. "So, I want to thank very much, first of all, his parents, those [third person, polite plural] who are deceased [his father] and those still alive [his mother]. A great 'Thank you!' to his father-in-law, and his mother-in-law, and probably (ironic smile), to D. [his wife], because now I have my wonderful friend–RIK." A thirty-six-year-old woman offered a toast at her mother's birthday party: "I owe my mother for everything I have, and for my becoming a human, forever, until the end of my life."

FAMILY RELATIONS AND GENDER IN KHUJAND

In Khujand, the practice of ethics and the expression of cultural identity start with daily politeness and continue with a deep, complex hierarchical system of family/clan/professional group relationships. The responsibilities of parents and children are usually clearly determined, but deviations (norm breaking) can be observed. Children have to take care of and look after their parents until the latters' death. There are forms of social control of the family and *mahalla*, including the "watching" of people to see whether they follow the rules. Breaking the rules (not taking care of parents or burying them without necessary respect) may cause social disregard. On the other hand, in a case when a parent does not fulfill his or her responsibility as a "good" parent, he or she may be condemned by the community. Traditional ties and responsibilities between sisters and brothers also have certain weight and become important when various events are held.

In Khujand, women have played a central role in the family and the private sector. For example, it is not rare for the mother to control the family budget constituted by salaries of almost all family members. More informal relations occur between mothers and children than between fathers and children. A well-known saying from the Qur'an illustrates this point: "Bihisht zeri poi modaron ast" (Paradise is under the mother's feet). One may address one's mother familiarly as "*tu*" ("you" in a single form), but respect for the mother is still strictly required, because "Vai shiri safed dodagi ast" (She has given white milk). Yet in popular belief, a mother's curse is not so terrifying and awful as a father's because a mother's milk given to the child prevents the mother's curses from being realized. Children may pass their requests or needs to their father through the mother. When a father swears at or beats a child, the child can find shelter only under "the mother's wing."

It is not surprising in Khujand when a son keeps a very trustful, intimate, and close relationship with his mother for life. He may come to her and ask advice, telling her all his problems and expecting her guidance. Such a relationship between a mother and son is most frequent with the youngest sons who care for the parents. Even when a son gets older and becomes a head of his own family or a whole clan, he cannot claim to be above his mother. AJK, who occupies a high social position, confessed that in critical moments of his life, he appealed to his mother and would invariably do everything she recommended. In many families, women directly or indirectly lead family decision making, such as money management, planning events, and of course marriage strategies and negotiations. A stereotype held by outsiders and supported by various ethnic jokes suggests that women in Khujand possess special status and power within the family. A thirty-five-year-old male non-Khujandi interviewee said: "Dar inja Modarshohi agar guem ham, khato namekunem" (We would not be wrong to say that there is a matriarchy here [in Khujand]).

Familial respect relations affect and interconnect with professional respect and responsibility relations. It is appropriate in Khujand for an employee to make courtesy visits to the boss's mother, so that she will know that her child has good workers. In one case, a man who was fired from his job was then rehired because the boss's mother insisted on her son taking the person back, and this type of advice from a mother is not regarded as unusual. It is also an index of a good attitude in the boss if he or she visits an employee's parents at least once a year and/or during the main holidays and family events.

THE *MAHALLA* AND GENDER IN KHUJAND

The *mahalla* is a community/neighborhood, either urban or rural, that reflects the extended family grouping of the Tajik *avlod* (Poliakov 1992, 76). Official Soviet policy had to legalize *mahallas* because it was more convenient to preserve them as social units in the cities and countryside than to create new forms of social organization. A *mahalla* is a community comprising from as few as 15 to up to as many as 300 households.

Mahallas in Khujand keep traditional ways and principles of life and social communication. This is reflected, first of all, in the lifestyles and traditional roles in the family and within the community. The *mahalla* phenomenon deserves closer attention by scholars studying Tajik society because it still remains an authoritative form of social control with its own rules and laws. The old part of Khujand is divided into more than 250 *mahallas*. People now living in new microdistricts of Khujand have moved there mostly from *mahallas* as a result of the division of big families, and they are expected to keep their relationship with their *mahalla*, since that relationship is a part of their identity.

Within the city, several areas are considered to be main villages, or *qishloqs*, each of which contains several *mahallas* that constitute the old city: Rumon, Razzoq, Panjshanbe, Chuqurak, and others. People usually designate each other and themselves using the names of their *qishloqs*—for example, Rumoni or Razzoqi. Each *qishloq* has an image—for instance, a stereotype of cunning and success in trade applied to people from Rumon, while the people from the Panjshanbe section are assumed to be wealthy.[6] The identity of a person depends on age, gender, and professional affiliation, as well as on elements such as parents'/ parents'-in-law social status, profession, position, and previous accomplishments, including even the number of children and, not incidentally, *mahalla* affiliation and/or original place of birth (if one now lives at another place).

A fifty-three-year-old female inhabitant of one *mahalla* describes a rather ideal picture of *mahalla* education and collaboration, which nonetheless reveals the values now at stake under conditions of change. Her description also suggests how much of ethical and social learning is a matter of participation and habits, rather than of verbal instruction:

> First, kids who grow up at the *mahalla* are different. They—the kids—are educated not only by the family—the whole *mahalla* educates them. For example, traditions existing in *mahallas* [involve] the *mahalla* [as a whole]. For example, in burying the deceased (person), the whole *mahalla* comes together and takes responsibility for taking (the deceased person) to the last point (i.e. burial and all the subsequent memorial events), or if there are sick people, bedridden, bedridden elderly, of course, they are visited. These are considered *mahalla* traditions. Those elders who live in the *mahalla* never feel deprived, they don't consider themselves to be without people (alone), because everyone, no matter whether young or old, sympathizes with them and helps them, goes and visits; if there is something to be done (housework), they (visitors) would help, like this. . . . Kids also are different, in the sense of ethics and behavior, greeting and addressing first, of course, in each family, [in the] *mahalla* from the beginning they meet and see older people, they get used to the *mahalla* traditions. Their education starts with greeting-addressing (*salom-alek*), of course, then, since they "sit-and-stand" (interact) with the older people, they learn *mahalla* traditions not by being told, but by watching. They see in their family first, then—at the public events, then—at the funerals, some *mahallas* have tea-houses, (where there is) "sitting-and-standing" for kids [young men]; all these constitute education for kids. From the first day, when they bring the baby [home], *mahalla* kids come together, strap (the baby) to the cradle, do "*ui-ui*" (rock to sleep), even while small he/she comes out and plays with (the *mahalla*) kids. He/she grows up within that environment, the environment of the *mahalla* itself.

During the research, an interesting case emerged. There are certain *mahallas* in Khujand located close to the central market; the main occupation of those *mahallas*' residents is activity within the bazaar. In some of these *mahallas*, significant parts of wealthy families are headed by women, and they are able to do charity work, donating money and giving entertainments to the *mahalla* mosque. The mosque clergy confessed that they pray for those "good sisters and their business success" because they have been generous and kind. One cleric also admitted that the women could attend *mahalla* sessions if they want to. This example suggests that economic empowerment of women can affect their participation in public life and their public recognition, at least at the local level.

Women also exercise their agency in public life during holidays and important life events at which different groups of people and families interact. Almost no event (except birthdays and jubilees) can be held without the presence of Muslim clergy. It is becoming more popular to invite female clergy to an event, especially for female gatherings. Our research uncovered the phenomena of *otunbucha* (female clergy) and *folbin* (shaman or fortune teller), which in their different forms exist in other parts of Tajikistan, but in Khujand they have special significance because almost no event can be held without *otunbucha,* and many people of different social groups apply to *folbin* in order to solve life problems and receive directions to make life better. These phenomena are an important form of female identity and a form of social representation.

Otunbucha and Gender in Khujand

Otunbucha are very popular in Khujand and are invited for almost every kind of life-cycle event and for major religious feasts. The *otunbucha* opens an event, and she closes it with *du'o* (prayer). Only one *otunbucha* presides at each event, but she may bring her students as well. She usually reads religious texts at the events, but the most important part of her performance is the exhortation of moral advice (*pand o nasihat*). I attended the Forty Days' death memorial that was held by my neighbor for her mother. During and after the readings of a religious text about Ali's exploits and his heroic death, the *otunbucha* kept saying:

> It is a main duty of the children in regard to their parents to weep intensely. They (mullahs) say "*ovoz naburoreton!*" (do not weep!). They (parents) raised you, gave you their love, lives, invested in you, and when they die, you won't weep? No, you should do this, because it is the least you can do for your parents after they die. Mullahs say that one should not hold all these events (referring to Shabi Siyoh [Dark Night, taking place the first evening following a burial], Begoh Okhir [the Last Night occurring three days after a burial], Chillai Khurd [Small Forty marking twenty days and twenty nights of grieving] and others). They are wrong! One should hold all these events, for it is a minimum one can do for one's parents

after they die. They (mullahs) talk, let them talk, but we will do what we do, and nobody can turn us from this way.

Thus, official clergy attached to mosques, appointed by the government, exert pressure against expensive rituals as an antipoverty strategy, but this pressure is viewed at the folk level as negative pressure against family responsibility and solidarity.

The government in Tajikistan has been encouraging the reduction of the expenditures for weddings, funerals, and other events, and official Islam supports the idea. Mullahs do the propaganda work, persuading people to cut expenses and not hold the whole set of events. But the propaganda is not always effective because people are concerned about social opinion—"what people would say." Thus, we can see that sometimes cultural identity and traditional values represented by female clergies are stronger and more influential than orthodox Islamic ideas and economics.

Otunbuchas cast judgment on people during events in trenchant terms, advocating vigorous participation. One recalled, "I attended an event where one son was as silent as a cow." This sort of comment motivates those attending to make sure they live up to the expectations of the clergy. In 2003, the maximum payment for this service was 10 somoni (US$3); now the minimum is 30 somoni ($10), while the audience also, then and now, may give small offerings of 1–2 somoni (around 50 cents), at which the *otunbucha* will add prayers for their parents as well. Any comments an *otunbucha* makes about a previous event she attended, in another house, are important in establishing that family's reputation. A government-appointed local mullah may be asked to do this service, but generally will be paid less for these events than an *otunbucha* of similar local reputation. *Otunbuchas* are also normally asked to lead prayers and make a statement at the wedding Salom, giving a more religious context to this smaller, home-based event.

Another activity of *otunbuchas* is the ritual called Mushkilkusho ("resolving difficulties"), which a woman dedicates and organizes to address a family or personal problem: for example, struggling with financial difficulties; calling back a husband who has gone to Russia for work and lost contact with the family; seeking get a better job; finding a marriage partner for herself, a daughter, or sister; or dealing with some non-life-threatening illnesses. The supplicant achieves an ongoing client relationship with supernatural allies who protect and help herself or her family, through repeatedly undergoing the ceremony and making its offerings.

At this event, bread, sweets, *hazor isfand* (wild rue, the dried stems, leaves, and seeds), *maviz* (black raisins), a lighted candle, dry tea leaves, salt, water, and cotton are assembled on a *sofreh* (clean eating cloth), possibly along with a plate or bowl of cooked food such as *osh, pilmini,* or *pirogi.* At one event, the sponsoring women put folded dresses on the cloth as well. The objects placed on the *sofreh* are blessed and given protective power by the rite that follows. The cotton is divided into small pieces, one for each participant, along with a portion of the raisins. The *otunbucha* recites a combination of praise for and narratives about powerful holy persons, perhaps also the legend that retells the origin of the rite itself in the votive actions of a poor girl. She offers general wishes in the form of prayers for the participants ("By God, may you receive and not have things taken from you by others"; "May you live long and happily with your husband"; "May God give to everyone, and particularly to us"; "May God give you no grief, but legitimate and ample reward for your work"; "May you be happy").

While the *otunbucha* is doing this, each participant removes the stems from her raisins, cleaning them one by one and placing the removed stems on the cotton. At the end of the final prayer, the participants hold their hands over the candle, palms downward, and then say "Amen," brushing their open hands downward over their faces. By this gesture, the participants' "faces are warmed" (*ru-garm*), the result of being the object of goodwill and help from everyone. The cotton and raisin stems will be disposed of after the ceremony in running water, taking with them all the participants' problems. The dried, cleaned raisins, bread, and other sanctified objects go home with the participants, who eat the food items or give them to friends and relations to share the blessing. The dried rue herb is used as a fumigant to protect against evil spirits.

This custom, widely practiced in Khujand, is popular all over the country. While it is often held at home by individual women who all know and invite one another reciprocally, there are also some very public venues for the event, where women may join a ceremony without prior acquaintance, but the ceremony remains in its nature and ethos a group event. In Dushanbe, at the shrine of Hazrat Maulana Hamadani, every Wednesday, perhaps two dozen different *otunbuchas* each occupy their own individual carpeted space, side by side in the small bazaar outside the shrine. Women come, usually in groups but in some cases individually, to sit down with their choice of *otunbucha* in a gathering of perhaps eight to twelve women, and place their own raisins, bread, and so forth on the *sofreh*. The *otunbucha* initiates a more or less elaborated ceremony as soon as a group assembles. It may last fifteen to twenty minutes or longer, with or without singing in the recitation, with or without candles, and so forth. After the main ceremony is completed, the leader may be asked to offer individual prayer/blessings over individual participants. Each participant gives 1 somoni or so to the practitioner for her services. Small chapbooks outlining the ceremony for the use of participants in either Tajik or Uzbek are available for purchase at bookstands outside mosques and shrines where inexpensive religious books and booklets are sold. One *otunbucha* interviewed in Khujand said that wealthy people should try to hold such a ceremony at least seven times a year. The supplicant's relationship with the helpful supernatural power is ongoing, with obligations; in Mushkilkusho and related rites practiced elsewhere in the wider cultural region, the votive, sustained, reciprocal nature of the relationship is even more explicit.

Folbin and Gender in Khujand

Folbin (literally, "fortune telling") is a form of supernatural intervention and in certain ways shares elements with shamanism, but it also has its own specific features. The term "*folbin*" designates a person, either male or female, who offers magical help to people. Male and female *folbins*, both urban and rural, have similar methods and tools, but each individual has different supernatural allies, *azizon* (deceased loved ones). A man or, more often, a woman accepts clients in his or her house or apartment on certain days (often three or four days a week, excluding Friday). Sometimes one can see a long line of people waiting, clients at a popular *folbin*'s door.

In the *folbin*'s house, a special room is set aside for clients, where there is little or no furniture except for a small table for the *folbin*'s books, notebook, pen, and other tools. *Kurpacha* (floor seating mats) rest against the walls for visitors. Male and female *folbins* wear white clothes. A female folbin wears a dress and trousers and a white headscarf; a male *folbin* usually wears a white shirt and pants. The *folbin* asks the visitor about his or her problems and issues to be solved and listens with attention. Then the *folbin* opens the book, usually the Qur'an, reads for two to three minutes, and then rolls his or her eyes back or closes his or her eyes, and starts a "conversation" with an "*azizon*" (supernatural associates or patrons such as well-known saints, spirits of ancestors), who are not visible to the visitor. The *folbin* may combine this effort with quick questioning of the visitor about details of the problem, possible obstructive people, family members, and other matters. Finally, the *folbin* asks the *azizon* to help, to advise, to solve the visitor's problem(s), and/or to show the way to solving them. Then the *folbin* offers an *Omin* (a final prayer), and blows into the visitor's water, dry tea, picture (sometimes), or other small objects like keys, pens, handkerchief, and so forth, which, used by the client, become tokens of the ritual's effect. The relationship is ongoing: the *folbin* will guarantee the result only if a visitor will follow all advice, and after some time (varying from forty days to three months) will repeat the ritual.

People seek to control their lives, to protect their achievements, wealth, and positions. In Khujand, people prefer to seek specific, practical ways of solving problems, including applying to mullahs and those who promise practical supernatural interventions (magic) in the daily problem-solving process. During the Soviet period as well, it was usual to visit a mullah, a *folbin*, or a *bakhshi* (local variety of shaman) in order to receive magical help or healing, especially in rural areas where medicine is not well developed and no hospitals are available. People may visit a *folbin* for social control, to get more power, to influence specific people, perhaps to make people "close their mouths" (to silence gossip), or to "close their eyes," so that they would not see certain activities.

When I asked two respectable and wealthy women why they visit a *folbin*, they said that the main goal is protective (rather than diagnostic, as the name *folbin* might imply), to keep a wealthy and prosperous life and to prevent the evil eye. OMK, a thirty-five-year-old woman who is having problems with her unfaithful husband, says:

> What would a *domullah* say: "Go, do your prayers (*namaz*), fast, behave well, do not fight, take care of your husband, do not listen to what people say." As to the *folbin*, he/she says exactly: "That person has done that activity, that person is your enemy." ... But, basically, what is good about *folbins* is that they will show (you) a way, will give (you) a recipe.

Even some prominent businessmen, male political leaders, and/or their wives visit *folbins* on a regular basis. There is a belief that if a person is successful, with a flourishing business or a stable leadership position, the person "does/ makes something," that is, regularly visits a "strong" mullah or *folbin*. Nobody, however, would confess that he or she visits a *folbin*; the very issue of *folbins* is considered to be closed, and people would not publicly discuss the issue.

A different situation exists with mullahs, who speak on behalf of official Islam and have a negative attitude toward *folbins* and *otunbuchas*. The act of making donations (mainly food and money, but sometimes clothes) to the mosques is highly valued, and people try to do so publicly in order to show how religious they are. For such local traditional events as Shabi Siyoh (Dark Night) and Begoh Okhir (Last Night), people invite both mullahs and *otunbuchas*, but a mullah's duty is to read, briefly, basic suras from the Qur'an, make the final prayer among males, and finish within a maximum of one hour. The *otunbucha* usually is supposed to give a performance for females; she will not be in a hurry, and she knows about her significance in the host house. Mullahs may criticize *otunbuchas*, doing it indirectly by advising families not to spend money on some events, but often the mullah and *otunbucha* coexist. My informant, mullah IKK, age forty-seven, said that he would never let a *folbin* or an *otunbucha* enter his own house, and he would not let anybody from his family apply to them because they demoralize the society.

In Khujand society, a sort of opposition between official clergies and nonofficial ones exist, and the mullahs are not always "the winners," because traditional, cultural expectations and demands are often not similar to those advocated by official Islam. People try to meet the expectations of their community and their culture rather than follow the mullah's advice. Thus, the phenomena of *otunbucha* and *folbin* provide evidence of women's status and power in two ways. First, women themselves choose whom to share their private problems with and how to solve those problems. Second, women seem to have their own way of understanding Islam, its foundations and history, and do not always conform to the Islam that mullahs offer.

Conclusion

Many factors affect gender roles and identity in Tajikistan today. These include the legal, political, economic, and social circumstances at both the national and local levels under which citizens carry out their daily lives. This chapter is based on a study of the circumstances in Khujand and surrounding areas. Khujand, of course, is an indissoluble part of Tajikistan as a whole, and Khujand people are similar to other Tajik people in many features. However, each region in Tajikistan has its own identity and peculiarities, and Khujand is no exception.

From the legal point of view, Tajik laws are not discriminatory. The government and the president have been undertaking major efforts for several years to raise women's participation in public life and politics. In the political sphere, the Soviet system of quotas for women was inherited and has had positive results, such as the comparatively high level of women representatives in Parliament and in middle management. In contrast, gender inequality still exists in the economic sphere. The recession in production increased unemployment and underemployment, spurred emigration, and brought about a drastic deterioration in the material situation and standard of living of the country's population in general. Poverty has undermined traditional roles (for example, the role of a man as the main breadwinner, which is essential for Tajik culture). The economic crisis has forced many women to start their own small businesses, selling goods in the bazaars and stores near their own houses or traveling to neighboring countries for goods. As the research shows, despite the traditional negative view of businesswomen, independent women are gaining more support and authority within the society and small communities.

The social sector also reflects new gender roles and identities. During the Soviet period, such professions as education and medicine were considered privileged. Although nowadays they are not well paid, women continue to occupy these professions. Social status and respect do not necessarily depend on salary; the very titles *muallima* (teacher) and *dukhtur* (doctor) still remain honorable. Globalization affects young people; people, especially young people, are accepting the new images, ideologies, and ideals that are being established. The term "businesswoman," for instance, is not a synonym for bad woman anymore, as it used to be five or six years ago.

The spread of NGOs and international organizations in the country has led to increasing numbers of women working for those organizations and gaining recognition for being economically independent, smart, and well educated. These women are well paid (by Khujand standards) and recognized because the city is small; they often serve as models for their neighbors and relatives. In Khujand, one-third of the interviewed young women, age twenty-one to thirty-five, would like to get a job "at a good NGO or international organization." A twenty-eight-year-old woman, an international organization employee, told me that she pulled her family out of poverty and earned the respect of the *mahalla* for the entire family after her father left the family eight years ago. Thus, during the transition from Communism, social and economic diversity has been increasing, as has its influence on the weakening of and even ignoring of patriarchal relations. Yet as I have shown, women's agency is exercised in more traditional realms as well. The phenomena of *otunbucha* and *folbin* demonstrate the involvement of women in public life and their ability to exercise influence in the family and in the community within the constraints of traditional cultural and religious values.

NOTES

1. This research was based on a U.S. Department of State Title VIII Special Initiatives Fellowship for Policy-Relevant Research project: *Social and Ethical Values in Tajik Everyday Speech and Oral Tradition: An Ethnographic Assessment*. Margaret A. Mills, Ohio State University, Columbus, Ohio, Principal Investigator. With the permission of the editor, Margaret Mills, portions of this chapter have been drawn from the volume being prepared on the basis of that research project.

2. Jamoat is a regional government unit, combining several *mahallas* and villages.

3. Of course, not all women suffer from economic uncertainty. A small group of women comes from wealthy families or has been married to wealthy and/or authoritative men. Although it was difficult to access this group of women in my research, some of them enjoyed having discussions with me in fashionable salons. For ordinary people, these women's lives seem like those of Hollywood stars. They may drive a car or have a personal driver; they do not usually work "for the state," as they like to emphasize; some of them "work for themselves," own shops, own salons, and have property elsewhere in Tajikistan and abroad.

4. Traditionally, the highest levels of employment of women have been on peasant farms, where the entire family does various types of work.

5. Kasimova, however, argues that the post-Soviet economic and social crisis stimulated the involvement of women in the public sphere. She claims that women have joined the labor market as an extra labor resource because most men did not have enough potential. Consequently, more women have been becoming heads of enterprises, markets, and plants (Kasimova 2005, 186).

6. All are names of villages that constitute the old part of Khujand city.

WORKS CITED

Falkingham, Jane. 2000. *Women and Gender Relations in Tajikistan.* Http://www.adb.org/ Documents/Books/Country_Briefing_Papers/Women_in_Tajikistan/women_in_ tajikistan.pdf.

Harris, Collette. 2004. *Control and Subversion: Gender Relations in Tajikistan.* London: Pluto Press.

Kasimova, Sofia. 2005. *Gender Order in Post-Soviet Tajikistan* . Dushanbe: Optima.

Khotkina, Zoya, and Galiya Rabieva, eds. 2003. *Tajikistan on the Way to Gender Equality.* Http://www.untj.org/files/reports/On%20the%20way%20to%20the%20Gender%20 equality_Eng.pdf.

Mills, Margaret A. N.d. *Social and Ethical Values in Tajik Everyday Speech and Oral Tradition: An Ethnographic Assessment*. U.S. Department of State Title VIII Special Initiatives Fellowship for Policy-Relevant Research.

Poliakov, Sergei P. 1992. *Everyday Islam: Religion and Tradition in Rural Central Asia*. Ed. Martha Brill Olcott. Trans. Anthony Olcott. Armonk, N.Y.: M. E. Sharpe.

Safarova, Marina, Anjelika Abdurakhmanova, and Rano Kasymova. 2007. *A Gender Analysis of EU Development Instruments and Policies in Tajikistan, Representing Central Asia*. Network of East-West Women. Http://www.neww.org.pl/download/EU_Gender-Watch_Tajikistan.pdf.

Notes on Contributors

Mary Buckley is a fellow and director of Studies in Politics, Psychology, Sociology and International Studies at Hughes Hall, University of Cambridge. She is author or editor of ten books, which include *Soviet Social Scientists Talking* (1986), *Women and Ideology in the Soviet Union* (1989), *Redefining Russian Society and Polity* (1993), and *Mobilizing Soviet Peasants* (2006). She has recently coedited three volumes on global perceptions of NATO intervention in Kosovo, 9/11, and the Bush Doctrine. Her wide research interests focus on the history of Soviet and post-Soviet politics and society, including foreign policy.

Barbara Einhorn is professor of Gender Studies, Department of Sociology, University of Sussex. Her research interests include citizenship, civil society, and gender politics, with special reference to mass dictatorships and to democratization in Central and Eastern Europe; identity, "home," and belonging in narratives of exile and return; and gender, nation, and identity. She is the editor of a special issue of the *European Journal of Women's Studies*, 5(3) 2008 entitled: "Questioning the Secular: Religion, Gender, Politics." She is the author of *Cinderella Goes to Market: Citizenship, Gender and Women's Movements in East Central Europe* (1993) and *Citizenship in an Enlarging Europe: From Dream to Awakening* (2006), as well as many articles, including, most recently, "Insiders and Outsiders: Within and Beyond the Gendered Nation," in *Handbook of Gender and Women's Studies*, edited by Kathy Davis, Mary Evans and Judith Lorber (2006); "Citizenship in an Enlarging Europe: Contested Strategies," *Czech Sociological Review* 41, no. 6 (2005);

and "Gender and Civil Society in Central and Eastern Europe" (with Charlotte Sever), *International Feminist Journal of Politics* 5, no. 2 (2003).

Ayça Ergun is assistant professor of sociology and vice-chair of Center for Black Sea and Central Asia (KORA) at Middle East Technical University. She also teaches in the Eurasian Studies Graduate Program. Her research interests include state-society relations, democratization, nation building, civil society formation, political elites, and human rights in the Southern Caucasus and Turkey. Her most recent publication is *Black Sea Politics: Political Culture and Civil Society in an Unstable Region* (coedited with Ayşe Güneş-Ayata and Işıl Çelimli) (2005).

Eleonora Fayzullaeva, Ph.D., is senior lecturer/reader at the Uzbek World Languages University and director of the Gender Program for the Embassy of Switzerland in Uzbekistan. She is the author of "Gender Based Violence," in *The Introduction to the Theory and Practice of Gender Relations* (2007), as well as papers on the development of gender and women's studies in higher education in the newly independent states of Eurasia. research interests also include gender aspects of labor migration, gender-based violence, and women's rights in the Muslim context.

Ayşe Güneş-Ayata is chairperson of the Center for Black Sea and Central Asia (KORA) and professor of political science at Middle East Technical University. She also teaches in the Gender and Women Studies Graduate Programme. She was a member of the Advisory Board of the Regional Bureau of Europe and Central Asia (RBEC) of the United Nations Development Program and has been responsible for the execution of various research projects on the region. Her research interests include gender, ethnicity, and migrant communities, as well as development of civil society, democratization, and political participation. Her recent publications are "Ethnic and Religious Bases of Voting," in *Politics, Parties and Elections in Turkey*, edited by Sabri Sayarı and Yılmaz Esmer (2002); "From Euro-skepticism to Turkey Skepticism: Changing Political Attitudes on the European Union in Turkey," *Journal of Southern Europe and the Balkans* (2003); and "Migration Poverty and Social Protection," in *Bridging the Gender Gap in Turkey: A Milestone Towards Faster Socio-Economic Development* (2003). She is the coeditor of *Black Sea Politics: Political Culture and Civil Society in an Unstable Region* (with Ayça Ergun and Işıl Çelimli) (2005) and *Gender and Identity Construction: Women of Central Asia, the Caucasus and Turkey* (with Feride Acar) (2000).

Timur Kocaoglu is associate professor of Turkic languages and Central Asian cultural history at the Center for Strategic Studies, Koc University (Istanbul, Turkey) and currently a visiting scholar at Center for European and Russian/ Eurasian Studies (CERES) and associate professor at James Madison College, Michigan State University. His interests include the political and cultural history of Central Eurasia and the Turkic languages. His books include *Turkish World Phrase Guide: Turkish, Azerbaijani, Turkmen, Uzbek, Uyghur, Kazakh, Kyrgyz, Tatar* (1992); *Reform Movements and Revolutions in Turkistan: 1900–1924* (2001); *Karay: The Trakai Dialect* (2006); and *A Comparative Grammar of the Turkic Languages* (forthcoming). Besides his academic writings in English and Turkish, his literary writings (poetry and short stories) in Turkish and Uzbek have been published in literary journals in both Turkey and Uzbekistan. He was the recipient of the Omer Seyfettin Best Short Story Award in 1999 in Turkey.

Enikö Magyari-Vincze is professor at Babeş-Bolyai University, Cluj, Romania, and director of the Centre for Gender Studies. Her teaching and research interests are in the domain of sociocultural anthropology and gender studies, particularly gender, nation, and sexuality in identity politics; reproduction; social inequalities and marginalization; and nationalism and feminism. Her recent publications include "Le patriarcat d'en haut et d'en bas en Roumanie," in *Nouvelles Questions Feministes, Postcommunisme: Genre et États en Transition* (2004); "Gender, Ethnicity and the Construction of the Social Order: A View from Below on Romania," in *Anthropological Yearbook of European Cultures, Gender and Nation in South Eastern Europe*, vol. 14 (2005); "Romanian Gender Regimes and Women's Citizenship," in *Women and Citizenship in Central and Eastern Europe*, edited by Jasmina Lukic, Joanna Regulska, and Darja Zavirsek (2006); *Social Exclusion at the Crossroads of Gender, Ethnicity and Class: A View through Roma Women's Reproductive Health* (2006).

Linda Racioppi is professor of comparative cultures and politics, and international relations at James Madison College, Michigan State University. Her current research focuses on gender and power; ethnicity, nationalism, and ethnic conflict; and film and nationalism. She is the author of *Soviet Policy Towards South Asia since 1970* (1994) and coauthor (with Katherine O'Sullivan See) of *Women's Activism in Contemporary Russia* (1997). She has recently authored or coauthored articles on engendering democratization, third party interventions in ethnic conflict, grassroots peace building and conflict, and interdisciplinary pedagogy.

Katherine O'Sullivan See is professor in the fields of comparative cultures and politics, and social relations and policy at James Madison College, Michigan State University. Her research interests include comparative race and ethnic conflict, gender and nationalism, social movements, and postconflict reconciliation. She is the author of *First World Nationalisms: Class and Ethnic Politics in Northern Ireland and Quebec* (1986) and coauthor (with Linda Racioppi) of *Women's Activism in Contemporary Russia* (1997). She has authored or coauthored many articles on gender and nationalism, ethnic conflict, race relations and conflict resolution.

Nadezda Shvedova, who holds a Ph.D. in history and a Doctor Degree in political science, is head of the Center of Socio-political Studies of the Institute of USA and Canada Studies, Russian Academy of Sciences, and a former Fulbright Scholar (August 2004–May 2005). She is the author or editor of more than 100 books and articles, including *Entrepreneurship and Women of the Indigenous Peoples of the North of the Russian Federation through Gender Education* (2007); *Obstacles to Women's Participation in Parliament: Beyond Numbers* (2005); *Simply About the Complex: Gender Education* (2002); *Health Care: The American Model* (1993); "Gender and Development: Problems and Achievements," *USA-Canada Economics-Politics-Culture* (2007); and "Gender, Democracy and Civil Society," in *Representative Power* 6 (2006), http://www.owl.ru/content/openpages/p59416. shtml. In 1999, she was awarded a Certificate of Merit by the Russian Academy of Sciences in recognition of her pioneering research, and in 2003 the Ministry of Labor and Social Development awarded her a Certificate of Merit in recognition of her activity to improve women's status in Russia.

Amanda Sloat is a professional staff member on the U.S. House of Representatives Foreign Affairs Committee. As a postdoctoral fellow at Queen's University Belfast, she was the academic coordinator of a ten-country research program on women's political participation in Central and Eastern Europe, which provided the basis for the chapter in this volume. She previously worked with the National Democratic Institute, European Commission, Scottish Parliament, and Northern Ireland Assembly. She has published *Scotland in Europe: A Study of Multi-Level Governance* (2002), as well as articles in the *European Journal of Women's Studies*, *Public Policy and Administration*, and *Regional and Federal Studies*.

Zulaikho Usmanova is senior scholar in residence at the Institute of Philosophy of the Academy of Science of the Republic of Tajikistan. She has served as the National Gender Officer in Dushanbe for the Organization for Security and Cooperation of

Europe (OSCE). An anthropologist by training, her research interests center on gender issues in Tajikistan, Islam and gender, and the anthropology of gender. She is the author of two books, *History of Tajik Culture* (with V. V. Vodnev and M. Karimov) (2003) and *Myth as a Phenomenon of Culture* (2000), as well as articles on Tajik national consciousness and on women's political leadership in Tajikistan. Her current research, supported by the CARTI program of the Open Society Institute, focuses on popular Islam in Tajikistan, with an emphasis on women.

Index